Darren Kerr and Donna Peberdy are senior lecturers in film and television at Southampton Solent University, UK. Darren is the co-editor of *Hard to Swallow: Hard-Core Pornography on Screen* (2012) and he has published articles on sex, horror, violence and adaptation. Donna is the author of *Masculinity and Film Performance: Male Angst in Contemporary American Cinema* (2011) and her research and publications focus on acting, performance, sex and gender.

TAINTED LOVE

Screening Sexual Perversion

Edited by

Darren Kerr and Donna Peberdy

I.B. TAURIS

LONDON · NEW YORK

Published in 2017 by
I.B.Tauris & Co. Ltd
London • New York
www.ibtauris.com

International Library of the Moving Image 16

ISBN (HB): 978 1 78076 195 4
ISBN (PB): 978 1 78076 196 1
eISBN: 978 1 78672 218 8
ePDF: 978 1 78673 218 7

A full CIP record for this book is available from the British Library
A full CIP record is available from the Library of Congress

Library of Congress Catalog Card Number: available

Typeset by Riverside Publishing Solutions
Printed and bound in Great Britain by T.J. International, Padstow, Cornwall

Contents

Contents

Illustrations

Illustrations

Acknowledgements

First and foremost we are indebted to our contributors for their unwavering support for this collection from inception to completion. Their commitment, generosity and patience has continually reaffirmed our faith in this project. Collectively, their insight offers an abundance of bold and thought-provoking conclusions that not only contribute to the field but challenge perceptions of what constitutes it. We are honoured to have had the opportunity to exchange ideas, engage in scintillating debate and publish their groundbreaking work here. Many thanks to the team at I.B.Tauris, and Maddy Hamey-Thomas in particular, for their valuable guidance and expediency when it mattered most. We are hugely grateful to Jeffrey Kusama-Hinte at Antidote Films and the wonderful Bill Sage for providing the necessary permissions to allow us to use such a striking image from *Mysterious Skin* (Gregg Araki, Antidote Films, 2004) to illustrate our cover. Thank you also to Bill's agent Rachel Sheedy at INSURGE-Ent and Jindra Span at Fortissimo Films. We are grateful to Southampton Solent University for supporting our work through Research and Innovation funding. This has enabled us to present our research to receptive audiences at SCMS, PCA/ACA, Cine-Excess and the *Film Studies* 'Sex and the Cinema' conference. We really appreciate the critically supportive environments and opportunity to test ideas before committing them to publication! Our colleagues and students in the Film Department at Solent continue to inspire and remind us of the value in a culture of research both outside and inside the classroom. We are especially grateful to David Alamouti, Mark Aldridge, Jacqueline Furby, Claire Hines, Simon Hobbs, Stuart Joy, Terence McSweeney, Angela Taylor and Russell White who keep the bar raised high. We would also like to thank the students of Sex on Screen and The Critic for having the enthusiasm, desire and will to challenge the normative and we encourage them to keep asking those difficult questions and pursuing the answers, even (especially) if that takes them into uncharted territory. This project has become much more than an edited collection. This year saw us launch *Screening Sex*, an academic blog and network, with the aim to share ideas, promote research and establish a diverse community of academics and creative practitioners working in the area. We would like to acknowledge current and future contributors for confronting and contesting matters of sexual politics, culture and representation in a valuable and accessible way. Finally, none of this would be possible without the love and support of our families. Thanks to our parents for their tolerance, encouragement and silence (at all the right moments). This book is dedicated to Alfie, Ben and Jude who make it all worthwhile.

Introduction: A Prelude to Perversion

Darren Kerr and Donna Peberdy

'The summer I was eight years old...'

Two boys are introduced near the start of *Mysterious Skin* (2004) – Brian Lackey (George Webster) and Neil McCormack (Chase Ellison) – narrated by their teenage selves (Brady Corbet and Joseph Gordon-Levitt). 'The summer I was eight years old', Brian recalls, 'five hours disappeared from my life'. Young Brian wakes up in a closet with a bloody nose. The last thing he remembers is sitting on the Little League bench as it starts to rain. From that moment, Brian experiences frequent nosebleeds, bed-wetting and passing out as he tries to make sense of his lost time. He later comes to believe that he was abducted by aliens who experimented on him. The juxtaposition of Brian's story with Neil's suggests a more disturbing explanation that is much closer to home. 'The summer I was eight years old', Neil narrates, 'I came for the first time'. Neil stands at his bedroom window, watching his mother (Elizabeth Shue) fellate her latest boyfriend up against Neil's backyard swing set. Moustached and rugged Alfred (David Lee Smith), Neil tells us, 'was all Marlboro Man [...] What I would years later come to call my type'. Neil licks his lips as Alfred moans in ecstasy. Alfred's orgasming face is interchanged with a close-up of another moustached man, who we later find out is Neil's softball instructor, referred to in the film only

1

as 'Coach' (Bill Sage). Neil screws up his face as he and Alfred climax simultaneously. Coach's satisfied, post-orgasm face once again flickers on screen as Neil exhales and inquisitively looks down at the floor. 'I'd been masturbating for years, but it wasn't until that summer that jizz actually squirted out of my dick when I came', Neil narrates. 'Couldn't wait to show Coach'.

Multiple sexually 'perverse' behaviours are presented to us in this early scene: the mother and boyfriend having sex outdoors; a prepubescent boy masturbating, while watching his mother, while desiring her boyfriend; a clear expression of child sexual awareness and admission of sexual desire for an adult; the implication that Brian's lost time is connected to Neil's story rather than a UFO; and the suggestion that something sexual has already happened between an eight-year-old boy and his Coach. It is a bold and controversial scene that establishes the tone for the wider film and establishes its 'refusal to tell a single story about the relation between childhood and sexuality'.[1] This is a film that will confront, challenge perceptions of sexuality, rupture reductive delineations between victims and violators and not be afraid to use explicit terms in a provocative manner. The confrontational scene and the wider film raise questions about what constitutes sexual perversion and the ways in which it is spoken. As Kathryn Bond Stockton asks, 'How do we see a sexual child as being something other than our own perversion?'[2] While Coach's latent sexual activity with a boy infringes widely acknowledged social, sexual and legal boundaries, Neil's confessional desire and actions present a lesser-known, but still uncomfortable, perspective on sexual agency that is often unrepresented, persistently silenced and culturally taboo.

With this scene, the film also establishes what it will not show. We see Neil masturbating from mid-shots, framed from the waist upwards, with beautifully lit close-ups of his flawless and cherubic face, point-of-view shots of the object of his desiring gaze and his lip-biting and grimaces as he masturbates. We do not see the ejaculation and semen – a shock tactic used in Todd Solondz's suburban satire *Happiness* (1998) six years earlier – but do see his quizzical expression as he looks at it. *Mysterious Skin* clearly makes choices about how it will depict sex, choices that explicitly set it apart from the depiction of adolescent sexuality in much of mainstream cinema. The combination of close-ups on Neil's face and pageboy haircut juxtaposed with his older self's dry and matter-of-fact narration shocks and confronts. The blunt voiceover means we cannot escape what Neil is saying. The 'underperformed emotion' or 'flat affect' creates 'an asterisk of uncertainty', to borrow from cultural theorist Lauren Berlant, where we might expect something more explicitly expressive or demonstrative.[3] Setting the two boy's introductions side-by-side has the effect of making Neil's affectless admission even more shocking in comparison with Brian's soft and vulnerable articulation. There are obvious ethical and legal implications in depicting sex involving children and Gordon-Levitt's voiceover is an important dramatic device utilised here and across the film to manage scenes of Neil, and later Brian, and Coach.

To 'protect' the child actors, director Gregg Araki — best known for his contribution to New Queer Cinema and the depiction of transgressive adolescent sexualities — had Webster and Ellison perform scenes on their own, without the presence of Bill Sage's Coach, and then relied on 'clever editing'.[4] 'I invented this whole separate movie that they were in to protect them from what the real movie was about [...] In truth they have no idea what they are acting', he noted.[5] The method of directing children out of the diegesis to achieve what is required within it gives some indication of the filmmaker's desire to capture troubling portrayals while carefully negotiating industry regulations and the ethics of child acting in what is otherwise an adult drama.[6] The cine-literate director noted: 'Those scenes are so critical to the story that I didn't want to make the movie if I couldn't include them'. He explained how he 'figured out a cinematic strategy' based on the Kuleshov experiment 'using subjective camera and point-of-view, and eyeline [whereby] meaning is created through the collision of images. It was possible to create those scenes by editing disparate shots together'.[7] Such a technique has ethical implications concerning the management of acting-out abuse and trauma, on the one hand protecting the child actors from exposure to provocative subject matter yet, on the other hand, problematic for the actor's lack of awareness of the wider context in which their performances will be seen by audiences.

Widely well received, *Mysterious Skin* inevitably opened to some controversy. The film was released without a rating in the US on a limited number of screens after an unsuccessful appeal by the filmmakers against the NC-17 rating the film received in the US. The Australian Family Association sought to have the film banned on the grounds that it could sexually arouse paedophiles or assist in grooming youngsters: 'Being able to get hold legally of a DVD where they can play a scene over and over again, showing the adult baseball coach fellating an eight-year-old boy', a spokesperson argued, 'could prove very helpful to some paedophiles'.[8] Conversely, President of the lobby group Watch On Censorship Margaret Pomeranz acknowledged Araki's careful handling of the subject matter and believed the film could actually be preventive in some way. 'This is a film about the damage that pedophilia creates. It has been so carefully filmed, the impact is on the audience', she stated, 'pedophiles could watch this film and be stricken by remorse. It could be a pedophile-curing film because they're confronted by the damage they do'.[9]

These opposing positions, revolving around the politics of controversial sexual identities on screen, have their foundation in just six minutes of screen time focusing on Coach. 'He haunts the movie like a ghost', commented Araki at the London Film Festival screening, 'he embodies that 1970s ideal of the sexy, blond, smiling guy'. The director went on to describe Bill Sage's 'textured and rich' performance, noting how the actor wanted Coach to be 'a complicated, conflicted human being not just a two-dimensional bad guy'.[10] Coach is markedly handsome, disarmingly charismatic and sexually omnipotent; we see him through Neil's yearning eyes, romantically lit and framed by a lingering, desiring camera (see Fig. 0.1).

Sage's depiction of Coach unsettles precisely for its departure from the tabloid image of the seedy predator and 'dirty old man'. The intent to look beyond the reductive discourses that inform moral panic is equally evident in Araki's aim to move beyond typical ways of producing narratives of sexual abuse:

> I really wanted the film to just give people something to think about and sort of feel this kind of empathy for those boys [...] The whole issue of child abuse is so sensationalised and so kind of saturated in the media today. The Michael Jackson thing and the Catholic Priests. It's all over everywhere. It has also become a cliché in TV movies and Hollywood dramas.[11]

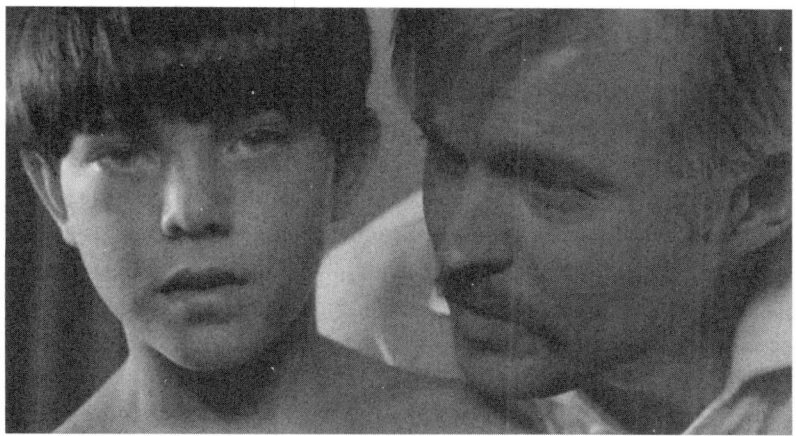

Fig. 0.1. Coach (Bill Sage) and Neil (Chase Ellison) in *Mysterious Skin* (Gregg Araki, Antidote Films, 2004)

Araki's 'modern masterpiece' embraces a poetic and aesthetically beautiful approach to culturally uncomfortable moments of desire alongside bleaker sequences of sex and sexual violence enacted on teenage Neil, encapsulating the ways in which the screen contests, challenges and interprets assumptions about sexual variance.[12] The film navigates the politics and poetics of representation to present a film that reveals and exposes our assumptions about normative and non-normative sexuality, a recurring theme across the essays in this collection.

Of course, the depiction of sexual perversion on-screen has a long, cautious and carefully managed history in Hollywood, a history characterised by principled regulation and creative interpretation. In 1927, 'The Don'ts and Be Carefuls' prohibited 'any inference of sex perversion [...] irrespective of the manner in which they are treated', sex perversion here referring to anything that went against the institution of marriage and heterosexual coupling.[13] The 1930 Motion Picture Production Code that was widely enforced by 1934 was more detailed about the 'moral obligation' of films, upheld the promotion of normative sexual relationships and maintained that the Hollywood screen was no place for 'impure love'.[14] The aim of the Production Code Administration was to clearly send the 'right' message to its mass audience. However, what was at stake was what that message should be. In spite (and arguably because) of the Code, the screen has always found a way to present and examine perversion, whether in coded performances found in studio pictures, quickly-produced B-movies or faux-educational exploitation films. Film genres and movements have repeatedly dressed their narratives in the sexually perverse, whether through motifs of sexual sadism in film noir, themes of deviancy and promiscuity in horror, explorations of reproduction in science fiction or experiments with sexual liberation in comedy. While they often contain an abiding morally condemnatory tone, accompanying and excusing the narratives for focusing on such dangerous endeavours, the attention to the way in which perverse pleasures have evolved on screen persists. It comes as no surprise that some of the more challenging depictions of sexual perversion on screen have taken place outside of the Hollywood mainstream and in the terrain of independent film, art cinema and other national cinemas that explore, more explicitly, alternative, marginalised and taboo sexualities. For all these reasons, film deserves close consideration and can be set apart from the mass media, which is often accused of perpetuating myths around perversion, conjuring hysteria and moral panic around atypical sexual behaviour and identities and perpetually reinscribing normative sexualities.

Interventions

The critical history of sexual perversion is a history of conflict, instability and plurality that has evolved from being defiantly classified and categorised by early sexologists to being rendered practically meaningless. The 'quagmire of phrases' invoked in discussions of perversion, as historian Julie Peakman notes, suggest that 'the time has come for a change – perhaps even an end to applying the word to any sexual behaviours [...] since many of our past sexual perversions have become our present sexual normality'.[15] Philosophy professor Igor Primoratz argues that the term 'perversion' is entirely negative, disapproving and used to condemn. 'It can safely be said that the term serves no useful purpose', he concludes. 'We should therefore simply drop it'.[16] An abbreviated overview of key interventions in the definition of perversion and resulting inquiry reveal the term and its variants to be discursively loaded, continually contested, often subject to contradictions, but with recurring commonalities that say as much about social and cultural constructions of normality as they do about departures from it.[17]

The 1886 publication of *Psychopathia Sexualis*, written by German forensic psychiatrist Richard von Krafft-Ebing, is seen by many as the founding text in defining sexual perversion that opened up 'a new continent of knowledge' regarding sexuality.[18] In his preface to the first edition, Krafft-Ebing observed a lack of knowledge, which he set out to address in what he described as his 'scientific study of the psychopathology of sexual life' rooted in the assumption that sexual desire was volatile and a clear distinction between the normal and the abnormal was required.[19] In his radical and seminal text, Krafft-Ebing sought to understand perversion as an illness rather than a crime, something to be treated rather than punished. He also maintained that *perversion* should be distinguished from *perversity* as a *disease* as opposed to a *vice*.[20] The publication was widely adopted by medical and legal professionals as well as lay-readers who sought to understand their own sexual behaviours and feelings in relation to the case histories. As Krafft-Ebing revised the text in later editions, his views, as historian Harry Oosterhuis points out, were revealed as 'far from static or coherent, and in many ways his scientific approach was ambivalent'.[21]

While Krafft-Ebing's work, along with that of early sexologists, was undeniably valuable in classifying sexual behaviour previously only considered in terms of immorality and criminality, its legacy is also in its pathologisation of non-normative sexuality and resulting normalisation of heterosexuality. As Kim M. Phillips and Barry Reay observe: 'The sexologists essentially created the pervert; there were no perverts before they were identified. And there was no normality before normality's other, perversion, was discovered'.[22] Other key first-wave sexologists including dermatologist Iwan Bloch, neurologist and psychoanalyst Sigmund Freud, physician Havelock Ellis, and second-wave sexologists such as biologist Alfred Kinsey began to chart a discourse that cumulatively ran from the culturally acceptable imperatives of reproduction to the necessity of sexual pleasure.[23] Their work accounted for sexual behaviour oscillating between lust and shame, examinations of the heterosexual norm and eventually the prevalence of sexually subversive behaviour in men and women in Kinsey's landmark reports *Sexual Behavior in the Human Male* and *Sexual Behavior in the Human Female*, published in 1948 and 1953 respectively.

The changing landscape around medical perceptions of perversion is encapsulated in the publication and ongoing revision of the *Diagnostic and Statistical Manual of Mental Disorders* (DSM), a 'catalyst for American psychiatry'.[24] Changes in terminology and categorisation of sexual pathology across the six editions and revisions reveal significant changes in psychiatric and medical discourse but they have also, in turn, influenced legal and cultural perceptions of sexual disorder and perversion. The 1952 first edition classified five 'sexual deviations': homosexuality, transvestism, paedophilia, fetishism and sexual sadism as personality disorders.[25] By 1968, the term was revised to 'deviant sexuality' – a seemingly significant move from act to identity – then to 'paraphilia' in the three subsequent editions, derived from the Latin *para* (other/outside) and *philia* (loving). With eight 'paraphilic disorders' detailed (exhibitionist disorder, frotteuristic disorder, sexual masochistic disorder and voyeuristic disorder joining fetishistic disorder, paedophilic disorder, sexual sadism disorder and transvestite disorder), the most recent fifth edition confirms a continual process of refining and locating the appropriate terminology, clarifying the distinction between pathological and non-pathological behaviours, shaping and being shaped by cultural shifts and legislative definitions of normative sexuality.

This medical history of perversion has been extended through the contentious place of perversion in sexual cultures. Georges Bataille's creative and critical outputs from the 1940s to early 1960s, as well as Michel Foucault's studies of sexuality in the 1970s and 1980s, in which he called for 'a different economy of bodies and pleasures', can be invoked to draw attention to philosophical, social, cultural and institutional ways of speaking perversion, in order to reclaim and re-evaluate sexual behaviours that are culturally, legally and medically regulated or contained.[26] The contestedness of sexuality and sexual perversion is captured in the writing of Robert Stoller and his psychiatric consideration of perversion as 'the erotic form of hatred'.[27] It informs Jeffery Weeks' sociological account of sexuality that calls for 'a politics around desire which is a politics of choice'[28] and it underpins Lisa Downing and Dany Nobus' psychoanalytic

8

reassessment that sets out to 'stage a serious dialogue' regarding the controversies of non-normative sexuality.[29] It is also evident in the development and reworking of Freudian and Foucauldian principles by queer theorists such as Judith Butler and Teresa de Lauretis, who expose and interrogate sexuality as political and as a discursive and performative sociocultural construct.[30] Indeed, invoking a model of 'perverse presentism' in *Female Masculinity*, Jack Halberstam invites us to question 'what we think we already know' in a way that 'avoids the trap of simply projecting contemporary understandings back in time but [...] apply insights from the present to conundrums of the past'.[31]

Regarding matters of screen representation more specifically, significant and notable interventions that have particularly influenced our approach to this collection have been made by Tanya Krzywinska and Linda Williams. Drawing from a 'wide spectrum' of examples across film history to consider sex and sexuality in narratives of adultery, bestiality, incest, BDSM and real sex, Krzywinska concludes: 'Of all the influences that prevail on cinematic mediations of sex and desire, it is transgression that proves to be a significant guiding factor'.[32] Her conclusions about the form and function of 'themes of transgression' are broad yet useful and a number are extended, tested and challenged in the following chapters. Linda Williams' *Screening Sex* features prominently across the collection. In our title, *Tainted Love: Screening Sexual Perversion*, we are inspired by Williams' identification of the double-meaning of *to screen* as both revealing and concealing. 'Sex is an act and more or less of "it" may be revealed but [...] it is not a stable truth that cameras and microphones either "catch" or don't catch,' she writes, 'It is a constructed, mediated, performed act and every revelation is also a concealment that leaves something to the imagination'.[33] As revealed in our opening discussion of *Mysterious Skin*, we believe this is no more true than in the screening of sexual perversion, which navigates legal constraints, ethical debates and the culturally confrontational.

For this collection, the point is to consider perversion in a film culture that demands dialogue and discussion, in spite of any 'corrective or containment element' that may be apparent in film narratives focusing on sexual transgression.[34] This enables us to consider the tension between terminology, classification and the discourses emerging through cultural approaches to perversion and screen representation. This tension between labelling, classifying and representing is encapsulated in the differences between diagnosis and debate, calling into question, for example, the approach that the DSM has had to perversion. What these definitions, categorisations and revisions illustrate is an understanding of perversion as measured against normative behaviour. By comparison, many of the films examined in this collection can be said to depict perversion by questioning what constitutes normative behaviour. In seeking to make sense of the depiction of sexual perversion on screen, the essays in this collection are informed by and extend the debates offered by these sexologists, psychiatrists and cultural theorists, alongside a wealth of others that cross numerous disciplines, who all share the common aim of seeking to understand sexuality and its social, cultural and physical manifestations. To return to Primoratz, while there may not be 'much chance of success in attempting to formulate a definition of sexual perversion that would capture the meaning of the term in ordinary discourse',[35] we would suggest film's various texts and contexts tackle ordinary discourses concerning perversion in thought-provoking and culturally meaningful ways.

In our usage, the multitude of perversions negates a single definition. This plurality also refers to the differing approaches on screen that can consider the same perversion but offer very alternative representations and readings. This attests to multiple identities, acts and actors and avoids making bold and sweeping claims that may apply to one perverse act or behaviour and not another. As an identity, then, perversion is considered in this collection as plural, fluid, changeable, socially determined and ascribed, culturally and historically mapped out. We are primarily concerned with the screen's engagement with such debates, issues and identities, as well as how it helps to formulate, make sense of and treat those identities in differing ways and with differing implications.

Screening Sexual Perversion

Tainted Love: Screening Sexual Perversion is divided into four parts that examine the imagined body and culture, anxiety through borders and boundaries, generational disquiet and the historical and cultural rewriting of perversion. Part One – 'Reviled Bodies: Fantasies, Realities and the Boundaries of the Explicit' – explores manifestations of problematic desire, beginning with Lisa Downing's essay on necrophilia as queer perversion in Lynne Stopkewich's *Kissed* (1996). Downing carefully considers the way in which female necrophilia unsettles perceptions of heterosexual desire and its potential to queer itself. This brings to attention assumptions we make about perversion, the gendering of deviant acts and expectations of pleasure. Dangerous pleasures and romantic obsessions inform John Mercer's account of the controversial *O Fantasma* (João Pedro Rodrigues, 2000). An imagined romantic connection between an individual and a stranger underpins erotomania in the film, which for Mercer eschews the argument of homosexuality as perversion and instead aligns gay desire with self-destructive tendencies. The struggle critics faced when attempting to position *O Fantasma* has also shadowed the work of Catherine Breillat – the focus of Helen Hester's essay on tensions found in the politics and perversions of the explicit. For Hester, Breillat purposefully revisits the work of *Romance* (1999) in *Anatomy of Hell* (2004) to further address the explicit as a political tool in rendering the sexual body as perceptible. In Breillat's films, the notion of the perverse is not just evident in the actions on screen but also produced through the limits of explicitness and how enhanced visibility can actually obscure, distort and defamiliarise. The ways in which sexual politics are written on the body influences Xavier Mendik's evaluation of social trauma in 1970s Italian pulp cinema. In opposition to the assumption that the sex comedies were apolitical and merely heterosexually conservative, Mendik demonstrates how these 'carnal dramas' co-opted sexual imagery and narrativised the traumas of the time.

Part Two – 'Too Close for Comfort: Mainstream Perversion, Marginal Tastes' – illustrates the proximity that perversion and various forms of transgression have to normative behaviour and sociocultural expectations of sexuality. Opening with 'A Dangerous Method: Provocative Performances of Perversion', Donna Peberdy considers the necessity of risk, hostility and normality when performing paedophilia and hysteria on screen. Peberdy's close analysis of Kevin Bacon's Walter in *The Woodsman* (Nicole Kassell, 2004) and Keira Knightley's Sabina in *A Dangerous*

Method (David Cronenberg, 2011) reveals ways in which performance can gesturally construct deviant characters while concurrently commenting on their respective sexual identities. Negotiating sexual identity drives the narrative of Steven Shainberg's film *Secretary* (2002) that, as Caroline Walters explores, reveals the ways sadomasochism (SM) is normalised through the conventions of romantic comedy. For Walters, contexts of marriage, therapeutic healing and courting risk seek to sanction the non-normative acts of SM in largely heteronormative ways. This assimilation encourages positive sexual practice, rendering SM as far from pathological. In 'Smutty Swedes: Sex Films, Pornography and "Good Sex"', Susanna Paasonen examines articulations of 'Swedish sin' through the competing discourses of sexual health and degeneracy. Paasonen explains how the US-produced *Swedish Erotica* series (circa 1977–2008) and the Super 8 films of Lasse Braun contributed to the tensions found in a perceived Scandinavian culture of sexual liberation and immorality. The transgressions of the sexually liberal also underpin Martin Fradley's account of cinema's fascination with 'socio-sexual conditioning'. In '"Does this look sexual to you?" Neoliberal Culture and Everyday Perversion in Recent Cinema', Fradley discusses a range of films from *The Girlfriend Experience* (Steven Soderbergh, 2009) to *A Serbian Film* (Srđan Spasojević, 2010), evaluating the ways in which cinema responds to sexualisation in culture under the conditions of neoliberalism.

Part Three – 'Coming of Age: Generational Encounters and Dangerous Liaisons' – focuses on the culturally contentious issues that discursively emerge through intergenerational desires, relationships and confrontations. In 'Larry Clark's Sex Education: Adolescent Sexuality and the Denial of Denial', Sarah Arnold asks us to reconsider the controversy that often encumbers Clark's aesthetic approach to representing teen sex on screen. Negating the politics of the liberal left and moral right, Arnold sees *Kids* (1995) and *Ken Park* (2002) as drawing attention to, as well as rejecting, the denial of adolescent sexuality. In 'The Age of Perversion: *L'ennui*, Erotic Combat and Intergenerational Existentialism', Beth Johnson examines how pitiless intimacy, sexual excess and boredom express the perverse relationship at the centre of Cédric Kahn's *L'ennui* (1998). The sexual bond between philosophy professor Martin (Charles Berling) and teenager Cécilia (Sophia Guillemin) acknowledges and unites generational differences in similar conditions of existential despair, boredom and abandon. The uninhibited and intemperate tone in Clark and Kahn's respective films often elicits unease, which Clarissa Smith notes is a defining quality of her experience writing about Christophe Honoré's *Ma mère* (2004). Evocative of a Bataillean sense of eroticism and death, Smith notes how the story of mother–son incest corrupts revered familial relationships in a culture of transgression, questioning the comfort of intimacy they ordinarily afford.

The final section – 'Sexual Infidelity: Adapting the Deviant, Re-imagining the Perverse' – presents ways in which perversion is managed through inter-dependent exchanges, which not only challenge fidelity debates in adaptation but also reconfigure perceptions of the original source material. In 'Perverting the Marquis de Sade', Sarah Taylor-Harman looks at the on-screen rehabilitation of the notorious libertine with particular focus on the displacement of his sexual violence in Philip Kaufman's *Quills* (2000). Taylor-Harman goes on to demonstrate how Sade is further re-imagined in subsequent erotic fan fiction based on the film, illustrating awareness of the fluid and complex sexual politics that circulate around him. The ability of adaptation to recover in order to discover, evident in Taylor-Harman work, also informs Guy Barefoot's essay, '"Something sweet": *Little Children*, the Sex Offender and Emma Bovary's Eyes'. While identifying significant omissions and alterations in the film adaptation, Barefoot is careful to note that this does not produce a poorer version of Tom Perrotta's novel but instead intentionally produces a new ambiguity that circulates around paedophile Ronnie (Jackie Earle Haley). Finally, the figure of the paedophile is also the focus of the last essay in the collection. In '*Let the Right One In* and the Wrong One Go: Paedophilia and Film Culture', Darren Kerr looks at how the erasing of one character's paedophilia in the process of adapting John Ajvide Lindqvist's novel draws attention to distinctions between sexual attraction and physical abuse. For Kerr, this illustrates the ways in which a marginal history of cinema has repeatedly reflected on the cultural need to confront demonisation, find a coherent language and present openly dialogic narratives tackling the politics of paedophilia.

In editing this collection of essays it is clear that the critical and cultural concept of perversion – contested historically, scientifically and theoretically – is repeatedly re-imagined and challenged on screen in inter- and extratextual ways. Many of the films at the centre of these essays were produced to provoke an audience into thinking differently about perversion, just as the writers of these essays, and the approaches they take, aim to similarly encourage the reader to look again. This has likewise informed our choice of cover image for this collection. With a finger to his lips, Coach's hush not only asks for silence but quietly coerces, makes complicit and offers an articulation of perverse behaviours that, for the writers in this collection, demand to be spoken about, read and heard. The direct address of the image captures the necessity to engage an audience directly in the various modes and methods of theorising, historicising and analysing the representation of perversion on screen.

Notes

1. Vicky Lebeau, *Childhood and Cinema* (London: Reaktion Books, 2008), p. 129.
2. Kathryn Bond Stockton, *The Queer Child, or Growing Sideways in the Twentieth Century* (Durham, NC and London: Duke University Press, 2009), p. 121.
3. Lauren Berlant, 'Structures of unfeeling: *Mysterious Skin*', *Journal of Politics, Culture and Society* 28/3 (September 2015), pp. 191–213.
4. Peter Bowen, 'The wonder years', *Filmmaker Magazine* (Spring 2005).
5. Ibid.
6. Lenny Abrahamson used a similar method when directing eight-year-old Jacob Tremblay in *Room* (2015). See Kermode and Mayo's Film Review, 'With Leonardo DiCaprio and Lenny Abrahamson', BBC Radio 5, 15 January 2016. Available at http://www.bbc.co.uk/programmes/b06vfcqk (accessed 27 January 2016).
7. S. F. Said, 'Close encounters', *Sight & Sound* 15/6 (June 2005), pp. 32–4.
8. Garry Maddox and Alexa Moses, 'Pedophilia theme sparks film ban call', *The Sydney Morning Herald*, 19 July 2005. Available at http://www.smh.com.au/news/film/call-for-film-to-be-banned/2005/07/18/1121538915851.html (accessed 12 April 2013).
9. Ibid.
10. Said, 'Close Encounters', pp. 32–4.
11. Peter Knegt, 'Decade: Gregg Araki on *Mysterious Skin*', *Indiewire*, 19 December 2009. Available at http://www.indiewire.com/article/decade_gregg_arak (accessed 12 April 2013).
12. B. Ruby Rich, 'Beyond Doom: Gregg Araki's *Mysterious Skin*', *New Queer Cinema: The Director's Cut* (Durham, NC and London: Duke University Press), p. 95.
13. Reproduced in Jon Lewis, *Hollywood v. Hard Core: How the Struggle Over Censorship Created the Modern Film Industry* (New York and London: New York University, 2002), pp. 302–7.

14. Ibid.
15. Julie Peakman, *The Pleasure's All Mine: A History of Perverse Sex* (London: Reaktion Books, 2013), p. 8.
16. Igor Primoratz, *Ethics and Sex* (London: Routledge, 2003), p. 65.
17. Andreas De Block and Pieter R. Adriaens provide an excellent and detailed historical review of how sexual deviance has been categorised in 'Pathologizing sexual deviance: A history', *Journal of Sex Research* 50/3–4 (2013), pp. 276–98.
18. Harry Oosterhuis, 'Richard von Krafft-Ebing's step-children of nature: Psychiatry and the making of homosexual identity', in Kim M. Phillips and Barry Reay (eds), *Sexualities in History: A Reader* (New York: Routledge, 2002), p. 277.
19. Richard von Krafft-Ebing, *Psychopathia Sexualis: A Medico Forensic Study*, translated by Franklin S. Klaf (New York: Arcade Publishing, 1965), p. vii. Originally published 1886.
20. Ibid., p. 54.
21. Oosterhuis, 'Richard von Krafft-Ebing's step-children of nature', p. 277.
22. Kim M. Phillips and Barry Reay (eds) *Sexualities in History: A Reader* (New York: Routledge, 2002), p. 13.
23. Iwan Bloch, *The Sexual Life of Our Time in its Relation to Modern Civilization*, translated from the sixth German edition by M. Eden Paul (London: Rebman, 1909); Sigmund Freud, *Three Essays on the Theory of Sexuality*, translated by James Strachey (New York: Basic Books, 1962), originally published 1905; Havelock Ellis, *Sex in Relation to Society* (Philadelphia, PA: F. A. Davis Company, 1913); Alfred C. Kinsey and the Institute for Sex Research, *Sexual Behavior in the Human Male* (Philadelphia, PA: W. B. Saunders Co., 1948) and *Sexual Behavior in the Human Female* (Philadelphia: Saunders, 1953).
24. Steeves Demazeux and Patrick Singy, 'Introduction', *The DSM-5 in Perspective: Philosophical Reflections on the Psychiatric Babel* (New York: Springer, 2015), p. xiii.
25. American Psychiatric Association, *Diagnostic and Statistical Manual of Mental Disorders* (Washington, DC: Author, 1952), pp. 38–9. Homosexuality was removed from the DSM by the American Psychiatric Association in 1973. Later editions and revisions were published in 1968 (DSM-II), 1980 (DSM-III), 1987 (DSM-III-R), 1994 (DSM-IV), 2000 (DSM-IV-R) and 2013 (DSM-5).
26. Key works include Georges Bataille's *L'Erotism*, originally published in 1957 and Michel Foucault's three volume *History of Sexuality*, originally published in 1976 (volume 1: *The Will to Knowledge*) and 1984 (volume 2: *The Use of Pleasure* and volume 3: *The Care of the Self*). See Georges Bataille, *Erotism: Death and Sensuality*, translated by Mary Dalwood (San Francisco, CA: City Lights Books, 1987); Michel Foucault, *History of Sexuality. Volume 1: An Introduction*, translated by Robert Hurley (New York: Pantheon Books, 1978).
27. Robert Stoller, *Perversion: the Erotic Form of Hatred* (New York: Pantheon Books, 1975).
28. Jeffery Weeks, *Sexuality and Its Discontents* (London: Routledge and Kegan Paul, 1985), p. 13.

29. Lisa Downing and Dany Nobus (eds), *Perversion: Psychoanalytic Perspectives/ Perspectives on Psychoanalysis* (London: Karnac, 2006).

30. See, for example, Judith Butler, *Gender Trouble: Feminism and the Subversion of Identity* (New York: Routledge, 1990); Judith Butler, *Bodies that Matter: On the Discursive Limits of 'Sex'* (New York: Routledge, 1993); Teresa de Lauretis, *The Practice of Love: Lesbian Sexuality and Perverse Desire* (Bloomington, IN: Indiana University Press, 1994).

31. Judith Halberstam, *Female Masculinity* (Durham, NC and London: Duke University Press, 1998), pp. 52–3.

32. Tanya Krzywinska, *Sex and the Cinema* (London: Wallflower, 2006), p. 229.

33. Linda Williams, *Screening Sex* (Durham, NC and London: Duke University Press, 2008), p. 2.

34. Krzywinska, *Sex and the Cinema*, p. 115.

35. Primoratz, *Ethics and Sex*, p. 50.

I

Reviled Bodies: Fantasies, Realities and the Boundaries of the Explicit

1

Straight Necrophilia as a Queer Perversion in Lynne Stopkewich's *Kissed*

Lisa Downing

Introduction: From Mimetic to Queer in One Short Century

When Hallward claims that 'Love is a more wonderful thing than art' in Oscar Wilde's *The Picture of Dorian Gray*, he is immediately corrected by Lord Henry, who states that 'they are both simply forms of imitation.'[1] A century later, postmodern aesthetic theories draw attention to the hollow at the centre of imitative theories of art; they point to a proliferation of simulacra, which have no original meaning or foundation in the 'real' world. Such logic is also prevalent within theories of gender and sexuality. Judith Butler is primary among those thinkers who aim to destabilise ideas of natural and original 'femininity' and 'masculinity'. She writes, '*gender is a kind of imitation for which there is no original*; in fact it is a kind of imitation that produces the very notion of the original as an *effect* and consequence of the imitation itself'.[2] Rejecting the Platonic idea of mimesis still visible in Wilde, Butler foregrounds gender as a series of self-perpetuating repetitions and identifies 'performativity' as the means by which (gendered) identities are shored up and come to pass as natural.

The loosening of concepts of masculinity and femininity from a pre-existing reality is equalled by a systematic denaturalisation of sexual identities. Butler goes on to note that 'there are no direct expressive or causal links between sex, gender, gender presentation, sexual practice, fantasy and sexuality. None of these terms captures or determines the rest.'[3] Such Butlerian soundbites have had wide-ranging political implications. In recent years, a shift in ideological focus has occurred within gay and lesbian studies from identity politics (positive identification within an oppressed group) to queer theory. Queer theory posits, after Michel Foucault, that identifying too closely with the terms 'gay' and 'lesbian' may be dangerous as it implies the existence of essential identities reducible to these names.[4] Rejecting this essentialism, queer theory calls for a plurality in the expression and understanding of desire; a mode of sexual *becoming* rather than *being*. It seeks not to replace heteronormativity with 'homonormativity', but, in Alexander Doty's words, to 'challenge or transgress established *straight or gay and lesbian* understandings of gender and sexuality'.[5]

Some theorists, mostly notably Calvin Thomas, have already begun to ask, in this age of postmodern gender studies, whether 'queer' ways of representing and conceptualising identities and practices might be applicable to heterosexual, but non-hetero*normative*, modes of desire.[6] What of sexualities between men and women that exclude reproduction and even genital sexuality? Can representations of such sexualities challenge the containing framework – or only the content – of dominant models of relationality and sex? Other theorists, especially Lacanian queer theorist Tim Dean, have suggested that *desire itself* might be essentially 'queer'. Dean theorises that desire has no aim other than its own satisfaction and that any object – 'the gaze, the voice, the phoneme, the lips, the rim of the anus [...] the slit formed by the eyelids' – is as 'proper' a target of desire as genitality.[7] In this understanding, it is the heteropatriarchal order, rather than 'nature', which demands that heterosexuality reproduce itself. And, moreoever, in light of this understanding, the practices of the subject that clinical sexology would term the 'paraphiliac', 'pervert' or 'fetishist' become exemplary forms of desiring.

Keeping in mind this understanding that heterosexual desire may queer itself and that perversion may, in short, offer a paradigmatic model of sexuality, I explore Lynne Stopkewich's *Kissed* (1996), which uses female necrophilia to disrupt and subvert conventional assumptions about male/female and masculine/feminine desires and sexual behaviours. The film displaces meaning and import away from sexual difference and onto the difference between life and death as the marker of desire. The focus on the desire of a living subject for dead matter in the film suggests a disruption of the order of 'reproductive futurism', as described by Lee Edelman in his manifesto of 'antisocial' queer theory, *No Future*.[8] By focusing on a female pervert, moreover, the film potentially goes a step further than Edelman's work, which uses, as its case studies, non-reproductive males, including Ebenezer Scrooge and a selection of Hitchcock's marriage-dodging men. *Kissed* thereby offers a filmic version of queer that is gender-transgressive and paradoxically both 'straight' and 'perverted' for a nascent *fin-de-siècle* twentieth-century audience.

Kissed and the Construction of Default Modes of Sexuality

Kissed focuses on Sandra (Molly Parker), a practicing necrophiliac, who embarks on a relationship with a medical student, Matt (Peter Outerbridge). Their relationship becomes impossible, as he is unable to accept her continuing desire to make love to the corpses at the funeral home where she works. The film ends when he commits suicide by hanging himself, in order to make a 'gift' to her of his corpse. 'I love you', she assures him, seconds before he dies. 'No you don't', he replies, just before he kicks away the chair, 'but you will'.

As well as being directed by a young woman and centring on a young female protagonist, *Kissed* is based on the 1992 short story 'We So Seldom Look on Love' by the female Canadian author Barbara Gowdy. This three-woman show is a deliberate directorial choice. In an interview featured on the video release, Stopkewich comments:

> I liked the idea that this necrophile was a woman. Given that
> men are generally portrayed in film as sexual aggressors, I

21

> thought that a female protagonist in charge of her own sexuality
> was an idea I wanted to work with, despite the taboo nature of
> her particular predilection.[9]

This statement firstly suggests that the reversal of gender roles is itself a powerful strategy for transforming an apparently sclerotic, immovable ideology. Secondly, however, it implies that what is at stake is an individual, unified 'sexual subject', rather than the 'impersonal' workings of desire in line with Dean, or the occupation of the 'position' of cultural death drive that Lee Edelman advocates. This attempt to shed different light on the category 'woman', without collapsing the stability of that category, might suggest a less-than-queer agenda. However, this caveat in place, I am persuaded that the film's internal logic nevertheless succeeds in refusing positivistic models of sexual identity in several ways.

The film in fact demonstrates in a particularly striking way how the construction of sexual and gendered identity functions by constituting a series of scenes from Sandra's life that reveal, through juxtaposition, the social implications and rituals of her sexuality. The film opens with scenes of Sandra's childhood, overlaid with an autobiographical voiceover, in which we witness her preparing the bodies of dead animals for burial, rubbing their blood on her face and body and, finally, cutting into their bodies. The film depicts the elaborate codes and ceremonies that she constructs to symbolise her desire for death, in conscious parallel with the more usual representations of girlish rite-of-passage experiments with boys, make-up and clothes.

While a myth of the neoliberal individual – 'choosing' from a range of options with regard to gender presentation and sexual 'lifestyle' – is perpetuated in these images of personal growth and individual fantasy, the importance of the social milieu is also highlighted. On leaving school, Sandra takes a job at a funeral home, where she goes on to have sexual contact with human corpses. The funeral home functions as a perverted microcosm of mainstream society, as the employees are all revealed to be practicing necrophiles. They are also portrayed as fitting certain stereotypes of the sexual pervert recognisable to the student of sexuality and gender. Jan (James Timmons) is a romantic idealist who worships the bodies of middle-aged mother figures (the Freudian pervert). Mr Wallis (Jay Brazeau) is pragmatic and prolific in his sexual consumption of the bodies of young boys, dismissing them as 'meat' (the stereotypical gay male predator). Sandra describes her orgasms, achieved by rubbing her clitoris on the faces of corpses, as transcendental experiences (the hysterical mystic). Thus, the lexicon of sexual perversion recognisable from mainstream sexological discourse is put under the deconstructive lens by means of its displacement into the context of an imagined necrophile community.

The members of this 'community' both do and do not have more in common with each other than they have with the sexual majority – what we might call, after Erich Fromm, 'biophiles'.[10] Fromm claims that necrophilic (or necrophilous) is the opposite of biophilic (or biophilous). He uses the terms to describe personality types, rather than sexual preferences or positions. However, in the case of *Kissed*, 'biophilia' can be deployed to refer to a pro-reproductive, pro-intercourse heterosexual positionality that is in contradistinction to Molly's anti-reproductive, necrophilic desires. The fractures and dissents within the group of necrophiles depicted in *Kissed* (Sandra and Jan assert, sentimentally, that a corpse is aware when you make love to it; Mr Wallis retorts that it is just insentient flesh) reinforces with dark humour the idea that a common object-choice is not enough to ensure a stable group identity. The sex of the object of desire is certainly an important factor – Sandra only loves young dead males, Jan old dead females, Mr Wallis dead boys – but the fact of their shared necrophilia makes the question of sexual difference (for once) into a *secondary* characteristic.

In some scenes, the codes of this alternative 'community' and the codes of the living heterosexual society are put into direct – and uneasy – dialogue. One of the central sequences of the film shows Sandra having sex with Matt for the first time. She lies flat on the bed as he makes love to her. Most of his body is out of shot, and we are presented with a close-up focus on her face, revealed to be passive, poised, disinterested and with closed eyes. The scene then cuts to a high camera angle shot of the double bed in a darkened room. A restless Sandra, unable to sleep, rises from the bed and leaves Matt still sleeping. We then cut to a shot of her running through a forest. The next scene – lasting

Fig. 1.1. Sandra (Molly Parker) caresses the object of her desire in *Kissed* (Lynne Stopkewich, Boneyard Film Company, 1996)

more than three minutes of real time – is of Sandra in the morgue of the funeral home, making frenzied love to the corpse of a young man (see Fig. 1.1).

Stopkewich's use of lighting in these scenes is both significant and problematic for the current reading. The interior of Matt's bedroom is dark and shadowy, in stark contrast to the light that floods the scenes of Sandra in the mortuary. In Gowdy's short story, the narrator describes having seen 'cadavers shining like stars'.[11] When filming Sandra's orgasm with a corpse, light is used to suggest transcendence as well as pleasure. The scenes of Sandra's orgasms on top of the corpse are sometimes five stops overexposed, suggesting a supplanting of the naturalistic everyday with some extraordinary flight of consciousness.[12] Similarly, in scenes of Sandra's everyday life, she is often the only character who is back-lit.

This cinematic language of enlightenment is ambiguous. This repeated association of Sandra with light functions to foreground her as the centre of consciousness. This would suggest the upholding of the rationalistic (masculine) model, which holds that 'truth' is attainable through the assertion of subjective identity. However, there is perhaps something self-conscious and ironic in the dull obscurity that is shown to characterise heterosexual sex and the 'clarification' offered by alternative perverted practices. Thus, the filmic language of light may become a way of playing on existing associations and epistemological frameworks concerning sexuality.

The sequence described above highlights the way in which Sandra's sexual relationship with the living medical student is to be read as a mere hiatus in her necrophilic lifestyle. Sex with Matt is shown to be innocuous but wholly unfulfilling. Importantly, it is not shown to be demeaning, humiliating or violent, merely uninteresting and 'straight'. This inverts the discourse that has heterosexual sex as the default paradigm of desire. It is possible to read this as an allusion and response to the masculine conceit of the myth of the healing rape, the act of sexual intercourse that puts the deviant female back on the sexual straight-and-narrow.

This conceit is surprisingly common, even in apparently 'progressive' filmmaking that is contemporaneous with Stopkewich's film. In Kevin Smith's *Chasing Amy* (1997), for example, Alyssa's (Joey Lauren Adams) 'lesbianism' is revealed as a temporary blip when she finds and embarks on a sexual relationship with Holden (Ben Affleck), the 'man of her dreams'. While her history of lesbianism does not disturb him, it is only when he discovers that in high school she experimented with male sexual partners – sometimes several at the same time – that he proclaims himself unable to carry on their relationship. I would suggest that the implicit misogyny of this film is not political but ontological. It lies not in the undermining of Alyssa's 'stable lesbian position' when she is shown having sex with a man, but in the underlying assumption that the meanings attributed to types of sexual activity by the masculine-heterosexual economy reveal a fundamental 'truth'. The film is reactionary in its belief that Alyssa's sexual identity is reducible to her hidden desire for a specific act and object choice and – more importantly – that this 'sexual identity' reveals the whole of her subjectivity. In *Kissed*, on the other hand, the signifying power of sexual intercourse is wholly defused. Sandra's necrophilia goes unchallenged, while it is Matt's male heterosexual 'biophilia' that is called into question by his encounter with otherness. Indeed, his final gesture is to die, to become a corpse, which effectively means transforming himself into an object with value in her sexual economy. This is a dark and transgressive twist on the cliché of the dowdy woman who transforms herself into a 'vamp' in order to signify within the heterosexual language of desire.

I have hinted above that there is a constant implicit tension between the film's tendency to assert Sandra's subjectivity as a stable centre of consciousness and a contradictory vein that is parodic and self-deconstructing of notions of identity. One way of reconciling these elements is to suggest that Stopkewich playfully demonstrates the extreme outcome of the logic of solipsistic subjectivity. This sexual subject, defiantly defining her worldview, ends by watching her lover sacrifice himself in the interests of her pleasure. Matt's suicide in the hope of being posthumously loved by Sandra is one of the most controversial elements of the film. Critics are extremely divided on the effectiveness of this conceit. In a very 'straight' reading of the film, Erwan Higuinen comments on the 'paradoxical normalisation of deviance to which the script's impasse bears witness in making of necrophilia a mere obstacle to conjugal happiness'.[13] However, according to Charlotte O'Sullivan, the *dénouement* is the most successful part of the film. She suggests that, following Matt's suicide, 'suddenly this corpse of a movie comes to life'.[14] She goes on to describe the motif of male-suicide-as-gift as simultaneously repulsive and pleasure-giving to the spectator.

These opposing reactions from a male and female critic are telling. I would suggest that the pleasure O'Sullivan draws attention to comes from the skewing of audience expectations regarding the gender of desire and death. In *Narcissus and Echo*, Naomi Segal analyses the narrative tradition in which a woman's death is narrated and given meaning by a surviving male protagonist. She writes that such a story's significance belongs 'to the hero who speaks, not to the heroine who dies'.[15] Guy Austin has recently taken up Segal's model and shown that it applies to a tradition of (mainly French) cinematic narratives as well as to the *récit*, the literary genre that Segal analyses.[16] In *Kissed*, the gendered relation of speaking agent and dying object is certainly inverted. However, more radically, the positions of necrophile and corpse (representing life and death) are made to signify, in place of the more usual terms 'masculine' and 'feminine', as the default figures for activity and passivity. Moreover, the victim here is a willing, consensual one, making his death into an unorthodox gift of love. Thus, traditions and stereotypes are repeatedly instated and reversed, systematically undermining sexual semiotics. This suggests a mobilisation and an abstraction of desiring positions, creating a cinema in which possibilities of identification are both liberated and made problematic.

It may, at first, seem that a necrophilic protagonist would be an unlikely figure with which to challenge attitudes towards (female) sexuality, the desire type being such an extreme and unusual one and spectator identification being, perhaps, significantly challenged by this. However, I would like to suggest that necrophilia may offer the best of all paradigms with which to draw attention to the traditional relations of gender and desire at work in cinema. Laura Mulvey's canonical article – on the way in which the woman is constituted as spectacle for the male gaze in narrative cinema – makes mention of the qualities of fixity and one-dimensionality of the female icon, in contradistinction to the male protagonist on screen and the masculine spectator, who produce action and make meaning.[17] Much has been written after Mulvey, suggesting the freeing-up of her positions of identificatory activity and passivity from notions of feminine/masculine, including works on queer spectatorship that focus on the potentiality of a series of 'identifications which are multiple, contradictory, shifting, oscillating, inconsistent and fluid'.[18]

Maleness and femaleness, masculinity and femininity, offer pale shadows of the ideas of activity and passivity. They wear them awkwardly and under constraint. If the object of the gaze in cinema has to be a fetishised, reified object, what could be a better representational form than the radically immobile corpse? It is overdetermined, literalised. Moreover, just like cinema, necrophilia involves a radical play with mobility and immobility. The lively, desirous imagination of the necrophile and the contrasting stillness of her objects that are rendered beyond the point of desiring have a paradigmatic quality. The extent to which the default model of desire – heterosexual genitality – is a complex construct, an interested ideology rather than a natural or original phenomenon, is revealed in the film by the intimate focus on the series of stages by which a new default model – love of the dead – takes precedence.

Necromantic Comedy

In *Kissed*, death functions to disrupt the traditional gendering of desire, both in terms of inverting mainstream heterosexual norms in which the subject of desire is male and the object female, and in undoing the longstanding psychoanalytic and sexological assumption that perverts, especially fetishistic ones, are always male. Hence, the filmic point-of-view and locus of consciousness are, unusually, female[19] and the default sexual paradigm presented is one of perversion.

In terms of genre, *Kissed* is recognisable as a romantic comedy. As one reviewer comments, 'the plot [...] couldn't be simpler: necrophiliac girl meets boy; boy dies'.[20] The generic form is recognisable, but the content is radically skewed, such that our expectations are destabilised. We think we are on familiar territory, but each time the apparently banal becomes uncanny. In *Kissed*, the cliché of a girl's first kiss in the back of a car is given a darkly humorous treatment, as we witness Sandra's compulsion to embrace her first corpse as the hearse goes through a car wash. Familiar cinematic tropes and conventions are thus played with, collapsed and emptied out, just as stereotypical ideas regarding gender are in turn cited, inverted and parodied.

Most significantly, the traditional romantic comedy ends with marriage and the implicit promise of children – the third term that both interrupts and cements the union of parents and ensures the continuation of reproductive futurism. Stopkewich's narrative, on the other hand, experiments with configurations of a woman's desire for a male bodily object outside of prescribed heterosexual marriage and reproduction. The third term around which desire is structured is the non-return of death. Death functions both to disrupt expectations and to signal, perhaps, the abyssal void at the centre of the myths according to which society functions. When read in this light, the film certainly offers a critique of compulsory heterosexuality and reproduction, which it replaces with death-driven perversion.

A question that subtends my thinking in this chapter has to do with the extent to which cinema – by nature a medium involving performance – can be in a position to say anything valuable about 'performativity' in the Butlerian sense, and thereby contribute to the denaturalisation of 'identity'.

At the most basic level, all narrative film works by seducing its watcher. If we were not a little bit captivated, if we were not ready to suspend disbelief, our interest in the images on screen could not be sustained; the spectacle would appear silly or dull. The images shown are always already mediated by directorial decisions and by the very artificial, manipulative processes that are camerawork and editing. Despite my attempts to demonstrate the ways in which this film self-consciously plays with the traditions it is working in, it nevertheless retains the power of the cinematic medium to seduce the spectator. This is acknowledged by Stopkewich. She comments, 'I didn't want viewers to pull back and intellectualise the scene, or think, "I can't believe what's happening!" I wanted to seduce the viewer as much as possible'.[21] It is by filling the familiar frame with subject matter that is deviant, disturbing and gender-unconventional that Stopkewich makes this seduction into a queer, perverse one.

The film thus allows us to view the object of cinema differently, just as queered perversion offers a different way of imagining desire. The cold, controlled hermetic vision of *Kissed* allows us to slip seamlessly into Sandra's inner world. The aestheticisation of the filmed images may risk anaesthetising a viewer to ethically problematic content.[22] It is almost impossible to know to what extent this manipulation of the audience is in the service of demonstrating the way in which cinema persuades and captivates, and to what extent these experiments collude with the traditions they comment upon. I would argue that the film is self-aware and deconstructive, yet charged with sexually potency. If desire is automatically aroused by the cinematic medium, what sorts of desirous identifications does this film invite the viewer to make, and what are their implications? By foregrounding emotional motifs such as self-sacrifice in the case of Sandra's boyfriend, as well as taboo and transgression, Stopkewich makes acts that are apparently morally dubious or violent become radically ambiguous as their gendered meanings are transformed. Thus, the cinematic narrative plays with conventions of representing desire in such a way as to make moral and political commentary difficult.

Unlike Laura Mulvey and Peter Wollen's experimental film *Riddles of the Sphinx* (1977), which aimed to exclude scopophilic pleasure altogether, *Kissed* clearly retains the traditional structural relationship between the viewer and the pleasurable spectacle, even as it problematises straightforward expectations of pleasure by including material that may evoke shock or disgust. Indeed, it draws on our very familiarity with this mechanism, but replaces the habitual, accepted content (an eroticised living female body presented for the 'masculine' gaze) with perverted content (a dead male body presented in a context of active female desire). It therefore makes visible the habitual gendered politics underlying the deployment of the mechanism. Following the logic of thinkers such as Butler, an artistic product that reveals, by its very construction, the lack of inevitability or 'naturalness' of the 'founding myths' of sexuality would be truly, and radically, queer. And, in light of the work of perversion theorists such as Joel Whitebook (1995), who argues that perversion marks a creative or utopian alternative to stagnant narratives of inevitable heterosexual desire and reproductive instinct,[23] we can contend that Lynne Stopkewich's film innovates by casting a queer eye on heterosexual ambition and deliberately perverting socially meaningful sexed relations as well as conventional gender positions.[24]

Notes

1. Oscar Wilde, *The Picture of Dorian Gray* (Oxford: Oxford University Press, 1974), p. 84. Originally published 1890.
2. Judith Butler, 'Imitation and gender insubordination', in Henry Abelove, Michèle Aina Barale and David M. Halperin (eds), *The Lesbian and Gay Studies Reader* (London: Routledge, 1993), p. 313. Original emphasis.
3. Ibid., p. 315.
4. Michel Foucault, *Histoire de la sexualité 1: La volonté de savoir* (Paris: Gallimard, 1976).
5. Alexander Doty, 'Queer theory', in John Hill and Pamela Church Gibson (eds), *The Oxford Guide to Film Studies* (Oxford: Oxford University Press, 1998), p. 149. My emphasis.
6. Calvin Thomas, *Straight with a Twist: Queer Theory and the Subject of Heterosexuality* (Urbana and Chicago: University of Illinois Press, 2000).
7. Tim Dean, *Beyond Sexuality* (Chicago: Chicago University Press, 2000), p. 194.
8. Lee Edelman, *No Future: Queer Theory and the Death Drive* (Durham and London: Duke University Press, 2004).
9. Lynne Stopkewich, Interview, *Kissed*, Tartan Video (1998).
10. Erich Fromm, *The Anatomy of Human Destructiveness* (London: Cape, 1973).
11. Barbara Gowdy, 'We So Seldom Look on Love', in *We So Seldom Look on Love: Stories by Barbara Gowdy* (Toronto: Somerville House, 1997), p. 170.

12. See Michael X. Ferraro, 'Passion, postmortem', *American Cinematographer* (April 1998), p. 66.
13. Erwan Higuinen, '*Kissed* de Lynne Stopkwich', *Cahiers du cinéma* (April 1998), p. 81. Author's translation.
14. Charlotte O'Sullivan, '*Kissed*', *Sight and Sound* (January 1998), p. 48.
15. Naomi Segal, *Narcissus and Echo: Women in the French récit* (Manchester: Manchester University Press, 1988), p. 12.
16. Guy Austin, *Contemporary French Cinema* (Manchester: Manchester University Press, 1996), p. 55.
17. Laura Mulvey, 'Visual pleasure and narrative cinema', *Screen* 16/3 (Autumn 1975), p. 20.
18. Caroline Evans and Lorraine Gamman, 'The gaze revisited or reviewing queer viewing', in Paul Burston and Colin Richardson (eds), *A Queer Romance: Lesbians, Gay Men and Popular Culture* (London: Routledge, 1995), p. 45.
19. See Lucy Bolton, *Film and Female Consciousness: Irigaray, Cinema and Thinking Women* (Basingstoke: Palgrave Macmillan, 2011).
20. O'Sullivan, '*Kissed*', p. 47.
21. Cited in Ferraro, 'Passion, postmortem', p. 66.
22. Lisa Downing and Libby Saxton, *Film and Ethics: Foreclosed Encounters* (London and New York: Routledge, 2009).
23. Joel Whitebook, *Perversion and Utopia: A Study in Psychoanalysis and Critical Theory* (Cambridge, MA: MIT Press, 1995).
24. I wish to thank Sue Harris, Robert Gillett, Alison Martin, Donna Peberdy and Darren Kerr for their suggestions, advice and comments on this piece of work at different stages of its development.

2

The Love That Dare Not Speak Its Name: *O Fantasma* and Erotomania

John Mercer

The final scene of João Pedro Rodrigues' arresting feature film debut *O Fantasma/Phantom* (2000) presents a dystopian vision of an isolated young gay man, increasingly removed from the world of human interactions, living an existence of almost complete silence by night. Sérgio (Ricardo Meneses), the lonely, alienated and sexually ambiguous protagonist of the film, finds himself rejected by the object of his romantic obsession. The rejection that Sérgio experiences has dramatic consequences for all concerned, with the protagonist becoming a fugitive after the culmination of his sexual fixation with a stranger who he abducts in a manner that is simultaneously extreme and futile. Finally alone in the alien landscape of a landfill site, reduced to living an asocial existence, Sérgio's story offers a stark and pessimistic picture of the outcomes of the extremes of obsessive behaviour and an over-investment in the possibility of gay romance.

This chapter discusses the theme of sexual and romantic obsession in gay cinema and, in particular, the most extreme variant of romantic obsession: erotomania. In J.C. Bucknill and D.H. Tuke's nineteenth-century *Manual of Psychological Medicine*, prefaced with a vignette of photogravures illustrating 'types of insanity', the condition is defined as being:

> restricted to those cases which are characterised by excessive love for an object, whether real or imaginary. In this disorder [...] the imagination alone is affected; there is an error of the understanding; it is a mental affection in which amatory delusions rule [...] In erotomania, the sentiment which characterises it is in the head [...] The erotomaniac is [...] the sport of the imagination.[1]

Erotomania, then, is a form of psychosis where an individual believes a romantic connection exists between them and an individual who is often a complete stranger. This delusion leads to obsessive behaviours including stalking and potentially abduction and harm. *O Fantasma* clearly articulates the extremities of the condition for dramatic purposes.

Sexual and romantic obsession is a recurrent narrative trope across a wide range of cinemas. From examples as diverse in content and form as the many versions of Charlotte Brontë's *Wuthering Heights* (1847) to thrillers such as *Play Misty For Me* (Clint Eastwood, 1971) and *Fatal Attraction* (Adrian Lyne, 1987) to the art cinema of *Last Tango in Paris* (Bernardo Bertolucci, 1972) and *In the Realm of the Senses/Ai no korîda* (Nagia Ôshima, 1976), we discover that powerful feelings of sexual attraction, the over-investment in romance or an ideal of romance often lead to tragedy. The obsessed figure of the erotomaniac is, more often than not, situated as a marginalised and demonised figure because of their overwhelming and disruptive sexual drives and therefore positioned as a threat to normative sexuality. The consequences of their actions often result in death and almost always in their expulsion from the narrative in order for equilibrium to be re-established. In cinema that focuses on heterosexual romance, this is naturally just one (though perhaps the most lurid and sensational example) of the many narrative constructions that frame our understanding of the nature of sex and romantic attachment. By contrast, in this chapter I argue that this trope is one of the central narrative themes of cinema that deals with homosexuality and gay desire and I use the controversial example of *O Fantasma* to explore this assertion. To situate and make sense of this claim, the chapter places the film within a lineage of cinema either made by, or speaking to, a gay audience that attempts to articulate the extremes of gay romantic passion.

I should clarify at this point that the purpose of this chapter within the context of this collection is not to argue that homosexuality is a perversion. This is not to say that there are not many examples in the history of cinema where the figure of the homosexual has been deployed to epitomise perversion and sexual depravity. This is a subject discussed at some length in Robert Hilliard's *Hollywood Speaks Out* and more specifically (and pointedly) in Robin Wood's essay 'The murderous gays: Hitchcock's homophobia'.[2] Instead, this chapter looks at a particular narrative and discursive tendency in cinema made by or for gay audiences that frequently equates gay desire and romantic love with an unhealthy and ultimately self-destructive obsession. This extension of the romantic notion of doomed or unrequited love seems central to articulations of gay desire.[3] In this chapter I ask the question, why is it that, in cinema, gay desire is so often positioned as an impossibility?

Uncomfortably Numb

O Fantasma is the story of refuse collector Sérgio, whose isolated and alienated nocturnal existence collecting the waste of the residents of Lisbon is divided between time spent at the Department of Sanitation depot and his clandestine sexual encounters in the back streets and public toilets of the city. Sérgio lives in a sordid rooming house and is invisible to everyone apart from co-worker Fatima (Beatriz Torcado), whose attempts at intimacy he repeatedly rejects. His only friend and apparent focus of identification is Lorde, the dog housed at the depot.

During his nightly collection rounds, Sérgio has a chance meeting with João (Andre Barbosa), a handsome, motorbike-riding suburbanite, and becomes sexually fixated with him. Sérgio follows João around the streets of the city and visits his home nightly, stealing swimming trunks and gloves from his garbage as his fixation escalates. By contrast, João is scarcely aware of the existence of the person who takes away his waste until Sérgio's stalking becomes apparent in a scene where he makes an abortive attempt at communicating his feelings. Rejected by João, Sérgio substitutes the emotional attachment he seems to desire with a sequence of anonymous sexual encounters with men on the city streets. From pick-ups in public toilets to sex with security guards and policemen, these encounters are cold, transactional and emotionally detached. His visits to João's home become more frequent and more insistent until he breaks into his home and marks the territory of his chosen mate by urinating in his room and on his bed. Finally, Sérgio is arrested. His capture acts as a catalyst for his final descent into his most extreme behaviour. Handcuffed, he escapes detention, returns to the depot and tries to enlist Fatima in breaking open his chains. The woman he has so insistently rejected now rejects him and Sérgio runs into the Lisbon backstreets to hide.

In a disruptive leap in the narrative, the next we see of Sérgio is in a reprise of the scene that opens the film, involving the protagonist dressed as the latex-clad 'Phantom' of the film's title, presumably at the home of the pick-up who has relieved him of his handcuffs in exchange for fetishistic sex (see Fig. 2.1). The pick-up lies prone on the bed while a dog howls at the bedroom door. We are left with the uncertain feeling that the anonymous male could either be sleeping or dead. Sérgio, apparently transfigured by

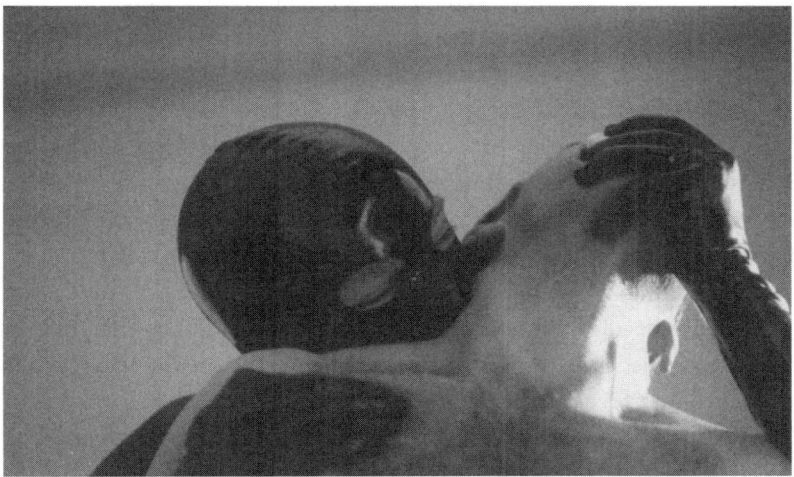

Fig. 2.1. Sérgio (Ricardo Meneses) as the 'Phantom' in *O Fantasma* (João Pedro Rodrigues, Rosa Filmes, 2000)

this experience and his new persona, returns to João's home, breaks into his room and abducts him, dragging the bound and gagged object of his affection through the night-time streets like a prized item retrieved from the garbage. Once again, we are uncertain as to what Sérgio's intentions may be and, when he finally deposits his terrified abductee in a back street and begins to beat and taunt him, we expect that his desire must be rape and murder. However, at the final moment, he appears to have some change of heart and runs away, leaving João bound but unharmed. With the object of his affections left behind and the possibility of a return to normality gone, Sérgio stalks the night streets in the manner of a dog and rides in the back of a refuse van to a landfill on the edge of the city. In this alien landscape he seems finally and curiously in his place.

O Fantasma was the first feature film made by João Pedro Rodrigues, a director who has attracted critical attention for a relatively small body of work since the initial controversy that the film attracted, both in his native Portugal and internationally. The controversy around the film focused on two interrelated issues: the sex and the conditions of production. The film's graphic depictions of real sex acts (including a brief but notorious scene of fellatio in a public toilet) were a topic of discussion when the film was in competition at the Venice Film Festival in 2000. Similarly, the film was criticised in Portugal on two counts. Firstly, and unsurprisingly, the film attracted attention because of its explicit sex scenes and sensational subject matter. Secondly, its production context was the cause of some controversy, in particular because it was partly funded by Rádio e Televisão de Portugal RTP, the Portuguese state-funded public service broadcaster, and by the Institute of the Cinema Audiovisual and Multimedia, a government body.

While popular reception of the film was coloured by the furore surrounding the delicious collision of sexual depravity and public money, critical reception was additionally inflected with ambivalence. Critics struggled to decide what kind of film *O Fantasma* was and how to position it. For example, on its American release, Dennis Lim in *The Village Voice* described the film as 'the artiest queer stroke movie of the year', whereas in *The New York Times* A.O. Scott criticised the film for being 'both grueling and dull' and as a 'glum, numb experience'.[4]

The range of, sometimes contradictory, responses that the film has provoked emerge exactly because it is a text that does not allow for easy sense-making. In fact, as I will explore subsequently in this chapter, the film denies it. This is not least because of the uncomfortable, ambiguous and often problematic representations of gay desire, articulated through the psychopathology of erotomania that the film offers. Critical and popular responses, oscillating between titillation, outrage and boredom, reproduce the responses that the text itself seems designed to elicit.

Cursed Fantasy

O Fantasma can be situated and understood within three traditions or cinematic practices. Firstly, it evidences a stylistic mode that is characteristic of aspects of Portuguese cinema. Rodrigues' cinematic output self-consciously references a range of sources. While the connections to the touchstones of gay film are perhaps more directly evident and relevant, it is also important to connect the film to a style in Portuguese cinema that uses non-professional actors and a realist or documentary aesthetic. The most obvious point of connection is the work of Pedro Costa and it is clear that in both style and content *O Fantasma* references *Ossos* (1997) and can be compared to *In Vanda's Room* (2000), which was released the same year. The grimy urban locations of these films – their darkness, the untrained performances that contrast the austere formality of their compositional strategies – are very similar. A less obvious connection also exists between this dark, urban aesthetic and the work of the most celebrated of Portuguese filmmakers, Manoel de Oliveira, who often elides documentary and fiction as generic and formal categories in order to call into question their 'ontological status'.[5]

Secondly, the film can be regarded as a contemporary addition to the canon of texts that might be organised under the collective category of *'films maudits'*. Originating from the 1949 Biarritz event *Le Festival du Films Maudits*, organised by the group *Objectif 49* (that included Cocteau, Bresson and Bazin, among others), the term refers back to nineteenth-century French poets Rimbaud, Verlaine and Baudelaire, known as the *poetes maudits* for their commitment to living outside respectable society and to challenging social mores. The term *'films maudits'* – which literally translates as 'cursed film' – designates a cinema that might, in a similar vein, be considered 'beyond the pale' on grounds of subject matter, narrative construction or mode of representation. Long before the more recognisable categories of cult cinema or paracinema, *films maudits* were those examples of films that were at the periphery of respectability and morality. In all cases, *films maudits* are distinguished by being the subject of controversy or an ambivalent reception. The films of the 1949 Biarritz exhibition included work such as Bresson's *Les Dames du Bois de Boulogne* (1945), dealing with prostitution, and Kenneth Anger's *Fireworks* (1947) with its experimental structure and homoerotic iconography.

Most of the examples of gay cinema that I will subsequently discuss in this chapter can be described as (and have at points been understood as) *films maudits*. Similarly, many of the films discussed in this edited collection would easily fit within the category of *films maudits*. Therefore it is important to acknowledge that even in an époque where homoerotic and homosexual images are no longer axiomatically taboo there are still instances (as in the case of *O Fantasma*) where the depiction of gay sexuality is so problematic that a film offers representations that situate it within the realm of the *maudit*. The *maudit* epitomises cultural production and modes of expression that are at the margins of acceptability and the images that *O Fantasma* presents are a vivid example of that.

Thirdly (and aligned to the previous categorisation), the film can be understood as belonging to the body of work labelled as gay or queer cinema. There is a very clear lineage and set of reference points that *O Fantasma* can be situated in relationship to, some of them very direct and self-consciously deployed by the director and some of them less so. In all cases it is very clear that the pivotal narrative thematic of gay desire and its articulation in terms of obsession, desperation, and even psychosis, is a recurrent motif across a range of texts understood as constituting a strand of gay cinema.[6]

Most obviously, the film alludes both to the literature of John Rechy and Jean Genet and the film *Un chant d'amour/A Song of Love* (1950). Genet belongs firmly within the tradition of the *poetes maudits*, whose episodic narratives and milieu of petty thieves, policemen, prostitutes and sailors, elevated through a language that finds beauty in degradation, is a key point of narrative and stylistic reference for *O Fantasma*. The prisoners and prison guards of Genet's *Un chant d'amour*, who are physically and psychically distanced from each other, long for emotional and sexual connection while lost in their own fantasies. They clearly find their contemporary articulation in Sérgio, the 'invisible' refuse collector. Rechy's highly sexualised 1970s accounts of the urban gay male experience similarly (though in a much more direct and less poetic way) deal with the potency of passionate gay desire. In his 1977 publication *The Sexual Outlaw: A Documentary*, during a passage that illuminates and reflects upon the same predatory sexual territory that *O Fantasma* covers, Rechy describes the gay experience as 'liberating, adventurous, righteously daring, revolutionary and beautiful in its sexual abundance. At its worst it is a stark vision of hell.'[7] The narrative of *O Fantasma*, then, elides the promiscuous urban gay male's experiences in the work of Rechy with the elevation of the criminality and debasement of Genet.

Similarly, Rainer Werner Fassbinder's elaborate cinematic realisation of *Querelle* (1982) deals with the nature of obsessive love, depicting the seedy underworld of the streets and repressed sexuality of macho environments in the most stylised manner. Lieutenant Seblon is obsessed with the cruel and emotionally detached Querelle, who is both obsessed with an idea of himself reflected in others and the subject of an obsessive focus for all of the key figures within the narrative. In *Querelle*, we can see a blueprint for the character of Sérgio: physically beautiful and yet psychically detached.

Less directly, we can see the work of both Kenneth Anger and Derek Jarman as belonging to the same lineage. While both filmmakers at points traverse a similar terrain, their means of expression and their modes of articulation are quite different. In the case of Anger, we see in his early films *Fireworks* and *Scorpio Rising* (1964) the use of experimental film strategies to eroticise the iconography of masculinity and youth culture, respectively. As Richard Dyer observes, the films are 'dreamlike in their handling of time and space' as their focus is the sexualised power of their iconography.[8] It is hard to underestimate the importance of Anger's stylistic vision and Jarman's work owes an evident debt to Anger just as it is possible to see *O Fantasma* as drawing on the same shared reference points in terms of the deployment of homoerotic iconography and dreamlike narrative pace. Jarman's films, of course, are divided between narrative cinema and the experimental and non-narrative. In Jarman's hands, the story of Saint Sebastian in *Sebastiane* (1976) is transformed into a narrative of gay obsession resulting in the saint's martyrdom. Even in the case of his adaptation of Marlowe's *Edward II* (1991), it is the King's fixation with Gaveston that brings about his downfall and ultimate execution. Jarman's painterly and contemplative style and his poetically erotic consideration of the male body are echoed in the preponderance of lingering, silent shots of Sérgio in repose.

Finally, the most attenuated link is to the work of Pedro Almodóvar, whose baroque narratives in almost all cases revolve around the figure of the crazed and obsessive lover who is driven to extremes out of an overwhelming passion. In Almódovar's case, the obsessed can be straight, as in *Matador* (1986) and *Tie Me Up! Tie Me Down!* (1989), gay, as in *Law of Desire* (1987), or sexually ambiguous, as in *Labyrinth of Passion* (1982) and *Talk To Her* (2002).

In the case of *O Fantasma* and the lineage of gay cinema that is identified here, fantasy plays a key role, as these are examples of cinema that either represent gay desire or intend to articulate fantasies of gay desire. I am arguing here that in and across these films (and specifically in *O Fantasma*) there is an attempt to deploy narrative constructions and an aesthetic of fantasy that connects the interior life of the characters and (or to) the audience. However, this is far from a straightforward relationship. Instead, it is both complicated and mutable. As Linda Williams notes in her discussion of the structures of fantasy in cinema:

> Fantasies are not, as is sometimes thought, wish-fulfilling linear narratives of mastery and control leading to closure and the attainment of desire. They are marked, rather, by the prolongation of desire and by the lack of fixed positions with respect to the objects and events fantasized.[9]

Throughout *O Fantasma*, our relationship to Sérgio as protagonist remains unclear. He is silent and unknowable, his desires and practices seem extreme and disturbed. Simultaneously, the *mise-en-scène* presents his body as an object of erotic desire. He is physically beautiful and Ricardo Meneses' startling physical performance makes his screen presence all-the-more compelling. Similarly, João, the object of Sérgio's erotomania, is sexualised, as are the succession of anonymous 'tricks' that Sérgio encounters. This results in a situation where the audience's position seems unstable, in line with Dyer's observation that 'a characteristic feature of gay/lesbian fantasy is the possibility of oscillation between wanting to be and wanting to have the object of desire'.[10] Both in terms of narrative and style, *O Fantasma* situates Sérgio as the estranged and lonely 'sad young man' that Dyer acknowledges is a recurrent trope across gay culture, connecting 'urbanism with alienation [and] the tradition of perceiving the city as a world of loneliness, loosened moral order, fleeting, impermanent contact and love for sale'.[11]

While Sérgio's sexual encounters punctuate the film's narrative with consistent regularity, they are always presented as having the flat, mechanical feel of transactional sexual exchanges and as a consequence are markedly not titillating in spite of their explicit nature. They are not presented as acts of connection but instead as enactments of sexual 'performance' implicitly bound up with power relations. In the notorious fellatio scene, Sérgio pushes away the gay man who wants to give him sexual pleasure, resulting in a scene of aborted sexual exchange. The scenes that bookend the fellatio sequence demonstrate instead that Sérgio's sole concern is to perform sexual acts on, or be used by, those who want to take pleasure from him.

Silence and Rejection

The challenge of the gay filmmaker has always been to find a language (or at the very least an appropriate register) through which to articulate gay desire and gay sexuality. As I have argued elsewhere, this has resulted in recourse to a range of expressive codes and generic formations as diverse as experimental and art cinema, pornography and melodrama.[12] I would argue, drawing on Janet Staiger, David Bordwell and Kristen Thompson, that narrative cinema is marked by a limited representational language that is pinned to an attendant narrative/discursive framework or logic; a structure that aims towards resolution and is focused around heterosexual romance.[13] This inevitably situates representations of homosexuality as problematic. Although one objective of the New Queer Cinema movement was to present unapologetic representations of gayness, it would be difficult to argue that a new rhetoric to situate gay desire has emerged. This means that the gay filmmaker has to mobilise and adapt an existing cinematic vernacular in order to articulate gay sexuality. In the case of *O Fantasma*, and indeed many of the other films mentioned in this chapter, this has been achieved by drawing upon two familiar filmic/stylistic registers: pornography and melodrama.[14]

While it is not a film that would necessarily be described as a melodrama per se, *O Fantasma* very clearly draws on a range of stylistic devices and melodramatic tropes to situate gay desire and to articulate the obsessive extremes of the erotomaniac. This means that the body of literature that deals with melodrama in film opens up a reading of *O Fantasma* that enables us to draw some conclusions. Most obviously, in the first instance, there are elements of a Sirkian *mise-en-scène* throughout the film. Sérgio is often depicted framed in doorways, peering through fences and bars, his alienated gaze caught in the reflection of mirrors. These distanciating techniques so characteristic of Douglas Sirk's films are filtered, in this case, through Sirk's acolyte Fassbinder and, consequently, the film seems to more obviously reference Fassbinder's strategic deployment of Sirkian style.

Unlike Sirk's films or any other example of Hollywood melodrama, *O Fantasma* is marked by a peculiar silence. Sérgio is an unusual protagonist in the sense that we know so little about his motivations since they are expressed by actions rather than words. This, as Peter Brooks notes in *The Melodramatic Imagination*, is characteristic of melodrama as a theatrical genre, which mobilises a 'dramaturgy of inarticulate cry and gesture'.[15] He argues that muteness is a key mechanism of melodrama as a mode of representation, substituting language for 'gestures which fill the gap [...] toward other meanings which cannot be generated from the language code' and that 'mute gesture is an expressionistic means, precisely the means of melodrama, to render meanings which are ineffable [...] it is the fullness, the pregnancy of the blank that is significant: meaningful though unspeakable'.[16] In the case of *O Fantasma* though, rather than producing the pathos that is the intended affective response to melodrama on the stage (and in cinema), it produces a sense of alienation and isolation. Sérgio's silence is asocial and potentially predatory; the film produces an uncomfortable, expectant silence.

There is a further way in which this muteness can be understood in *O Fantasma*, which draws on Geoffrey Nowell-Smith's essay 'Minnelli and melodrama', in which he suggests:

> The undischarged emotion which cannot be accommodated within the action, subordinated as it is to the demands of family/lineage/inheritance, is traditionally expressed in the music and in the case of film, in certain elements of the *mise-en-scène*.[17]

Nowell-Smith observes that the ideological contradictions contained in the family melodrama were so marked at moments of high tension that narrative coherence breaks down. Drawing on this argument, the muteness of *O Fantasma* can be regarded as a dramatic and stylistic device that forces the narrative and mode of representation towards extremities – in this case the overwhelming emotions associated with romantic obsession and erotomania. The sheer force of what is not, and cannot, be expressed by words in the film is instead articulated by the performance of extreme behaviours and by extreme modes of representation. It is notable that, at several points in the film, Sérgio has sexual encounters where either he or his partner is bound and/or gagged. The performance of sex here and the way it is presented suggests that the prospect (and indeed the fear) of reciprocation or rejection is so fraught with risk that a vocalisation of gay sexuality has to be denied. Gay desire in *O Fantasma*, then, can only be situated in extreme places and articulated through extremes. This is what is at stake in the film and this is what I suggest results in the hysterical recourse to melodramatic and pornographic representation here, problematically positioning gay romance as a perversion.

Building on the work of Carol Clover, Linda Williams draws useful connections between horror, pornography and melodrama as genres that are concerned with producing an effect in their audiences that she describes as a 'form of ecstasy'.[18] She notes that 'the success of these genres is often measured by the extent to which the audience sensation mimics what is seen on the screen'.[19] There is a very clear sense in which we can see that, in terms of narrative, style and representation, *O Fantasma* exists at the nexus of these three genres and could therefore be read as the embodiment of the 'body genres' that Williams discusses. Yet the film completely denies the ecstatic, mimetic response that Williams describes. The muteness of the protagonist, the stylistic devices of the *mise-en-scène* and the alienating treatment of the subject matter all conspire to create a critical and emotional distance between what we see and how we feel. So the effect that the film produces seems curiously at odds with the story and the set of generic expectations that it is drawing on.

What is most notable about *O Fantasma* is that rather than a particular effect, the film produces a series of denials. In the cold and unknowable Sérgio we are denied a point of identification or recognition within the text. We are denied words, emotions and the emotive cinematic devices that enable us to make the sequence of events easily legible. This in turn means that we are denied a moral compass to navigate us through this ambiguous narrative and in which to situate our responses. We are denied a narrative resolution as the film ends in a manner where outcomes are uncertain. As a result of this denial, we are finally denied the redemptive consolation of love. This denial is really what the film offers us and is the thematic lynchpin around which the narrative is organised and the protagonist's actions are given motivation. Sérgio's erotomania emerges from, and is fed by, denial.

Ultimately then, *O Fantasma* could be regarded as little more than an uncomfortable viewing experience. It seems to present a vision of gay existence that is as far away from a 'positive' representation as one could imagine, connecting gay sexuality to alienation and psychosis. I, however, believe that the film is offering something altogether more complex that builds on a long tradition within gay culture of exploring the nature and limits of emotion and desire. *O Fantasma* is a film that engages with, produces and expresses obsession. It emerges from the obsessive desire of the gay filmmaker to develop a cinematic language, rhetoric and narrative to situate gay desire. Finally, *O Fantasma* speaks to the obsessive desire of audiences to witness staged depictions of the extremes of sexuality in order to make sense of their own. The representation of perversity in the film can be seen as having some normative function. The staging of taboo practices and perverse desires offers the audience both the potential for titillation and the paradoxical reassurance of alienation; a window into a world that we are curious to witness but do not want to inhabit.

Notes

1. J.C. Bucknill and D.H. Tuke, *A Manual of Psychological Medicine* (Philadelphia: Blanchard and Lea, 1858), pp. 212-3.

2. Robert J. Hilliard, *Hollywood Speaks Out: Pictures That Dared to Protest Real World Issues* (Oxford: Wiley–Blackwell, 2009); Robin Wood, 'The murderous gays: Hitchcock's homophobia', in Alexander Doty and Corey Creekmur (eds), *Out in Culture: Gay, Lesbian, and Queer Essays on Popular Culture* (Durham, NC: Duke University Press, 1995), pp. 197–215.

3. See Vito Russo, *The Celluloid Closet: Homosexuality and the Movies* (New York: Harper and Row, 1981).

4. Dennis Lim, 'Bow wow wow', *The Village Voice* (2002). Available at http://www.villagevoice.com/2002-11-19/film-bow-wow-wow/1/ (accessed 8 June 2011); A.O. Scott, 'Garbageman collects guys, then throws them away', *The New York Times* 152, 22 November 2002, pp. B19, E18.

5. Randal Johnson, *Manoel de Oliveira* (Champaign, IL: University of Illinois Press, 2007), p. 73.

6. I am borrowing my working definition here from Richard Dyer. In the introduction to the second edition of *Now You See It*, Dyer summarises some of the issues at stake here with customary clarity. Extending Dyer's consideration of his own process of definition of a field of enquiry, Brett Farmer discusses the relationship between gay men and cinema in an especially informative chapter on the processes of gay spectatorship. It is important to note that gay cinema marks out a broad and not necessarily clearly defined terrain and therefore is to some extent a contested category. I use the term advisedly here as it is one that is both deceptively simple and yet fraught with potential epistemological problems. Is gay cinema describing, for example, a body of films made by gay men or women? Or perhaps the term refers to films in which homosexuality is a narrative theme? Indeed, can the term be applied to cinema (such as the work of John Waters) that often does not feature gay characters nor explicitly engage with homosexuality? Boundary-marking is important even though it may be arbitrary and even while the definition of gay cinema is not the focus of this chapter it is inevitably a consideration. So for my purposes I use the term gay cinema in the context of this essay to refer to films that are made by (and speak directly to) gay men and lesbians about their sexuality and existence. Richard Dyer, *Now You See It: Studies in Lesbian and Gay Film*, second edition (London: Routledge, 2003), p. 6; Brett Farmer, *Spectacular Passions: Cinema, Fantasy, Gay Male Spectatorships* (Durham: Duke University Press, 2000), p. 25.

7. John Rechy, *The Sexual Outlaw: A Documentary* (London: Futura, 1977), p. 242.

8. Dyer, *Now You See It*, p. 122.

9. Linda Williams, 'Film bodies: gender, genre, excess', in Leo Braudy and Marshall Cohen (eds), *Film Theory and Criticism* (Oxford: Oxford University Press, 1991), p. 736.

10. Richard Dyer, *The Culture of Queers* (London: Routledge, 2002), p. 133.

11. Ibid., pp. 116, 121.

12. See John Mercer and Martin Shingler, *Melodrama: Genre, Style, Sensibility* (New York: Columbia University Press, 2004).

13. David Bordwell, Janet Staiger and Kristen Thompson, *The Classical Hollywood Cinema: Film Style and Mode of Production to 1960* (London: Routledge, 1985), p. 16.

14. The film's DVD release made unambiguous value of the pornographic elements of the text. The film is described as the 'original uncut version!' Quotes describe it as 'sexually explicit' and as the 'pure libido film of the year.' DVD special features even include Meneses' 'spicy' audition interview and 'specially isolated "eye candy" moments.'

15. Peter Brooks, *The Melodramatic Imagination: Balzac, Henry James, Melodrama, and the Mode of Excess* (New Haven, CT: Yale University Press, 1976), p. 66.

16. Ibid., pp. 72–3.

17. Geoffrey Nowell-Smith, 'Minnelli and melodrama', in Christine Gledhill (ed.), *Home is Where the Heart Is* (London: BFI Publishing, 1987), p. 73.

18. Williams, 'Film bodies', p. 729. Carol Clover, *Men, Women and Chainsaws: Gender in the Modern Horror Film* (New York: Princeton University Press, 1993).

19. Ibid., p. 730.

3

Perverting the Explicit: Catherine Breillat's Visual Vocabulary of Desire

Helen Hester

The French filmmaker Catherine Breillat is a figure widely perceived to be at the very centre of a contemporary cinematic attitude that 'seeks to dismantle the prohibition regarding the exposure of the body and of "real" sexual activity in narrative film'.[1] Lisa Downing suggests that her films represent 'the most talked about of the new generation of films to gain notoriety for their excursion into explicit sexual representation'.[2] Critics such as James Quandt, meanwhile, argue that Breillat has 'made a career out of erotic provocation'.[3] It is this sustained and urgent interaction with the realm of the explicit that will be the focus here. For, despite the rope bondage, promiscuity, masturbation, rough sex and other 'perversities' dealt with in the director's work, it is perhaps her struggle to make things 'maximally visible', to borrow from Linda Williams, that represents her most perverse tendency.[4]

Breillat's explicitness – her desire to reveal and display that which is usually hidden – can be seen as perverse in the popular sense of being non-normative, contrary or unexpected. After all, by screening authentic sexual acts and graphically depicting sexual bodies, she makes public that which is conventionally thought of as more properly belonging to the private sphere. As Tanya Krzywinska suggests:

> In presenting what is expected to be privately intimate for mass consumption, making money out of it, and the act of making sex a spectator entertainment, the representation of sex in cinema challenges some of the basic principles that are perceived to order a civilised society.[5]

In this sense, we may position Breillat's explicit filmmaking as disruptive, as undermining certain received social assumptions and thereby demonstrating the possibility of less culturally visible ways of being. Indeed, as we shall see, her work at times gestures toward the idea of the explicit as a kind of political tool, one which might encourage more ethical modes of interaction between gendered individuals.

However, Breillat's project of making public and maximally visible can itself be positioned as perverse. Her engagement with the explicit, while at first glance appearing to advocate the importance of a bold and unwavering look at the conventionally obscene, can in some ways be seen to perpetually complicate, undermine and deviate from itself. In other words, the director's explicitness continually turns away from its own apparent course and agenda. Breillat endeavours to represent the sexual body in a manner that is visually perceptible yet remains elusive and inaccessible. Even the most graphic of her on-screen representations are to some extent obscure and resistant to interpretation, and the more explicitly such bodies are depicted on screen, the more illegible they appear. Using two of Breillat's more sexually graphic films – *Romance* (1999), an account of a young school teacher's quest for erotic fulfilment, and *Anatomy of Hell* (2004), a cinematic meditation upon desire, sexuality and relations between cisgendered men and women – this chapter will explore how the director works to generate a sense of the political potential of the explicit, before moving on to discuss how her work perverts and undermines this idea. For those of us in Breillat's audience, I suggest, the closer we look, the less we see.

The Political Explicit

The two films I am discussing in this chapter can be thought of as companion pieces. Breillat has stated that she made *Anatomy of Hell* because of a feeling that 'in *Romance* I didn't go to the extreme limit because courage failed me'.[6] Film critic Geoffrey Macnab suggests that '*Anatomy of Hell* does not really function as a sequel but instead pushes some of the 1999 movie's key themes to new extremes'.[7] Indeed, the shared themes of sexuality, recognition, violence, shame and the body do work to unite the films, as does the casting of the well-known porn star Rocco Siffredi, whose very presence invites us to think about how Breillat's work differs from (and implicitly critiques) the conventions of pornography. More than this, though, I would argue that the two works sometimes appear as reflections of one another. Indeed, two crucial scenes from *Romance* and *Anatomy of Hell* – one depicting a couple examining a used condom, the other depicting reactions to a used tampon – appear intended to act as mirror images of one another.

In *Romance*, immediately prior to a key sex scene between the protagonist and her Italian lover, Marie (Caroline Ducey) and Paolo (Siffredi) discuss the issue of contraception. Breillat depicts the couple in a mid-shot as they sit naked on the bed, with Marie positioned on the left of the screen and Paolo on the right. Paolo, referring to condoms, states that 'Once they've been used, they're revolting. Not very pretty'. Marie then reaches beneath the bed to pick up a used and semen-filled condom. Returning to her relaxed position facing Paolo, and holding the condom so that it is visible to him, she agrees: 'They are rather disgusting. It's like a Tampax. To screw, you take it out discretely, hide it under the bed so the guy's not turned off. Guys are easily disgusted. Later, you have to get it back'. Returning the used condom to the floor, she declares, 'I quite like disgusting things', and the two proceed to have sex.

Douglas Keesey considers this an important scene in terms of the treatment of gender relations within the film. He argues that Paolo's aversion to used condoms represents 'a moment of bodily self-loathing', and suggests that, by having Marie examine the object and compare it to tampons, Breillat is depicting 'each gender fearing the other's disgust and here helping each other to overcome it'.[8] This scene can be viewed as an instance of affinity and mutuality between the lovers, one which, significantly for our purposes, is founded upon a shared act of perverse viewing, a making-visible and an unflinching examination of that which is usually discarded, hidden or ignored.

It is through an act of making explicit that Marie engages with Paolo and encourages him to surmount his anxieties regarding his body and the abject substances that it produces.[9] The form of this encounter works to draw the viewer's attention to the potential interpersonal and political implications of explicitness itself; the possibility that turning one's gaze upon the obscene – in the sense of that which is typically or conventionally 'off (*ob*) the public scene'[10] – might facilitate greater levels of communication and understanding between self and other. In this sense, the scene acts as a commentary upon, and an oblique defence of, the confrontational nature of Breillat's defiantly explicit filmmaking and her investment in rendering hidden things visible.

This important moment from *Romance* appears to be intertextually referenced, or to some extent even restaged, in *Anatomy of Hell*. Developed from Breillat's 2008 novel *Pornocracy*,[11] this later film depicts the peculiar relationship between a female character, credited as The Woman (Amira Casar), and the person she hires to study her naked body and genitalia, credited as The Man (again played by Siffredi). On their third evening together, as a growing sense of intimacy begins to soften The Man's initial feelings of horror and disgust towards his companion, the protagonists sit facing one another on the bed in a mid-shot. As with the scene from *Romance*, the woman's naked body occupies the left hand side of the screen, while the body of Siffredi (fully clothed this time) occupies the right. The Woman, who is menstruating, instructs her partner to remove her tampon: 'I wore it to keep the blood off the sheets in your absence. But now that you're here ... Pull. Pull. It comes out easily'. We see The Man reaching towards her before the shot cuts to a close-up of the bloodied tampon.

Not only is the *mise-en-scène* comparable to that of the scene in *Romance*, and not only does this scene display a similar interest in emitted bodily substances, but it also features a common emphasis upon the importance of explicitness for overcoming a tenacious disgust. The Man and The Woman in *Anatomy of Hell* act out something akin to a gender-inverted version of the encounter between Marie and Paolo, with the tampon that Marie merely mentioned now being displayed in frank and graphic detail. In *Anatomy of Hell*, it is the male character who is asked to face up to a conventionally abject or obscene aspect of the other's body, and who, after being perversely impelled to look at that which typically remains out of sight, finds himself newly capable of experiencing what Breillat refers to as 'an indescribable mingling' with the gendered other.[12] Later, The Man goes so far as to drink from a glass of water in which the used tampon has been submerged. The explicitness of these perverse acts, then, is a tool for dismantling disgust, and this dismantling represents both an overcoming of personal aversion and a breaking down of the norms surrounding the socially acceptable bourgeois body. After all, as William Ian Miller notes, 'the gust in disgust was very early on, in both English and French, not a narrow reference to the sense of taste as in the sensation of food and drink, but an homage to the broader, newly emerging idea of "good taste".[13]

But the realm of the explicit is not, in practice, so easily converted or reduced to a political tool, and Breillat's project often seems to inadvertently pervert itself. The most remarkable thing about these scenes is that, despite advocating explicitness, they also draw our attention to the unavoidable constraints faced by the practice of *making visible*. That is, they serve to highlight the limits of the explicit. The contraceptive and sanitary devices upon which these scenes focus are necessarily hidden when being used for the purposes for which they were designed. We cannot, of course, typically see the condom at the moment it performs its chief function of acting as a barrier between ejaculated semen and the body's interior. Nor can we witness the soft cotton mass of a tampon absorbing the blood emitted during menstruation. Our view of these objects and their functionality can only ever be partial and provisional.

By focusing these two scenes upon objects that necessarily perform their primary functions in a manner that is visually inaccessible – scenes that act as indirect praise for the process of making visible – Breillat flags up the impossibility of true explicitness. These scenes are perverse in that they gesture toward the limits of their own arguments and suggest that the explicitness they advocate is inevitably incomplete and perpetually partial. Indeed, Breillat's films illustrate the failure of the explicit in a number of other, perhaps unexpected, places.

Extreme Close-ups: The Asignifying Explicit

Breillat's exploration of the possibilities of the explicit unsurprisingly includes detailed attention to the cis female body. Genitalia is depicted, sometimes hugely enlarged and in graphic detail. For example, we witness an unsimulated birth in unflinching close-up near the end of *Romance* and there are a number of explicit images of The Woman's vulva in *Anatomy of Hell*. Referring to her admission that she felt she had not been bold enough in her depiction of the vulva in *Romance*, Breillat has noted, 'I didn't shoot the female sex. I just shot the *triangle* so I was very prudish. I did not go to the final demonstration, the expression of which, as an artist, I should have'.[14] It is Breillat's attempt to 'go to the final demonstration' in her representation of the cis female body and the problems inherent with this that are significant in this regard. While the majority of *Anatomy of Hell* is aesthetically serene and almost painterly, the extreme genital close-ups, far from working to make their subject explicit, in fact register as disorientating, weird and profoundly bewildering; they enter a realm of asignification in which signs become elusive and resistant to immediate interpretation.

The first such shot comes as The Man explores the interior of The Woman's vagina for the first time and the viewer is suddenly confronted with an explicit, tightly-cropped image of his finger penetrating a vagina pearled with moisture. The feeling of strangeness that this sudden cut evokes may well owe something to the particular constraints that Breillat had to work within during filming. As the opening intertitles of *Anatomy of Hell* state, 'For the actress's most intimate scenes, a body double was used. It's not her body, it's an extension of a fictional character'. As Amira Casar declined to let her body be used for the genital close-ups, Breillat was forced to find an alternative. She explains, 'The body double wasn't a solution I was happy with, but at the same time I wasn't going to let the lack of an actress stop me from making my film. If you imagine me as a painter, then it's as if Amira gave me the red in my palette, but for other scenes I needed blue and I chose another body to supply it'.[15]

Somewhat ironically, however, the lead actress's refusal to provide Breillat with the graphic and wholly 'authentic' close-ups that the director desired works to create a greater sense of connection between *Anatomy of*

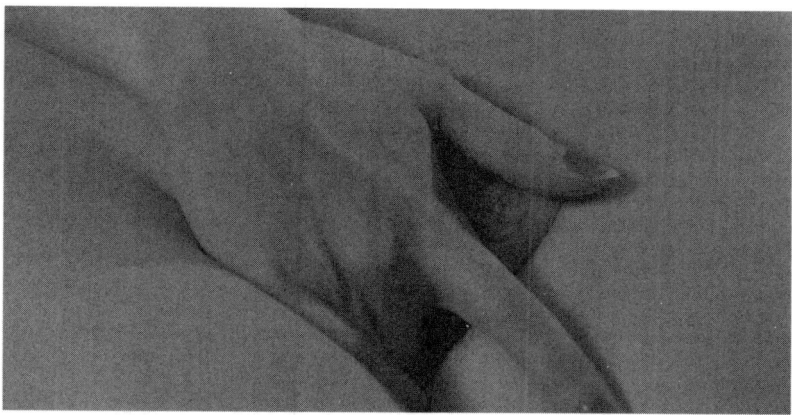

Fig. 3.1. Close-up of a vulva in *Romance* (Catherine Breillat, Flach Film, 1999)

Hell and that archetypal realm of the sexually explicit: the pornographic. Without Casar's whole body to connect to the sexual organs, the cis female form necessarily becomes fragmented. The long, uninterrupted takes that characterise some of *Romance*'s most significant sex scenes are replaced by blunt cuts to tightly-cropped 'meat shots' of genitalia being penetrated by fingers and sex toys (see Fig. 3.1). The spectator is therefore left with certain moments that are strongly reminiscent of some of the dominant conventions of mainstream hardcore. Breillat's attempts to go beyond the conventions of pornography – to allow her audience to 'really see sex in a movie that is not a pornographic one'[16] – are to some extent compromised here.

It is not only the pseudo-pornographic qualities of these vivid and striking visuals that is enhanced by their fragmented nature. I would contend that their affecting oddness and illegibility are also thereby augmented. That is, despite representing the sexual organs in graphic detail, these most explicit of images stubbornly resist the viewer's initial attempts to make sense of them or to recognise them as familiar parts of the body. Factors such as an abundance of dark pubic hair, the sudden jarring cut to an extreme close-up, the sheer size of the image and the stripping away of any context-providing bodily landmarks all work to render this first genital close-up peculiarly ambiguous.[17]

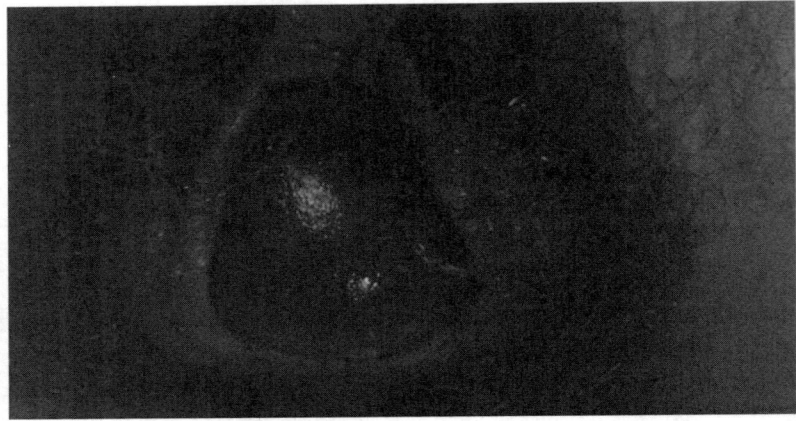

Fig. 3.2. Extreme genital close-up in *Anatomy of Hell* (Catherine Breillat, CB Films, 2004)

If anything, this effect of asignification and disorientation is even more pronounced in the second extreme genital close-up of the film (see Fig. 3.2), in which The Woman expels an object from her vagina. We initially see a shot of The Man's face, neck and bare shoulders, with The Woman's foot caressing him. 'See anything?' she asks. 'You can't see anything, right?' In mid-shot, we see her lying on the bed as The Man positions himself so that he can look directly into her vagina. 'I can hide it inside me for as long as I want', says The Woman, before the shot cuts to a medium close-up of her companion staring intently between her spread legs. There is then a very brief shot of The Woman's genitalia in extreme close-up. During the course of this fleeting glimpse of the sexual organs we see an object – curved, black and glistening – emerging from within the body's interior, spreading and opening the vulva in manner that recalls the full-frontal birth scene from *Romance*. 'I can also make it come out when I want', says The Woman, as The Man picks up and fondles the ejected object.

The strangeness of this image is maintained despite the spectator being primed for possible genital close-ups, and in spite of the context-giving shots and dialogue that indicate that there is currently an unidentified foreign object lodged within the protagonist's body. This effect is aided in part by the briefness of the shot, which does not give the viewer time to process or interpret that which is flashing up on the screen. The object itself is also somewhat unexpected, being as it is neither familiar nor easily identifiable; the novel on which the film is based describes it (rather unpleasantly) as 'a rounded oblong form, one of those black shiny stones, thick as a negro's penis',[18] while The Woman later refers to it as a 'stone dildo'.

Seeing this ambiguous object being ejected from the vagina is both disorientating and affecting. The extreme close-up resists absorption and explanation by the contextual events that surround it and remains somehow resistant to, and dislocated from, the narrative in which it is embedded. The audience is given all the requisite information required to read the image accurately, yet we remain somehow unprepared for it, taken aback by its strangeness and prompted to experience its impact upon our bodies more intensely than we are able to understand its role within the syntagmatic chain. The signs are present but the significance is lost. To borrow from Patricia MacCormack, the shot 'ruptures outward, organizing the image as connected to us rather than metonymically to the forms of the previous and following frame – the "what?" is simultaneous with the "wow"'.[19]

The genital images in *Anatomy of Hell* might therefore be said to defy, if only temporarily, our attempts to read them. The director's close-ups manage to be both compelling and repellent at the same time, working to momentarily transform the genitalia into a cipher that is both threateningly ambiguous and visually strange. Despite Breillat's attempt to show more in *Anatomy of Hell* than she did in *Romance* – that is, despite her attempts to be less coy about representing the vulva – these eminently explicit frames remain somewhat illegible. They mark two fleeting but powerful moments of asignification and perceptual uncertainty in the film. Indeed, on first encountering these shots, the viewer may not even immediately register that he or she is staring into hugely enlarged representations of a vulva.

What, then, are we to make of the function of the explicit here? That which is left unseen in the course of our everyday lives is indeed being made maximally visible. Breillat's attempt to bring the conventionally obscene *on*-scene and to make the traditionally private suddenly public appears to be flourishing.[20] And yet, there is an ambiguity at the heart of these close-up shots that cannot straightforwardly be reconciled with those ideas of the overt, the apparent, and the candid, which circulate around the concept of the explicit. Indeed, at the very instances when the director is engaging most obviously with the explicit, the viewer is confronted with images that exert a profoundly complicating influence and plunge the maximally visible into ambiguity. Once again, then, Breillat's perverse project perverts itself, as her attempts to visualise the sexual body become distorted and mired in perceptual uncertainty.

Making it Explicit, Making it Real

There are significant moments of mirroring in *Romance* and *Anatomy of Hell* where the importance of explicitness can once again be seen to make itself known. There are markedly similar shots of cis male fingers entering or withdrawing from the cis female protagonists' vaginas, for instance. In *Romance*, we see the hand of Marie's lover Robert (François Berléand) – the character responsible for her sexual salvation through BDSM – touching and penetrating her. He fastidiously binds Marie, before using scissors to cut an opening in the gusset of her underwear and inserting his fingers through this hole. We then see a close-up of his fingers, which Eugenie Brinkema describes as 'emerging, wet and sticky clear'.[21] *Anatomy of Hell*, meanwhile, features a similar depiction of penetration occurring around the time of the film's first extreme genital close-up. We see The Man's hand disappear between The Woman's thighs before resurfacing, the index finger tipped with a glistening, pearlescent residue.

Once again, then, making the conventionally unseen visually explicit appears to be part of a wider feminist agenda. The enormously enlarged depictions of vaginal wetness that confront the viewer suggest the possibility and importance of finding a visual logic for representing the materiality of non-phallic sexual pleasure. As Deborah Shamoon notes, 'depicting female arousal and orgasm proves problematic because there is less physical evidence; specifically, there exists no direct female equivalent to erection and ejaculation'.[22] However, in the Japanese 'ladies' comics of her study, 'vaginal wetness as a sign of female arousal [is] comparable to that of the erect penis'.[23] Indeed, for Brinkema, the importance of Breillat's utilisation of the sexually explicit in her films lies precisely here – in a politically-motivated attempt to visualise female desire. She argues that an understanding of this project should be central to any attempt to analyse Breillat's treatment of sexuality:

> the presence of unsimulated sex in her films, caught under the catchall term 'pornography', is absolutely significant [...] Breillat's foray into the ontological realism of the image is always and uniquely centred on the sticky production of wet female desire.[24]

Brinkema goes on to argue that this emphasis upon vaginal moisture in Breillat's work can be linked to the director's resistance to conventional pornography's generically limited vision of sex, claiming that the image of Robert's glistening fingers 'is a radical reorientation of pornography's classic male cum shot' and that the presence of female wetness must be understood as 'radically *othering* the image'.[25]

But again we are reminded of the perverted explicitness at the heart of Breillat's work. Elsewhere in her insightful discussion, Brinkema perhaps inadvertently complicates the idea of making perceptible. She argues that it is expulsion rather than penetration that represents the privileged moment of contact within Breillat's texts – that is, she suggests that the secretion of wetness takes priority over the insertion of fingers. She goes on to add, 'this is a depth model movement, in/out, very different from movements that dance across surfaces, faces, pubic hair, and privileged precisely because this movement calls out to the interior space that carries traces of the real'.[26] If, as Brinkema suggests, Breillat is in fact primarily interested in depth rather than surface, then we are no doubt approaching the key element of perversity within her explicitness.

As I have already suggested in relation to the condom and the tampon scenes, any attempt to visualise that which is visually inaccessible – the interior of a living and desiring human body, for example – will inevitably provoke a certain stylistic tension. It is testament to Breillat's ambition that she attempts to make even the unspectacular production of the concealed bodily interior maximally perceptible. Nonetheless, if depth *is* in fact privileged over surface in the director's work, then her somewhat discordant treatment of the explicit could easily be attributed to the impossibility of her ever successfully reconciling her method with her subject matter.

Brinkema's remarks regarding the bodily interior as a vehicle for 'traces of the real' take us in another direction, since there is something more profound at work in the presence of the asignifying explicit within Breillat's films. This gestures toward a Lacanian-inflected notion of the Real – an order from which the subject is both alienated and shielded by language and signification. Following this, Breillat's screen language distances us from the possibility of 'really seeing sex', a possibility that would at first glance seem to be at the heart of her cinematic project. Brinkema's commentary is particularly interesting in that it recalls what Slavoj Žižek has described as the 'authentic twentieth-century passion for penetrating the Real Thing (ultimately the destructive Void) through the cobweb of semblances which constitutes our reality'.[27] That is, it reminds us of the insatiable contemporary fascination with experiencing an affecting realm that exists beyond comprehension, representation and everyday social reality; a fascination Alain Badiou has labelled the 'veritable exaltation of the real, even in its horror'.[28]

Indeed, Brinkema's remarks provide us with a speculative metaphor for the operations of the Real. As we have seen, when Brinkema argues that the movement of insertion and expulsion – the movement of things into and out of the human body – is prioritised in Breillat's work, she attributes this to the ability of the bodily interior to communicate something of the Real. Breillat's films invoke the Real precisely through the bodily trace of vaginal residue, thereby positioning sexual wetness as the very image of the Real. But how might such an image reflect or illuminate the concept? And in what ways might it relate to and further our discussion of Breillat's explicitness? For Badiou, the Real is 'the source of both horror and enthusiasm, simultaneously lethal and creative', the void that is the irreducible other of our everyday reality.[29] It is in this sense of the Real as an elusive (non)presence that Brinkema's remarks about the Real within Breillat's depictions of wetness become instructive. Perceiving vaginal wetness as a manner of making explicit cis female sexual desire in no way exhausts its symbolic possibilities. As MacCormack notes, this 'sticky substance is a kind of visible which is never visible – indeed it is usually transparent – or only perceived as touch even while it is an image'.[30] The pearlescent traces that appear in *Romance* and *Anatomy of Hell* continue to unsettle ideas of the explicit, being as they are affecting yet barely perceptible (in)visible (non)presences. In this sense, then, they come to function as a potential image for the impossible Real, experienced only in the form of the residue or the ephemeral trace.

The detectable but transparent presence of non-phallic arousal in Breillat's films can in this way be read as a telling metaphor for the Real, something Žižek similarly calls attention to in his argument that 'when we get too close to the desired object, erotic fascination turns into disgust at the Real of the bare flesh'.[31] It illustrates the inaccessibility of a Real that we cannot help but be aware of and thereby suggests some of the deeper connections between this concept and that of the explicit. The explicit, as it functions within Breillat's texts, is elusive, mobile and continually gestured toward without ever being attained. Obscurity manifests itself at the very moment when things are most clearly put on display and perverts the would-be explicit image by turning it inexorably away from itself. In those moments when Breillat grants us full visual access, the Real makes its presence felt via that which we sense we are nonetheless unable to see – by our creeping awareness of the impossibility of Breillat's explicit.

Conclusion: The Perversity of the Elusive Explicit

As this discussion has shown, Breillat's filmmaking engages with the idea of explicitness through a series of perverse acts in diverse, nuanced and thought-provoking ways. Whether she is using scenes that display conventionally hidden objects of disgust as an indirect defence of the possibilities of cinematic explicitness, or attempting to utilise depictions of vaginal wetness in the cause of articulating and insisting upon the possibilities of developing a visual logic of a specifically non-phallic sexual desire, she acknowledges and exploits the complexity of this concept to the fullest extent.

And yet, the tension within Breillat's explicitness serves to add a further level to any discussion of her confrontational portrayals of gendered bodies and sexual acts. As the examination of asignifying genital close-ups and of vaginal wetness as a metaphor for the Real has suggested, there is a perversity at the heart of Breillat's use of the explicit, in that it relies upon the less-than-visible, or is transformed at the supposed moment of maximum visibility into something unavailable for interpretation or the easy attribution of meaning. In Breillat's work, perversity manifests itself not just in the sexual acts but also in the inextricable relationship between the explicit and the Real, so that the intended impact of the image consistently and provocatively escapes us. We are left disorientated, flailing and struggling to make sense. Her perverse explicitness taps into the obscurely compelling order of the Real, indicates the limits of our ability to see, interpret, and understand and demonstrates that the very act of attempting to make increasingly visible can work to further obscure.

This is not to say that the asignifying explicit is unique to Breillat's work. That her films engage with the explicit as an overt theme certainly works to render her output a particularly clear example of the functioning of this concept and yet her body of work illustrates only a more general operation, common to all attempts to screen sexual perversities. In the course of her examination of the history of sex and the moving image, Williams insists upon the 'double meaning of the verb *to screen* as both revelation and concealment'.[32] When contemplating the filmic representation of various forms of sexuality, we would do well to bear in mind the imperfect vision afforded by the act of screening. If we are tempted to reduce the asignifying explicit to a trait peculiar to Breillat's work, or to the various auteurist, art film genres to which her work belongs, then we must caution ourselves against assuming that there are any purer forms of the explicit available. No matter how clear or seemingly uncomplicated the cinematic view, any attempt to make maximally visible is bound to be complicated and compromised. The resulting explicitness is asignifying, elusive and arguably illegible, yet always illuminating.[33]

Notes

1. Lisa Downing, 'French cinema's new "sexual revolution": postmodern porn and troubled genre', *French Cultural Studies* 15/3 (2004), p. 266.
2. Ibid., p. 268.
3. James Quandt, 'Flesh and blood: sex and violence in recent French cinema', *Artforum* (February 2004). Available at http://artforum.com/inprint/id=6199&pagenum=0 (accessed 28 November 2010).
4. Linda Williams, *Screening Sex* (Durham, NC: Duke University Press, 2008), p. 4.
5. Tanya Krzywinska, *Sex and the Cinema* (London: Wallflower Press, 2006), p. 83.

6. Gabrielle Murray, 'When violence is an axe and romance is dark: an interview with Catherine Breillat', *Senses of Cinema* (13 March 2011). Available at http://www.sensesofcinema.com/2011/feature-articles/when-violence-is-an-axe-and-romance-is-dark-an-interview-with-catherine-breillat (accessed 15 July 2011).

7. Geoffrey Macnab, 'Sadean woman', *Sight and Sound* 14/12 (December 2004), pp. 20–2.

8. Douglas Keesey, *Catherine Breillat* (Manchester: Manchester University Press, 2009), p. 126.

9. William Ian Miller sees semen as a particularly abject substance for those who produce it: 'I am of the view that semen is of all sex-linked disgust substances the most revolting to *men*: not because it shares a pathway with urine, not even because it has other primary disgust features (it is slimy, sticky, and viscous), but because it appears under conditions that are dignity-destroying, a prelude to the mini-shames attendant on post-ejaculatory tristesse. The appearance of semen signals the evanescence and the end of pleasure'. William Ian Miller, *The Anatomy of Disgust* (Cambridge, MA: Harvard University Press, 1997), pp. 103–104. Original emphasis.

10. Linda Williams, 'Porn studies: proliferating pornographies on/scene: an introduction', in Linda Williams (ed.), *Porn Studies* (Durham, NC: Duke University Press, 2004), p. 3.

11. Catherine Breillat, *Pornocracy*, translated by Paul Buck and Catherine Petit (Los Angeles: Semiotext(e), 2008).

12. Ibid., p. 91.

13. Miller, *The Anatomy of Disgust*, p. 170.

14. Murray, 'When violence is an axe and romance is dark', original emphasis.

15. Cited in Geoffrey Macnab, 'Written on the body', *Sight and Sound* 14/12 (December 2004), p. 22.

16. Murray, 'When violence is an axe and romance is dark'.

17. Indeed, I would argue that this close-up recalls Cindy Sherman's murky, organic and enigmatically raw *Untitled # 190*, an artwork Hal Foster perceives as giving the Lacanian Real 'a horrific visage of its own'. Hal Foster, 'Obscene, abject, traumatic', *October* 78 (1996), p. 113.

18. Breillat, *Pornocracy*, p. 83.

19. Patricia MacCormack, *Cinesexuality* (Aldershot: Ashgate, 2008), p. 26.

20. For an enlightening discussion of the concept of 'on/scenity', see Linda Williams' excellent article 'Second thoughts on *Hard Core*: American obscenity law and the scapegoating of deviance', in Pamela Church Gibson and Roma Gibson (eds), *Dirty Looks: Women, Pornography, Power* (London: British Film Institute, 1993), pp. 46–61.

21. Eugenie Brinkema, 'Celluloid is sticky: sex, death, materiality, metaphysics (in some films by Catherine Breillat)', *Women: A Cultural Review* 17/2 (2006), p. 151.

22. Deborah Shamoon, 'Office sluts and rebel flowers: the pleasures of Japanese pornographic comics for women', in Linda Williams (ed.), *Porn Studies* (Durham, NC: Duke University Press, 2004), p. 91.

23. Ibid.
24. Brinkema, 'Celluloid is sticky', p. 149.
25. Ibid., p. 152, original emphasis.
26. Ibid., p. 166.
27. Slavoj Žižek, *Welcome to the Desert of the Real! Five Essays on September 11 and Related Dates* (London: Verso, 2002), p. 12.
28. Alain Badiou, *The Century*, translated by Alberto Toscano (Cambridge: Polity Press, 2007), p. 19.
29. Ibid., p. 32.
30. MacCormack, *Cinesexuality*, p. 82.
31. Žižek, *Welcome to the Desert of the Real!*, p. 6.
32. Williams, *Screening Sex*, p. 2, original emphasis.
33. I would like to thank Robert Duggan and Benjamin Noys for reading and responding to this article in an earlier form and Caroline Walters and Michael O'Rourke for informing and influencing my ideas regarding Breillat's work. Particular thanks are due to Diarmuid Hester for his patience, insight and boundless intellectual generosity.

4

From Sexual Perversion to Social Trauma: Titillation, Terrorism and Italian Erotic Cinema During the *anni di piombo*

Xavier Mendik

> The long unacknowledged persistence of the *anni di piombo* in the collective psyche suggests that Italian culture developed in relation to the political violence and terrorism of the 1970s a defensive amnesia symptomatic of an experience of psychological trauma or wound.[1]

In recent years, critics and theorists have begun to re-examine how 1970s Italian pulp (or *filone*) cinema developed, evolved and responded to the so-called *anni di piombo*, or 'years of lead', which lasted from 1969 to 1983. Here, a decade of violent revolt, terrorist activity and militant sexual politics created a context of trauma that impacted on the Italian collective and celluloid consciousness. Some of the most memorable markers in this decade of the macabre included train station bombings by clandestine fascist groups (the Piazza Fontana in Milan in 1969 and Bologna in 1980), as well as sustained violent activity by leftist collectives such as The Red

Brigades (*Brigate Rosse*), which culminated in the spectacularly tragic kidnapping and murder of Christian Democrat Premier Aldo Moro in 1978. Beyond these headline grabbing atrocities, Alan O' Leary's recent work on the era has identified over 14,000 terrorist attacks upon Italian citizens between 1969 and 1983, resulting in 374 deaths and more than 1170 injuries.[2]

Due to the sheer scale and duration of this sustained period of urban violence and insurrection, it is possible to argue that the *anni di piombo* provided a traumatic social and psychic imprint, which was replicated in a variety of sex and death cycles that proliferated in Italy during this time. For instance, the Italian *poliziotteschi* (or rogue cop) cycle of the 1970s seemed to tap directly into the nihilism of the decade. Via a sustained series of brutal narratives, wayward cops or vigilante citizens were forced to resort to extreme methods to combat the unrestrained lawlessness prevalent in the urban sphere. Titles including *Street Law/Il cittadino si ribella* (Enzo G. Castellari, 1974), *Italy Armed to the Teeth/Italia a mano armata* (Umberto Lenzi, 1976), *The Big Racket/Il grande racket* (Enzo G. Castellari, 1976) and *Live Like a Man, Die Like a Cop/Uomini si nasce poliziotti si muore* (Ruggero Deodato, 1976) often employed the evocative visual index of suffering synonymous with the *anni di piombo*. Such films featured quasi-realist newspaper reportage of metropolitan atrocities and repeated scenes of fatal female hostage-taking, to the sinister assassinations of police commissioners and magistrates, as well as unpalatable images detailing the sexual brutalisation of minors. Although *poliziotteschi* has been seen as one of the most iconic cycles to directly reflect the wider Italian traumas and tensions of the era, it is interesting to note how other popular cycles and formats also responded to the wider feel-bad impetus of the decade. Indeed, given the traumas associated with transportation and urban violence outlined above, even pre-existing horror cycles such as rape and revenge dramas were remarketed in Italy to become railtrack-rape-and-revenge narratives. A new range of titles were devised to detail the sexual indignities meted out to a cross-section of Italian citizens by the countercultural thugs they encountered on ill-fated public transportation outings, most notably *Don't Ride on Late Night Trains/L'ultimo treno della notte* (Aldo Lado, 1975) and *Terror Express/La ragazza del vagone letto* (Ferdinando Baldi, 1980).

In their recent studies of cultural representations of the *anni di piombo*, authors including Beverly Allen and Ruth Glynn have identified the importance of narrativising the traumas inherent in 1970s Italy, which they see as annexing fears of political violence to unsettling scenarios of compulsion, repetition and unresolved infantile desire. For Allen, the influence of these leaden years could be seen in the growth of what she terms 'terrorist fictions', in which tales of disenchanted leftist males merged with wider fictional considerations of erotic tensions within the Italian family unit.[3] Glynn's work is even more significant for annexing the sociocultural to the psychosexual. She links a range of recent accounts aligning the study of individual malady associated with the psychoanalytic study and clinical case study to the consideration of collective distress associated with terrorist acts or natural catastrophes. By devising the term 'insidious trauma', Glynn notes 'how acts of terrorism may traumatise people who have no direct encounter with these acts', thus producing 'the lateral spread of traumatic symptoms beyond those immediately affected by the trauma inducing event'.[4] The author proceeds to chart the insidious impact of these fears across both the collective and individual psyche via the analysis of a range of diaries and unpublished memoirs from 1970s Italy. Here, widespread reporting of terrorist bomb blasts, staged assassinations or politically motivated car-jackings merged with more individualistic fears around corporeal corruption, castration anxiety and fearful fantasies of the female body.

Arguably, it is readings by authors such as Allen and Glynn that have begun to apply innovative sociocultural and psychoanalytical methodologies to the study of the *anni di piombo*. The aim of this chapter is to expand the recent interest in representations produced during these leaden years and to apply them to the erotic cycles that also flourished during the decade. Although often dismissed for their seemingly conservative and apolitical renditions of desire and heterosexuality, I aim to show how Italian erotic cinema of the 1970s also functions as a kind of trauma narrative, which employed paradoxical and phantasmagorical representations of female sexuality to expose both the collective 'socio-political trauma of terrorism',[5] as well as the unrepressed libidinal desires within the family.

Although Italian cinema has long traded on images of female sensuality, these representations are often conveyed by coded mechanisms (such as dialogue, costume and bodily gesture), in a variety of flamboyant postwar populist formats. For Mary P. Wood, the postwar economic miracle further accentuated an interest in the '*maggiorate fisiche* (the physically well endowed)', with representations of the fuller female form coming to further convey the nation's emergent interest in consumption (both of products and sexed bodies).[6] During the 1960s, Wood has argued that more explicit representations of female sexuality remained the preserve of auteur-based cinema, with art house directors such as Luciano Visconti and Michelangelo Antonioni employing images of estranged female sexuality to 'shock and sometimes provoke statements about contemporary society'.[7] Arguably, it was the political turmoil of post-1968 Europe that extended explicit imagery into more populist cinema, ensuring that the resultant outrageous iconography could be read through a darkly pessimistic social and nationalistic lens.

The explosion of erotic cinema during this decade has been termed by author Rémi Fournier Lanzoni as *filone erotico*, an essentially generically impure set of representations with their own specific industrial, cultural and historic considerations.[8] Although Lanzoni's insightful analysis focuses on the so-called comic considerations of the era, he does note how the established traditions of *commedia all'italiana* (or the nationally defined comedy of manners) markedly shifted during the 1970s to accommodate an unnerving emphasis on death and the grotesque, which can be linked to wider social discontents from the 1970s. These fears related to the ever-present threat of terrorist intervention (from both neo-fascist and leftist collectives), as well as gender-based phobias reflecting the changing status of Italian women during the period. As the author notes, these fears resulted in convoluted and confused narratives that addressed social malaise and psychodrama in equal measure. In the 1970s:

> as the visually erotic element pervaded all genres of cinema without exception [...] One of the early characteristics of erotic cinema was its element of the so-called 'schoolboy point of view', evolving quickly towards a provocative voyeurism.[9]

Lanzoni notes a connection between the male teen-oriented erotic material of the *anni di piombo*, as well as the potentially perverse forms of voyeurism they convey. A manifest plot device of many Italian erotic titles produced during these years was a focus on young schoolboys who become erotically obsessed with surveying the private activities of mature female authority figures. It is also interesting to note how these culturally defined imperatives were frequently annexed with psychic considerations that frequently sought to eroticise familial relations. By annexing contemporary Italian fears with libidinal tensions, the *filone erotico* also provide a crucial index of how fantasies and fears of female domination function on both social and psychic levels of disturbance.

A Carnal Counterculture: Comedy, Copulation and the *anni di piombo*

Although defined by a decade of militant terrorist activity and the all-pervasive influence of the *Brigate Rosse*, the rise of Italian feminism was seen as an equally disruptive political discourse, even to those male figures advocating radical countercultural change.[10] Indeed, as Lanzoni has argued, although feminism was one of the later radical movements to develop during the *anni di piombo*, it remained one of the most significant. Female interventions in the economic and political sphere represented one of the most significant revolutions of this decade, both in the workplace and the private sphere. As Lanzoni has commented:

> These initiatives included a wide range of requests such as legalizing divorce and abortion, establishing equal rights between both partners within marriage contracts, promoting awareness for sexual freedom, contraception and finally the creation of women's commissions in factory councils.[11]

While these struggles confirmed that, in Italy, 'a true "women's liberation" phenomenon stood against a fossilised patriarchal-dominated society',[12] this contradiction extended to splits between many feminist groups and the (male-dominated) countercultural movements of the period.

While advances were made during this era (such as the 1968 repeal of female adultery, which had been punishable in law since 1930), Lanzoni has noted the potentially contradictory 'consumption' of female sexuality that accompanied these legal changes. Sexual imagery was often co-opted to connote unabashed feminist emancipation while retaining the vicarious thrills so popular with heterosexual audiences:

> It was during these years of sudden sexual freedom that one of the most visible manifestations of the decade began to surface with the advent of graphic eroticism and ultimately pornography (1966 saw the first erotic publication for men in Italy). However, the phenomenon did not explode until the seventies with the first *luci rosse cinema* (red light district theatres began to screen pornographic films in 1977), which eventually deeply divided the feminist movement.[13]

If the explosion of sexually explicit material during the 1970s revealed a contradictory construction of the liberated and libidinous female, then it also rendered male representations as equally ambiguous. Faced with a new set of male-defined but overtly desiring female types, Lanzoni identifies the importance of new strategies of grotesque and comedic representation, which often used humorous tropes to short-circuit masculine fears around a newly enlivened female sensuality. These tropes feature in one of two dominant erotic Italian traditions that came to dominate during this turbulent period: the erotic comedy and morbid sexual dramas.

In its comic variant, 1970s Italian erotic cinema often annexed social fears of female liberation to libidinalised familial tensions by detailing faulty patriarchal models whose desires undercut moral value systems within the nuclear unit. Despite their appeal to 'comic' strategies, this erotic variant relied heavily on a troubling preoccupation with 'graphic incest related scenes', which depicted the illicit relations between a sexually charged teenager and an older parental figure with authority over them.[14] The moral tensions implicit in these couplings were often diffused by the introduction of a comedic element (the so-called *commedia sexy all'italiana* that remains the focus of Lanzoni's study).

The dystopic family dynamic that the author identifies in the Italian erotic comedy seems replicated in some of the key erotic films produced in 1975 alone, such as: *Erotic Games in a Respectable Family/Giochi erotica di una famiglia per bene* (Francesco Degli Espinosa), *My Father's*

Nurse/L'infermiera di mio padre (Mario Bianchi), *Intimate Relations/ La nuora giovane* (Luigi Russo), *A Virgin in the Family/Una vergine in famiglia* (Luca Degli Azzeri) and *Vice in the Family/Il vizio di famiglia* (Mariano Laurenti), all of which promote a clear fixation with eroticising clandestine relations within the family unit.

These narratives, which deal centrally with illegitimate desires between teenage and mature siblings, extended beyond a single year of Italian production to become a key erotic marker between the years of 1975–80. This coincided with *both* a heightened period of terrorist insurrection and the emergence of the *luci rosse cinema* circuit.[15] Drawing on the gender paradoxes identified in Lanzoni's analysis of the *commedia sexy all'italiana*, it is unsurprising that issues of male debasement (either comedic or dramatic) are central to the *filone erotico* produced during this era. Punishment is attributed to male protagonists for illicit attempts to survey concealed scenes of sexual activity between family members. In its comic variant, the *filone erotico* used an extensive vocabulary of facial distortion and physiological discomfort, to convey how ill-fated attempts by male family members to exploit the sexuality of their siblings ultimately led to their own discomfort. An example of this can be seen in Alfonso Brescia's *Sweet Teen/L'adolescente* (1976), which features the Sicilian comic Tuccio Musumeci as Vito Gnaula, a sexually repressed husband whose markedly younger spouse Grazia (Daniela Giordano) refuses to consummate their marriage. Gnaula's resultant libidinal frustrations are expressed in a range of distorted facial displays, which follow the repeated pattern of the protagonist experiencing humiliation when his advances are comically rejected.

Echoing the troubled period of its production, *Sweet Teen* combines comedy with social commentary in the central scene, where Vito discovers that the physician, who has been supervising his wife's campaign of sexual abstinence, is in fact a radical separatist feminist who initiates a same-sex tryst at the same time as lecturing the ailing patriarch on his failings as a heterosexual male. This scene (along with a later segment in which Vito is wrongfully interrogated by the police for diarising references to the female anatomy under encrypted names such as *Brigande Rosse*, anarchists and fascists), indicates the extent to which the film's examination of sexuality is clearly wedded to countercultural activity. However, the introduction of Serenella (Sonia Viviani), Vito's alluring teenage niece, also shifts the narrative clearly into realms of incest fantasy, reproducing many of the boundaries of confused lineage that Freud identified in several of his accounts of primal sexuality.[16] For instance, although introduced as a distant sibling who has relocated into the couple's home following the death of her natural parents, the couple refer to the youngster in much vaguer familial terms, with comments such as 'Don't you think that our daughter is acting strange lately?'

These statements (and the conflation of sibling roles that they imply), add an additional level of perversion to Vito's frustrated libido, which is instantly redirected towards his new teenage guest. As he later comments during one of his many failed attempts to seduce the youngster: 'Who cares about kinship in front of those boobs!' This playful displacement of the incest drive also facilitates a number of illicit encounters in the film that, interestingly, involve several family members surveying other close relatives engaged in sexual activity. This strategy (which begins with both Grazia and Serenella peering into a room to watch Vito attempting intercourse with his secretary) gains an additional libidinal impetus when his niece finally agrees to have intercourse with him on the proviso that she can first watch her aunt being unfaithful with another suitor. Although Vito attempts to pay another man to seduce his wife in order to secure his own niece's virginity, the plan only facilitates further humiliation when the ill-fated male unwittingly ends up initiating intercourse with Grazia's male lover in a darkened room. This surprising same-sex interlude (along with Vito's highly feminised preparations of self-adornment prior to lovemaking) reiterates the policy of phallic debasement underpinning the comic *filone erotico*.

Such a scene of male debasement remains relatively rare within the confines of heterosexual titillation, indicative of Laura Mulvey's observation that 'the male figure cannot bear the burden of sexual objectification. Man is reluctant to gaze at his exhibitionist like.'[17] However, these strategies of male heterosexual humiliation exceed the example of *Sweet Teen* to become a key trope in many key examples of Italian erotic comedy produced during the *anni di piombo*. These strategies of male debasement were confirmed in a related comic cycle of Italian erotica whereby an emancipated external female figure (such as a tutor or work assistant) disrupts both familial and heterosexual boundaries by initiating sexual contact with both father and son, often with comic and chaotic results. As exemplified by *The School Teacher* films featuring the iconic 1970s starlet Edwige Fenech, this sub-cycle exploited what Lanzoni sees as 'the growing fascination of Italian popular audiences for erotic female teachers, female doctors or nurses, even nuns at times'.[18] While annexing tropes of terrorism to titillation as identified above, the cycle also uses interesting points of same-sex desire and transsexual masquerade in a policy of male humiliation, which stresses inadvertent or enforced feminisation as resulting in perverse familial bonds.

In *The School Teacher/L'insegnante* (Nando Cicero, 1975), Fenech plays Giovanna, the young tutor pressured by an older lover into giving private lessons (and sex sessions) to an industrialist's wayward son, Franco (Alfredo Pea). Her spouse's directives are premised on an unwholesome quest to achieve both financial gain and civic influence, which he hopes will enliven his chances of short-circuiting the chronic social housing applications in the province. These demands reflect the petty falsifications and municipal corruptions that come to define the other male protagonists' treatment of Giovanna in the film. Thus, when the industrialist expresses doubts surrounding his son's sexual prowess, he implores Giovanna to seduce the minor, commenting 'But you're modern, liberal. Think of all the peace of mind you can give to our son'. While phrases of such as 'modern', 'liberated' and 'teases' are used interchangeably to describe the apparent complexities of modern Italian womanhood, shrieks of 'mother, mother' or desperate cries to 'mama!' are the more-than-frequent words emitted by male tutors and the lacklustre school studs under Giovanna's charge.

The students' curious maternal pleas (often uttered by the rubber-faced and incongruously cast middle-aged comic Alvaro Vitali) once again relocate 1970s Italian sex comedy within the realm of the familial, echoing the perverse chains of illicit desire and confused lineage that I have identified. So while attempting to secure Giovanna's sexual services for their son, the industrialist confirms that his sibling needs 'A gentle hand, like a sister, a big sister', while the mother terms her son 'Little Franco' as a shy boy 'who has to be handled very gently'. These circuits of ambiguous desire are confounded by Franco's own perverse attempts to manipulate his tutor/sister surrogate's affections, and having taken advice on 'how do you fake being a fag' from Vitali's character and the other implausible male 'teens' in the school, Franco proceeds to enhance his already-feminised appearance via bouts of cross-dressing and enthusiastic nylon play. Although these extended scenes of comic sexual disguise are coded and contained as moments of 'queer passing', they cannot be divorced from wider strategies from grotesque feminisation and obsessions with anality and genital punishment that mark both the film and *The School Teacher* series as a whole.

Indeed, the 1978 sequel *The School Teacher Goes to Boys High/ L'insegnante va in collegio* (Mariano Laurenti) expands some of these same sex tensions in a narrative that pairs Fenech's habitual role as a desirable mentor with an industrialist's attempts to evade threats from trade unions and militants alike. Having declared himself bankrupt, this so-called 'Captain of Industry' (genre regular Renzo Montagnani) relocates to a provincial town where both he and his teenage son fall for Monica (Fenech playing the lone female language tutor at an all-male Catholic college). Courtesy of the usual confusions and thwarted couplings upon which Italian erotic comedies rely, repeated attempts by the student body to see Monica naked result in aroused pupils surveying a range of partly clad male bodies by 'mistake'. Their misinterpretation of the heroine's stage direction also renders the school's version of *Othello* as a same-sex romance sealed with an extended kiss between the two confused and semi-literate male pupils. The final image of the film depicts Monica chastising the industrialist's son for besmirching her feminist inclinations before seducing the visibly younger suitor at the point where his father is led away for punishment by the local *Brigade Rosse* faction. This moment of sexual and social incongruity adds an additional air of perversity, which cannot be divorced from the wider tensions at play within comic renditions of the *anni di piombo*.

Titillation as Trauma Narrative: Male Immobility and Morbid Infantilism

While the comic variant of 1970s Italian sexploitation cinema uses themes of perverse desire and heterosexual performativity to humorous effect, a series of morbid erotic dramas also flourished during the terrorist years.

These narratives replaced sexual incompatibility with themes of physical immobility, while once again addressing both the social and sexual annexes of trauma addressed above. In this second format, the trope of the politically attuned, but sexually vociferous, Italian woman was often recast as a potential vengeful and threatening figure, whose potency is sharply contrasted with images of male disability or incarceration. Appropriately, one of the earliest examples of this cycle was released in 1968, at the height of political unrest in Europe, and released under various titles that included *Grazie zia*, *Come Play with Me* and *Thank you Aunt*. Directed by noted erotic auteur Salvatore Sampiri, the film locates an incestuous relationship between the physically and mentally unstable teenage Alvise (Lou Castel) and his sexually unfulfilled older Aunt (Lisa Gastone), against the backdrop of student rebellion and the Vietnam War. News reportage and atrocity re-enactment frequently interrupt the erotic games between the two, establishing morbid overtones that result in alienation, sexual regression and ultimately death (see Fig. 4.1). Alvise's prepubescent angst is itself mirrored by his aunt's alienation from the male-centred political discourses that surround her, including a relationship with an older lover who would rather read the latest Umberto Eco article than to initiate intercourse with her.

Although clearly attuned to the political and sexual discontents of the era, the film remains interesting for its themes of morbid loving that are played out against the imperfect and immobile male form. *Come Play with Me* begins with a prolonged image of male suffering, as Alvise's body distorts from the electric shock therapy attempting to cure his paralysis, before detailing the various punitive, humiliating and wounding treatments imposed on this disabled form by his rich industrialist father figure.

What makes these acts of male humiliation against Alvise's body even more significant is that they are performed by actor Lou Castel, whose established persona as a virile icon from the Italian spaghetti western craze of the era is totally at odds with the immobile and infantilised vision presented in the film. Indeed, it seems appropriate that, having opened the narrative with the images of the inert male body in pain, *Come Play with Me* ends when Alvise's aunt administers a lethal injection to him, once all other taboos have been broken.

Fig. 4.1. Erotic games between teenage Alvise (Lou Castel) and his sexually unfulfilled older Aunt (Lisa Gastone) in *Come Play with Me* (Salvatore Samperi, Doria Film, 1968)

Rather than representing an isolated instance, the conflation of social and sexual trauma expressed in *Come Play with Me* were themselves reproduced in a range of carnal dramas, which further linked female erotic power and political awareness to male fatalism and regression. Arguably, these texts translate heterosexual erotica into a realm of male *neurotica*, by fusing gender fears surrounding the empowerment of women in a series of dark family dramas that flirt with incestuous content. Although these films were initiated during peak period of the *anni di piombo* in the 1970s, it is intriguing to note that the main period of production for this second, morbid strand of erotica came after 1985, immediately after the cessation of terrorist hostilities. The series included titles such as *The Trap/La gabbia* (Giuseppe Patroni Griffi, 1985), *The Dark Side of Love/Fotografando Patricia* (Salvatore Samperi, 1984), *Scandalous Gilda/Scandalosa Gilda* (1985) and *Evil Senses/Sensi* (Gabriele Lava, 1986), *Lady of the Night/La signora della notte* (Piero Shivazappa, 1986), *Desiring Julia/Desiderando Giulia* (Andrea Barzini, 1986) and *The Devil's Honey/Il miele del diavolo* (Lucio Fulci, 1986).

However, rather than representing any celluloid containment to the social and sexual contradictions endemic to the terrorist years, the continued proliferation of these dark erotic narratives act as a cinematic surplus to the larger framework of what Glynn has termed the 'wilful forgetting which has taken place in the meantime'.[19] As the author argues, although 1980s Italy was defined by an attempt to stabilise political, social and cultural relations following a decade of such profound instability, the psychic reverberations from these past acts of atrocity continued to function as a form of communal and individualised compulsive repetition. The effect is that:

> Italian culture as a whole will be seen to be trapped in a cycle
> of numbing and intrusion, of silence and re-enactment with
> respect to the experience of the *anni di piombo*.[20]

Indeed, as Glynn has further suggested in a related study of 'Terrorism, a female malady', the traumatic repetitions from the height of the 1970s terror campaigns were very much kept alive during the 1980s, through the trials of captured insurgents that became headline news during this period. She notes, 'Instrumental to the containment of terrorism was the legal-cultural innovation of *pentitismo*, a formal mechanism affording significant reductions in sentencing for prisoners who collaborated with the authorities by naming their fellow militants'.[21] These trials, which took on a confessional form, where past transgressions were placed in the communal (and conscious) sphere, have close connections with the psychic return of repressed and traumatic data outlined above. Indeed, as Glynn has suggested, the process of *pentitismo* in fact exacerbated the failure to foreclose these traumatic impulses when 'the information to which the public was exposed in the mid-1980s confirmed the alarming magnitude of the threat posed by political violence at the peak and, for the first time, shed light on the full extent and nature of women's involvement in acts of terrorism'.[22]

As the author suggests, the possible links between women and terrorism that emerged during the course of these trials fed into darker and more sexually vociferous representations of female Italian sexuality during the period. These tensions are most clearly reflected in the proliferation of dark sexual dramas during the mid-1980s. In this respect, these morbid Italian sexual tales contain a number of key repeated features worthy of consideration. Firstly, adapting some of the tragi-comic elements of thwarted male desire identified in the 1970s comic variants, these texts similarly focus on the trope of a violated male voyeur whose illicit gaze is punished by a woman or women within the text. In so doing, Italian erotic cinema both establishes and yet chastises the heterosexual male gaze of pornographic cinema. These works reproduce the 'challenges to gender and genre' that Linda Ruth Williams has identified in her recent work on 1980s American direct-to-video erotica.[23] Denied the direct, uninhibited and fleshy examination of the human body that hardcore cinema affords, these milder forms of titillation often code their moments of copulation via motifs of extratextual excess. Interestingly, Williams argues that the American variants she explores often fuse salacious content with an appeal to noir and horror thematics, thus conflating erotic intent with a range of dominant female figures that connote harmful intent towards the male.

By also terming these softcore thrillers as 'exercises in cinematic foreplay', Williams draws on Freudian notions of regression to indicate how such narrative deviations represent a deferral of desire, which finds its basis in infantile displeasure.[24] As with the concept of the primal scene that Freud identified in his classic 1918 study 'From the history of an infantile neurosis', Williams argues that the direct-to-video porn format reproduces the impotent gaze of the child to a scene of parental intercourse via its repeated trope of depicted male voyeurs, reduced to watching rather than enacting sexual activity. Alongside Williams' example of the American direct-to-video thriller, Italy's *filone erotico* format of the 1980s also appears to reproduce this primal scene structure, not only replicating the role of the on-screen male voyeur, but also allowing the actual film's viewer access to hidden and concealed scenes of sexuality. Indeed these titles frequently frame their sexual encounters via cameras hidden behind bed-posts, outside of doors and beyond window frames, as if to underscore that the viewer is accessing something 'forbidden'. Moreover, these Italian works confirm Williams' conclusion that 'although it is sexually exploited, voyeurism is also made to underpin the genre's punishment scenarios.'[25]

These so-called punishment scenarios are confirmed by the second key feature found in 1980s Italian erotic dramas. Themes of male immobility seen in titles such as *Come Play with Me* are reproduced in the repeated trope of enforced male infantilism, with an adult voyeur being bound and subjected to sexual indignities at the hands of more powerful and punitive female figures. This disconcerting feature was seen in a number of key entries, such as *The Devil's Honey*, which dwelt on images of a potent and vengeful heroine force-feeding dog food to the bound and defenceless surgeon who had earlier killed her lover in a medical blunder. *The Trap* replaced chastisement by canine chow with cruelty through chic cuisine. Here, middle-aged lothario Michael (Tony Mussante) has his chest sliced open by the mistress he spurned years earlier, who then pours fine red wine and caviar into the open wounds. This act forms one of many sexual indignities endured by the defenceless male lead. The film contrasts his present-tense punishment at the hands of Marie Colbert (Laura Antonelli) and her sexually sadistic teenage daughter Jacqueline (Blanca Marsillach) with an extended range of flashbacks detailing how, 15 years earlier, he inducted the younger and more impressionable Marie into a range of sadomasochistic games.

While these past-tense inserts indicate Michael's mastery over the sexual proceedings, the film's contemporary timeframe details a catalogue of masochistic humiliations that the protagonist endures, clearly linking his immobility to a process of enforced infantilisation organised by the vengeful female duo. This results in scenes of enforced toileting and bathing under duress, while Marie's punitive smothering of discarded food over the bound victim clearly evokes the abject imagery of waste matter that Julia Kristeva has associated with the pre-Oedipal stage of childhood.[26]

This unsettling process of infantilisation climaxes with the pair conducting a homespun operation on Michael's violated body, in order to suture the knife wound he has incurred from an earlier escape attempt. This highly evocative medical scene is shot from an overhead position, with the linen robe draped around Michael's genital area further evoking a coda of infancy through its similarity to a child's diaper. This scene and the larger context of enforced infantilisation in which it occurs confirms Glynn's comment that 'the subject is in a necessarily passive position in relation to the trauma as the traumatic image or event imposes itself on a subject incapable of *active* response'.[27] The traumas that the film details further confirm the morbid circuit of familial desire that runs through the other films under examination. This is evident in the unsettling theme of desire spanning differing generations, in a sexual tryst that binds mother and daughter to the captive male. As a result, the film contains a number of disconcerting scenes where the delirious Michael believes he has initiated intercourse with his former lover, only to discover it to be Jacqueline disguised in her mother's clothes. While *The Trap* strongly suggests the teenage girl to be the protagonist's own wayward female offspring, the finale of the film confirms the regressive circuit of desire underpinning the text; Jacqueline succeeds in binding both the fatally injured Michael and her own mother so that she can control the sexual relations between the trio.

Alongside the startling strategy of enforced infantilisation, *The Trap* also features a final key trope associated with the other Italian morbid erotic dramas. This is a complex and carnal cinematic style whereby flashbacks outlining prior sexual 'crimes' impede narrative progression. When quizzed about his memories of their earlier teenage encounters, Michael tells a forlorn Marie that 'I forgot you straight away, that's what's so strange, and after fifteen years you pop up out of nowhere'. However, the narrative prevents any such closure by the constant interruption of the past inserts, which eventually come to decide the fates of all three characters. Indeed, the film even splits the varied past inserts across gendered lines, counterbalancing Michael's erotic recollections with the traumatic memories of humiliation Marie endured during the couple's prior games. Even the film's closing scene, which fails to reveal either the full nature of the traumatic flashback scene or the final fate of the protagonists, points to a state of compulsive irresolution that binds individual malady to the unresolved traumas of the *anni di piombo*. As Glynn has commented, 'it is through the unconscious language of repetition – flashbacks, nightmares, emotional flooding and other forms of intrusively repetitive behaviour – that the wound cries out'.[28]

Other Italian erotic dramas also evidence a circuit of infantilism and regression underscored by traumatic flashbacks and back-plots, which reveal a past sexual transgression that functions as a present-tense trigger for gendered punishment. As one of the final titles produced during the *anni di piombo*, *The Dark Side of Love* also remains one the most nihilistic in its exploration of these regressive themes. Expanding on thematic interests from his earlier *Come Play with Me*, director Salvatore Sampiri revisits themes of punitive voyeurism within the near-incestuous relationship between a young male protagonist and a female parental substitute. The transgressive coupling is played out between the 16-year-old Emilio (Lorenzo Lena) and his sexually precocious older sister Patrizia (Monica Guerritore).

Indicating its basis in trauma rather than titillation, it is noticeable that *The Dark Side of Love* begins and ends with images of death and regression. The opening scene depicts the funeral of Emilio's mother and is intercut with his obsessive reviewing of home video tapes revealing the degree of demeaning control the deceased matriarch retained. Emilio suffers from a severe bone deformity that has 'trapped his body between childhood and manhood' (enforced male infantilism again), a permanent state of physiological regression that results in Patrizia returning from Venice to tend for her younger sibling. Sexual tensions soon come to the surface, however, when Patrizia organises a series of sexual encounters for her brother to watch, thus exploiting his desire and unease at viewing these taboo acts. It is only when the couple have re-enacted the heroine's first sexual encounter with an 'older' stranger in a movie theatre that the regressive circuit is complete, and the film ends with an unsettling image of the pair wrapped in a foetal death pose.

With its emphasis on an emancipated but destructive female who also acts as an agent of sexual regression, the ending of *The Dark Side of Love* confirms that Italian erotic cinema remains a stark and nihilistic sexual landscape in which the pleasures associated with the male pornographic imagination are either comically humiliated or rendered displeasurable via their connection with threat, violence or familial transgression. Thus, the films I have outlined indicate the extent to which erotic material evokes not only sensuality but also the potential trauma and suffering for the Italian sexual citizen of the *anni di piombo*.

Notes

1. Ruth Glynn, 'Terrorism, a female malady', in Ruth Glynn, Giancarlo Lombardi and Alan O'Leary (eds), *Terrorism Italian Style: Representations of Political Violence in Contemporary Italian Cinema* (London: IGRS Books, 2012), p. 318.

2. Alan O' Leary, 'Italian cinema and the "anni di piombo"', *Journal of European Studies* 40/3 (2010), pp. 243–57.

3. Beverley Allen, 'They're not children anymore: the novelisation of "Italians" and "terrorists"', in Beverly Allen and May Russo (eds), *Revisioning Italy: National Identity and Global Culture* (Minneapolis: University of Minnesota Press, 1997), pp. 63–7.

4. Ruth Glynn, 'Trauma on the line: terrorism, testimony in the *anni do piombo*', in Monica Jansen and Paula Jordão (eds), *The Value of Literature in and After the Seventies: The Case of Italy and Portugal*, Proceedings of the International Conference (2006), pp. 323, 320. Available at http://congress70.library.uu.nl/index.html?000004/index.html (accessed 22 January 2012).

5. Ibid., p. 324.

6. Mary P. Wood, *Italian Cinema* (Oxford: Berg, 2005), p. 166.

7. Ibid., p. 61.

8. Rémi Fournier Lanzoni, *Comedy Italian Style: The Age of Italian Film Comedies* (New York: Continuum, 2008), p. 182.

9. Ibid., p. 157.

10. See Paul Ginsborg, *A History of Contemporary Italy 1943–1980* (London: Penguin History, 1990).

11. Lanzoni, *Comedy Italian Style*, p. 148.

12. Ibid.

13. Ibid., p. 151.

14. Ibid., p. 159.

15. See Adrian Luther-Smith (ed.), *Delirium: A Guide to Italian Exploitation Cinema 1975–1979* (London: Media Publications, 1997).

16. Sigmund Freud, 'From the history of an infantile neurosis', *Three Case Studies* (New York: Touchstone, 1963), pp. 161–280. Originally published 1918.

17. Laura Mulvey, 'Visual pleasure and narrative cinema', in Constance Penley (ed.), *Feminism and Film Theory* (London: Routledge, 1988), p. 63.

18. Lanzoni, *Comedy Italian Style*, p. 159.

19. Glynn, 'Trauma on the line', p. 322.

20. Ibid.

21. Glynn, 'Terrorism', p. 119.

22. Ibid.

23. Linda Ruth Williams, *The Erotic Thriller in Contemporary Cinema* (Edinburgh: Edinburgh University Press, 2005), p. 331.

24. Ibid.

25. Williams, *The Erotic Thriller*, p. 338.

26. Julia Kristeva, *Powers of Horror: An Essay on Abjection* (New York: Columbia University Press, 1982).

27. Glynn, 'Trauma on the line', p. 325.

28. Ibid.

II

Too Close for Comfort: Mainstream Perversion, Marginal Tastes

5

A Dangerous Method: Provocative Performances of Perversion

Donna Peberdy

In 2002, Bill Pullman – perhaps most recognised for his heroic and honourable performances as the President of the United States in science fiction blockbuster *Independence Day* (Roland Emmerich, 1996) and average man-next-door in the romantic comedies *Sleepless in Seattle* (Nora Ephron, 1993) and *While You Were Sleeping* (John Turteltaub, 1995) – took to the Broadway stage in a rather different role. 'You have to realise that in the movie world, there's the belief that the parts you play are somehow who you are. In Hollywood, you're routinely told, "Don't play a pedophile"', the actor commented in one interview.[1] 'With this play the transgression is even worse', Pullman noted of Edward Albee's domestic melodrama, in which he appeared as a husband who admits to having an affair with a goat. Pullman was initially reluctant to take on the role of a zoophile in *The Goat, or Who is Sylvia?* since it was such a departure from the 'affable guy' he played on screen. But he also saw theatre as a space where risks could and should be played out and where it was possible to 'expand one's understanding of humanity'.[2] Hollywood, by comparison for the actor, was much more conservative in its treatment of sexuality. The risks were seemingly greater for actors playing sexually deviant characters on screen because taking on such roles may have a lasting impact on screen persona and reputation.

Given these ostensible risks, what is the attraction for an actor to take on such a role? For Pullman, playing a zoophile created a challenge to 'find the dignity in this character', in the hope that his performance would incite discussion and debate. The play's message, Pullman believed, was that 'we should feel compassion for those who have transgressed. We need boundaries, but sometimes we need to question those boundaries'.[3] Echoing Pullman, Dylan Baker, who plays a paedophile in independent film *Happiness* (Todd Solondz, 1998), has commented that he hoped he would not 'fall victim to typecasting' but found the experience of getting into his *Happiness* character cathartic: 'The ability to go in and really find the depths of this character was a little releasing and actually invigorating', he noted, 'it's a very disturbing film, but at the same time I enjoyed myself immensely'.[4] Similarly, Stanley Tucci has noted how 'exciting' he found the process of playing a child-molesting serial killer in *The Lovely Bones* (Peter Jackson, 2009). 'Your whole organism tells you that you don't want to do it', Tucci responded when asked how he prepared for the role, continuing: 'but you do want to do it, because it's a fascinating study, and you want to create a real person'.[5]

The three actors express a shared aim to find and present something meaningful in their characterisations, in spite of their characters' sexual perversions. The enjoyment and fascination in taking on such roles comes from playing characters who have transgressed social and sexual norms yet present the audience with a characterisation that may call into question previously-held assumptions and beliefs. The boundaries Pullman mentions refer to the boundaries of what is deemed normal and acceptable in terms of sexuality in society. But the roles also challenge the boundaries of representation and performance: what is at stake in playing a paedophile, a zoophile or other sexual perversion? The actors' comments demonstrate how performing sexual perversion is already provocative due to the ostensible 'risks' and impact on persona.

I am particularly interested here in the provocative potential of the performance of sexual perversion. That is, the extent to which performance can impact how we understand sexual perversion and perverse sexualities. Acting in this context becomes the negotiation of risk and the transgression of multiple boundaries in order to raise questions and provoke discussion. To examine the implications of performing sexual perversion in more detail, this chapter focuses on two quite different case studies: Kevin Bacon's performance of a convicted child molester in Nicole Kassell's poignant and understated independent drama *The Woodsman* (2004) and Keira Knightley's performance of sexual hysteria and sadomasochism in David Cronenberg's cerebral historical fiction *A Dangerous Method* (2011). The two films feature actors performing sexual perversion in leading roles but it is *how* they perform their respective perversions that is especially significant. Both performances overwhelm their narratives in terms of impact, commanding attention beyond the film diegesis. Bacon and Knightley's performances elicited more attention from reviewers than the films in which they appeared, which is unusual since acting is generally given short shrift in reviews. In this chapter, I explore how these performances not only engage with and challenge preconceived notions and stereotypes, but they also challenge the boundaries and norms of sexual identity and the performing body.

'When will I be normal?': Rehabilitating the Paedophile in *The Woodsman*

The Woodsman opens with convicted paedophile Walter's release back into the community after serving 12 years in prison for molesting girls. The children, we find out later, were aged between nine and 14. Now in his mid-40s, Walter moves into an apartment that just so happens to overlook a school playground, only marginally further than the required 300 feet he must keep from children. He manages to find a job at a lumberyard, cautiously embarks on a relationship with straight-talking co-worker Vicki (played by Bacon's wife Kyra Sedgwick), all the while being monitored by parole officer Sergeant Lucas (Mos Def) and counselled by therapist Rosen (Michael Shannon). The film follows Walter's rehabilitation from his perspective as he battles with both his sexual and social identity. His role clearly sits alongside other characterisations of sexual transgressors by the actor, including a child kidnapper in *Trapped* (Luis Mandoki, 2002), a gay prostitute in *JFK* (Oliver Stone, 1991), a stalker in *In the Cut* (Jane Campion, 2003) and a corrupt prison guard in *Sleepers* (Barry Levinson, 1996), who recurrently subjects the young male teens under his watch to verbal, physical and sexual abuse. In bringing its sexual transgressor centre stage, *The Woodsman* stands apart from these earlier films and others released around the time, such as *L.I.E.* (Michael Cuesta, 2001), *Mystic River* (Clint Eastwood, 2003), *Mysterious Skin* (Gregg Araki, 2004) and *Little Children* (Todd Field, 2006), that tell their stories from the perspective of the child victim or wider community. In doing so, *The Woodsman* gives space to explore a complex sexual identity typically presented as a straightforward stereotype.

'"The paedophile" is a concept', writes Jenny Kitzinger, 'enmeshed in a series of crass stereotypes which place the child sexual abuser "outside" society'. She continues, 'In the tabloid press abusers are "animals", "monsters", "sex maniacs", "beasts" and "perverts" who are routinely described as "loners" and "weirdos".'[6] The 'plethora of words' used to describe the paedophile, as Carol-Ann Hooper and Ann Kaloski argue, conceals a 'poverty of meaning'.[7] Nonetheless, the paedophile has emerged 'as arguably the most feared and vilified of all "predatory strangers"'.[8] The fictionalised paedophile has become increasingly visible on screen in the last two decades and is a character very much constructed and read via the popularised discourses presented to us by the mainstream media. He (rarely she) is most often a subsidiary figure, antagonist and villain, lurking in cinema's shadows and alleyways; never the protagonist. The mainstream screen has historically inscribed the paedophile with deviance, dysfunction and danger, projecting the 'unrepresentable' act of child sexual abuse onto a physical form.[9] He is rendered in narrow visual terms as an evil stranger, a predator prowling children's playgrounds and stalking internet chat rooms, a pathological other and modern-day folk devil. He is, simply, a threat to children and a threat to society.

The Woodsman was released amid tabloid name-and-shame campaigns and media vigilantism in response to high-profile sexual assault and murder cases in the US and UK involving 'known' paedophiles.[10] In many respects, the film conforms to the prevailing discourse around the 'paedophile in the community' and 'stranger danger' rhetoric that considers paedophiles as 'inherently recidivist' and 'beyond the capacity for rehabilitation'.[11] 'While popular knowledge jars with the relatively low re-offending rates of child sexual offenders', Simon Cross writes, 'public concerns about paedophiles have become absorbed within a rhetoric of contemporary punitive populism reinforced by the popular press and other agencies'.[12] The film knowingly constructs a familiar backdrop for its paedophile narrative in placing Walter literally overlooking a school playground, establishing him as a loner who keeps himself to himself at work, spends his time alone in his apartment or follows young girls he sees on the bus. He expresses his desire to 'be normal' in therapy sessions but he is not sure what that means or how to achieve it. Responses to Walter's rehabilitation are differently articulated through minor characters: a receptionist at the lumberyard discovers Walter's prior conviction and circulates his release sheet under the premise that 'people have the right to know'; he is vilified by his parole officer, who is convinced it is only a matter of time before Walter re-offends; his brother-in-law vocalises his support for Walter and his recovery but is not comfortable having Walter attend his daughter's birthday party.

Bacon's motivation in taking on the role directly engages with two competing discourses around the paedophile: the popularised image of the predatory stranger and the statistical reality that paedophiles are often close relations, acquaintances or known in some other capacity.[13] In an interview with the BBC, the actor noted:

> These guys don't have horns. If they were monsters we could send a superhero out to kill them, or a guy with a big sword – and that would make life a lot easier. The reality is much, much more frightening than that – they are friends of the family, in our churches, in our schools, riding on the bus next to us.[14]

Bacon commented in numerous interviews that his intention was to make Walter 'human': 'I didn't want anything sort of special about him, a crazy look in his eyes, a leer'.[15] His comments reveal an intention to present a provocative character, one that goes against the standard script for the sex offender and seeks to unravel the popularised image of the paedophile. If, as Anne-Marie McAlinden has argued, 'the fact child sex offenders may be "of us" rather than "other than us" is a deeply unpalatable truth for society to countenance', it is Walter's proximity, rather than otherness, that is the most disconcerting.[16]

Significantly, we find out very little about his character's motivations. We are not given a backstory that explains why Walter molested young girls. Bacon's performance is all we have in deciding whether or not Walter can successfully enter back into society. The actor worked with director Nicole Kassell in pre-production to strip back the dialogue from Steven Fechter's original play in order to allow emotion to be expressed via his gestures and expressions rather than words. 'I wanted to take his sadness, shame, history, his 12 years in prison, all that kind of stuff and put it in my belly and then find ways to let it out, through the eyes or voice or whatever', the actor noted.[17] His construction of an ambivalent, tormented man is all the more unsettling as a result.

Throughout the film, Bacon's performance is characterised by self-consciousness, awkwardness and torment. His eyes are often the locus of anguish; conflict is portrayed via searching glances, darting pupils and downward glances at the floor, suggesting shame and unease. The cinematography amplifies Bacon's performance of introspection, juxtaposing expressions of doubt and worry with close-ups of splashing water on his face and extended glances into mirrors. We wonder what Walter is thinking as we watch him silently watching himself. Vicki also watches Walter, trying to read him. 'I used to think you were shy but now I think it's something else', she tells him after giving him a lift home from work, 'something happened to you'. Her perceptiveness regarding Walter reveals her own past traumas and encourages Walter to disclose his 'deep, dark secret'. 'I'm not easily shocked', she states matter-of-factly, all the more intrigued after their first, 'intense' sexual encounter. When Walter later confesses that he molested girls, we read him via Vicki's reactions to his confession as she tries to comprehend the implications of what she is hearing. His confession is delivered calmly, his voice is measured but he avoids eye contact. 'It's not what you think', Walter says, 'I never hurt them. Never'. His response indicates how far he still has to go in his rehabilitation; Walter does not yet recognise his molestation as harmful. When Vicki is taken aback but responds calmly, trying to understand, Walter ejects her from his apartment. His shame and disgust at his past actions are directed at Vicki, punishing her for not responding in a way that he thinks he deserves. Walter's discomfort is palpable as he stands by the door as she leaves, awkwardly moving his hands in and out of his pockets.

During a therapy session, the camera stays on Walter and his reaction to Rosen's probing questions about his relationship with his sister when they were children. With his head down, Bacon's body language is closed and defensive. As Rosen encourages him to recall his feelings for his sister and what he might have experienced as a child, Walter recoils with a pained expression on his face: 'I liked smelling her hair. That's all'. His watery eyes and intermittent swallowing suggest his defensiveness masks a deep-rooted sadness and shame. In an intimate scene that immediately follows, Vicki sits on Walter's lap as he caresses her body. He stops her from reciprocating his touches, holding her hands down by her side and deeply inhales the smell of her hair, suppressing a cry with a look of anguish. Bacon presents a tormented man battling with his sexuality and trying to make sense of his past and present emotions.

Walter's interiority is interspersed with forceful eruptions of emotion. The range of his turmoil is evident when his parole officer visits his apartment to ask why he got off his bus at a different stop, using the opportunity to disparage him. He asks Walter if he believes in fairytales and, when he replies in the negative, Lucas recalls the character of The Woodsman, who cut open the stomach of the Big Bad Wolf to rescue Little Red Riding Hood. This is interspersed with Lucas recounting a recent visit to a man on death row for abusing and murdering a young girl. 'You ever seen a seven-year-old been sodomized in half?' he asks, rhetorically, before concluding: 'There ain't no fucking woodsmen in this world'. 'I don't know why they keep letting freaks like you out on the street', he says finally, 'It just means that we gotta catch you all over again'. Walter sits quietly through the parole officer's damning comparison and assessment of his ability to be rehabilitated. His face and body are uncomfortably stiff as he struggles to retain his composure. As soon as Lucas leaves, Walter falls to his knees, violently tearing pages out of the journal he has been keeping as part of his therapy. However cathartic keeping the journal may have been for Walter, he understands that the popular perception of the paedophile as predator persists regardless. With his hands to the side of his head, clasping his temples, Bacon visibly shakes and sobs into the strewn paper, pulling his head to his knees in a child's pose on the floor.

Fig. 5.1. Convicted paedophile Walter (Kevin Bacon) attempts to befriend 11-year-old Robin (Hannah Pilkes) in *The Woodsman* (Nicole Kassell, Dash Films, 2004)

Such moments of agonised introspection contrast scenes of Walter with Robin (Hannah Pilkes), an 11-year-old girl he sees on the bus home from work and follows to a park. In Robin's company, Walter is more relaxed and at ease; the constant sense of surveillance is lifted (see Fig. 5.1). His posture is looser and less guarded, his facial expressions are more open. His smile is easy, earnest and childlike. Later, Walter meets Robin again and asks her to sit on his lap. At first she declines but then asks, 'Would you like me to sit on your lap?' Walter looks hopeful and replies, after a pause, 'Yes, I would enjoy that'. Robin then reveals that her father also asks her to sit on his lap but she does not like it. Walter's face falls and there is a look of realisation as he comprehends her father's request, and therefore his own, as harmfully abusive. The exchange calls into question his earlier clarification to Vicki that he 'never hurt' the girls he molested; he realises the hurt caused extends beyond physical sexual violence. It implies that interactions with victims, not vilification from law enforcement, might be more effective in his rehabilitation.

It is a tense, uncomfortable scene and Bacon is the site of our unease. While it is not verbally articulated, the range of Walter's conflict is patently visible in Bacon's subtle gestures and expressions. Shaking his head, nodding, closing his eyes, looking at the floor and picking at his hands, his nuanced performance captures multiple, conflicting emotions, revealing Walter's gradual understanding about his past actions and that he must choose to either succumb to or reject his deviant sexual desires. Both here and throughout the film, Bacon's performance of Walter's desire is manifested in the sensory – the smell of hair, the sights and sounds of the school playground, the touch of skin – that normalises and demonises, comforts and taunts him. Bacon's performance plays with our expectations of where discomfort lies, inviting us into Walter's turmoil, giving us a glimpse of what attracts him but also his confusion and pain.

It is this repeated presentation of ambivalence that is most provocative about Bacon's performance. A presentation of a predatory paedophile without remorse or one who completely renounces his transgressive sexuality would perhaps be easier to comprehend. The predator is given to us in *The Woodsman* as a man Walter names Candy (Kevin Rice), who loiters around the playground and lures young boys into his car with sweets. We know even less about Candy than we do about Walter and he becomes the template for the cunning and calculated predator from which both Walter and Bacon are trying to distance themselves. The inclusion of Candy's character is a calculated move to establish Walter's complexity. When Walter sees a young boy emerge from Candy's car, he attacks Candy, repeatedly punching him in the face but, for a split second, Walter's face appears in place of Candy's bloody pulp. Candy is not simply the Big Bad Wolf to Walter's Woodsman; the two are interchangeable, as Walter's display of anger and loathing is directed as much against Candy as it is against himself.

By the end of the film, Walter is, for all intents and purposes, on his way to becoming successfully rehabilitated. He moves out of his playground-facing apartment and in with Vicki and meets with the sister who has refused to speak with him since he was convicted. Rather than provide a sense of comfort that Walter has been rehabilitated, however, the resolution calls into question the very concept of rehabilitation and Bacon's performance points to its impossibility. There is no return to or restoration of a normal, stable state; his new equilibrium is a constant battle. Through Bacon's introspective performance, we are asked to witness Walter's torment and conflict as he wavers between fascination and desire, confusion and clarity, repulsion and shame. His performance asks us to view Walter not as a predatory paedophile but as a man desperate to be 'normal', haunted by his past actions and tormented by his possible future desires. Bacon's performance presents Walter's battle with his sexuality; trapped between wanting and doing, his eventual decision to not pursue Robin does not negate his desire. His ambivalence is provocative because it does not present a paedophile who has been cured but one who has learned to perform in a way that allows him to 'pass' as normal. His socially deviant sexual urges have not been eradicated but need to be continually managed.

'Only the clash of destructive forces can create something new': Boundary Testing in *A Dangerous Method*

A Dangerous Method also explores the possibility of rehabilitation through a performance of repression, suppression and containment, although one characterised by corporeal excess rather than introspection. Based on true events, Keira Knightley plays Sabina Spielrein, a Russian woman admitted to the care of Carl Jung (Michael Fassbender) for the treatment of acute sexual hysteria in 1904. In consultation with Sigmund Freud (Viggo Mortensen), Jung treats Sabina with the infamous 'talking cure', the 'dangerous method' of the film's title. Her hysteria is revealed to be a response to her repression of sexually masochistic impulses that stem from being beaten by her father as a child and her subsequent shame and humiliation. She admits that her father's beatings – of herself and her siblings – sexually excited her to the point that embarrassment of any kind has become arousing. 'There's no hope for me', she despairs, 'I'm vile and filthy and corrupt, I must never be let out of here'. As her mental health improves, the doctor and patient embark on an extra-marital affair and she goes on to become a student and then practitioner of psychoanalysis, influencing both Jung and Freud's later theories on sexuality.

The representation of hysteria offers an intriguing counterpoint to the paedophile. The figure of the paedophile, although by no means new, is very much a modern-day folk devil, proliferating in the news media and fuelled by the pervasiveness of the internet. The sexual hysteric is a figure from the past, suffering from an archaic condition that is no longer recognised by medical professionals as a legitimate disorder and its verity has since been widely interpreted and challenged.[18] While paedophilia is predominantly associated with men, hysteria was considered an overwhelmingly female affliction. And while the popularised image of the paedophile is one of the active predator, the image of the hysteric is one who passively suffers as a consequence of her female body.

The 'conceptual catchall' of hysteria has been variously applied throughout history, from the 'wandering womb' of its literal translation relating to the uterus, to demonic possession and witchcraft, to sexual repression.[19] By the late nineteenth century and into the twentieth century, the period in which A Dangerous Method is set, it was a 'veritable phenomenon' and inextricable from female sexuality.[20] In Richard von Krafft-Ebing's 1886 publication Psychopathia Sexualis, hysteria was described as a neurosis, characterised by 'convulsive attacks' and 'abnormally intense sexual impulse'.[21] In keeping with Krafft-Ebing, in his 1905 publication Three Essays on the Theory of Sexuality, Freud considered hysteria a neurosis rather than symptom and therefore 'the negative of perversion', characterised by 'an immense sexual desire and a very exaggerated sexual rejection'.[22] A Dangerous Method and Knightley's performance of hysteria both confirm and challenge his conclusions. Rather than existing as opposites, hysteria and perversion are inextricably linked; sexual perversion becomes both a way of managing hysteria – Sabina discovers a sexual outlet in the form of a sadomasochistic relationship with Jung – and is explicitly manifested in Knightley's performance of hysteria and repression. While Knightley's role in Cronenberg's period drama is a transgressive variation on the assertive and audacious women who refuse to conform to convention – seen in the Pirates of the Caribbean action-adventure franchise (Gore Verbinski, 2003, 2006, 2007) and her period drama collaborations with director Joe Wright: Pride & Prejudice (2005), Atonement (2007) and Anna Karenina (2012) – her performance of hysteria offers a significant departure.

The film opens with Knightley's Sabina in a horse-drawn carriage, screaming and twisting her body to resist the restraining clutches of two men. With her face up against the glass window, she bares her teeth, wailing and growling as the carriage approaches the Burghölzli Clinic in Zürich. Three men carry her writhing body towards the entrance to the clinic. She launches her head back, kicking her feet and cackling demonically. The following day, Jung meets his new patient. Sat in a wooden chair with her elbows elevated, her wrists angled and upper body pushed forward, her lips tremble and her head shakes, her wide eyes are fixed on the doctor. Her breathing is laboured as she stutters, 'I'm not mad, you know'. She cowers when Jung walks past to sit in a chair behind her, protecting herself with a contorted arm, her eyes frantically darting left and right. When Jung asks Sabina if she knows what has brought on her attacks, she launches forward in her chair and splutters through bared teeth: 'humiliation … any kind of humiliation', violently jutting out her lower jaw and twisting her arms behind her back (see Fig. 5.2). Squirming, she pushes her hands into her groin area, an action she repeats when Sabina experiences humiliation in a later scene. The gesture is revealed to be a literal attempt at suppressing her sexual impulses as she is overcome with the urgent need to masturbate. The scene ends with Sabina admitting that after her father beat her and her siblings, they had to kiss his hand in a gesture of submission. Knightley's frenzied contortions and stuttering give

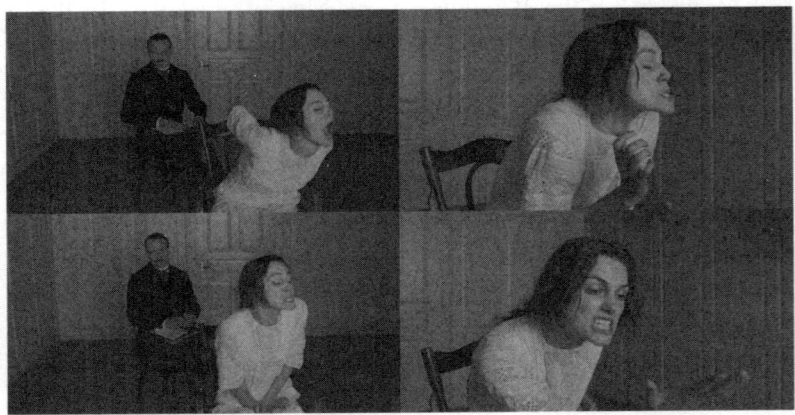

Fig. 5.2. Sabina Spielrein's (Keira Knightley) hysteria is played out on her contorted body in *A Dangerous Method* (David Cronenberg, RPC, 2011), observed by Carl Jung (Michael Fassbender)

way to trembling. She stares into her outstretched palm and curled fingers as her character tries to understand the impact of her father's actions towards her.

Knightley's performance divided critics, dominating both positive and negative reviews of the film. The actor was described as 'the film's most problematic element' in her 'brave but unskilled depiction of hysteria that leaves itself open to easy laughs'.[23] Reviewers criticised Knightley's 'unruly collection of yammering tics and starts [that] might veer close to parody at times',[24] stating that she 'extends her lower jaw like a demented snapping turtle [...] and making her already prominent eyes pop out of her skull.[25] Other critics praised Knightley's 'brave' and 'gutsy' portrayal, although acknowledging its potential to be divisive,[26] and *New York Times* critic Manohla Dargis even included Knightley in her 'Best Actress' top five for the year for her 'underappreciated performance' in the film.[27] The critical discordance highlights a challenge posed to the boundaries of normative and acceptable representation and, whether positively or negatively received, Knightley's performance of hysteria stood out to the extent that it overwhelmed the wider film narrative.

David Cronenberg found himself defending Knightley in promotional interviews as a result of the negative reaction the actor received. The director asserted that Knightley's extreme performance style was 'the whole point', since the actor was playing a character suffering from hysteria, her performance was grounded in extensive research and was, in fact, 'relatively subdued compared to the footage of actual hysterical patients' they had watched when researching the character.[28] The film's press kit describes the scenes of hysteria as 'direct interpretations of the hospital records' that note how the 'patient laughs and cries in a strangely mixed, compulsive manner. Masses of tics; she rotates her head jerkily, sticks out her tongue, twitches her legs [...] Cannot stand people or noise.[29] The justification highlights the problematic nature of Knightley's excessive performance. While it might be 'true to the clinical description of that earlier time',[30] the performance of a condition marked by excess is immediately complicated since excess and realism have historically been seen as occupying opposing ends of the performance spectrum.

Knightley's performative excess has a crucial function in the film, breaking the viewer's 'total absorption in the narrative'[31] and inviting the viewer to ask questions about the narrative in a way that would not be possible without such disruptions. Referring specifically to excess in relation to film acting, Carole Zucker notes that 'an unequivocal cleavage between the act and the actor' is created as a consequence of excess. 'And in that gap', she observes, 'there is a declaration of acting as an instrument of reflection, an arena of play and experimentation, and a forum for commentary'.[32] Knightley's sinuous, histrionic performance overstates and accentuates, demanding attention. Whether perceived positively or nega-tively, the excessive performance stops us in our tracks and invites us to make sense of it. Knightley's performance thus presents a challenging and provocative example of boundary-testing (to appropriate a psychiatric term) whereby the body becomes both the mechanism for and site of perversion.

Comparing Knightley's performance to another film performance of hysteria from the following year emphasises its distinctiveness. Loosely based on a true story, French drama *Augustine* (Alice Winocour, 2012) similarly focuses on the relationship between a medical professional treating a patient diagnosed with hysteria: neurologist Jean-Martin Charcot (Vincent Linden) and his prize patient Augustine (French singer-songwriter Soko), who is admitted to Salpêtrière Hospital after a paralysing attack. Charcot gained notoriety in the 1870s and 1880s for his use of photography and live demonstrations to document and showcase his treatment of hysteria with hypnosis. The film plays out the link between hysteria and performance through the staging of the live demonstrations, presenting the hysterical woman as spectacle. Soko's performance of hysteria is predominantly filmed in a series of long and wide shots, drawing attention to the entire body and its unnatural movements. Director Alice Winocour was inspired by horror films featuring possession and exorcism and manipulated Soko's body using ropes and strings to achieve unnatural, 'brutal movements' that were then digitally erased in post-production.[33] When Augustine suffers an attack, her body spasms, rapidly alternating between limpness, wild motions and an arched, rigid opisthotonic position. However, the performance of hysteria is unequivocally erotic rather than monstrous. Her hyperextended body is accompanied by orgasmic moans, pants and gasps, occasionally punctuated by exclamations of 'Oui! Oui!'. Her facial expressions convey pleasure and satisfaction as she pushes her hands in between her legs and clutches at her breasts. In contrast to Sabina's suppression of desire and denial of masturbation in *A Dangerous Method*, Augustine's hysterical attack is a display of uninhibited female sexual pleasure. If the sexual connotations were not obvious enough, the reactions of Charcot and the male demonstration audience are foregrounded on more than one occasion, their mouths agape in fascination and amusement. As Augustine's paroxysm finally reaches its climax, the men erupt in applause and cheering.

Knightley's performance of hysteria is ugly, animalistic and grotesque. Even though Sabina's hysteria is decidedly linked to the sexual, it is not a sensual or erotic performance. Knightley's movements defy normative bodily parameters in a physical act of contortion, without the use of ropes and strings. Close-ups and tight framing draw attention to the eyes, mouth, jaw and hands. With Jung sitting behind Sabina, Knightley's performance is presented direct to camera and is the spectacle. Occasionally we see Sabina from behind, from Jung's perspective, but reaction shots are entirely absent. Cronenberg wanted 'all the tension [to] be concentrated around her mouth'.[34] Not only was this in a bid to be faithful to the gestures and expressions of female hysterics in the early 1900s, but in baring her teeth, hyperextending her lower jaw and stuttering and spitting over her words, Knightley's method encapsulates Sabina's inability to articulate and verbalise her humiliation.

Cronenberg's films often reveal a fascination with transgressing the boundaries of the body, what Elisabeth Bronfen has referred to as a 'mutable corporeality'.[35] What we frequently see in Cronenberg's films, she notes, is a 'blurring of the boundary between internal and external body spaces'.[36] Cronenberg's fascination clearly extends to performance and how actors embody the struggle to contain and control the transforming, transgressive body. While *A Dangerous Method* might be Cronenberg's 'calmest and most cerebral film yet',[37] Knightley's corporeal excess place it somewhere between the body horror of *The Fly* (1986) and *Crash* (1996), and the bodies that 'speak' in *A History of Violence* (2005) and *Eastern Promises* (2007) via violence and tattoos, respectively. Projecting the inside out is evident in Knightley's exterior emotionalism as Sabina's repression is projected outward and her sexual humiliation is explicitly played out on the actor's face and body. It appears all the more excessive when framed against Fassbender and Mortensen's muted, introspective performances as Jung and Freud.

Instead of establishing an assimilation trajectory that seeks to move Sabina towards heteronormativity by alleviating or denying her perversion, hysteria is presented as a consequence of trying to repress non-normative desires. Sexual deviance becomes the cure, rather than symptom. The sadomasochistic relationship Sabina embarks on with Jung is cathartic and empowering. With Jung again positioned behind Sabina, the scenes of sadomasochism both mirror and subvert the therapy sessions. In therapy, she struggles to articulate her past traumas and her body responds violently at the confession of her repressed urges. In her sexual pursuit of Jung, she is confident and direct. 'With me, I want you to be ferocious. I want you to punish me', she demands. As Jung vigorously thrashes her rear with a belt, she watches herself in the mirror. On her knees with both hands tied to the bed in front of her, her composed and defiant gaze is locked on her reflection as she climaxes. The verbal recollection of her desire and shame that her body battles with in response to her father's beatings is exchanged for physical reenactment in which she has control, where 'loss of control as *memory* is mediated by a show of excess of control as *spectacle*'.[38] Her erratic movements, stuttering and histrionics dissipate as she embraces her masochistic desire. Previously dependent on Jung as both her doctor and lover, Sabina reaches the point where she can move on from the relationship and, in a reversal of roles, it is then Jung who cries at her feet, begging her not to leave. By the end of the film, it is not Sabina but Jung, muted and composed for a large part of the film, who has become unhinged by his sexual longing and tormented by his inability to make sense of sexual desire. We are left with an image of the psychiatrist staring vacantly into space on the cusp of a nervous breakdown. Sabina is asked to 'help' Jung and the doctor/patient relationship is inverted.

In her excessive and violent projection, Knightley's challenge to the boundaries of the body externalises Sabina attempts to first contain and then embrace her sexuality. It is a performance of hysteria made provocative by its excess but also in demanding release in sadomasochism, which inverts power and 'plays the world backwards'.[39] As with Kevin Bacon's performance in *The Woodsman*, the performing body becomes the site of unease. In challenging and defying the limitations of the normative physical and performing body and inviting questions about the relationship between realism and excess, Knightley's provocative performance – not the psychological 'talking cure' – becomes the 'dangerous method' of the film.

Acting and/as Transgression

The dangerous method that both Keira Knightley and Kevin Bacon embark on offers a direct challenge to the 'norm' and necessitates the negotiation of risk. Far from fearing being typecast, as Bill Pullman and Dylan Baker's earlier comments attest, Kevin Bacon commented in interviews that he was not worried about the impact of the role on his reputation. He perceived taking on such a role as all part of the job of being an actor:

> To me, an actor is someone who is not afraid to take risks; to put on different hats; to be a good guy, a bad guy, a victim, an abuser. There are all kinds of people in the world, and playing them is what acting is all about.[40]

His challenge instead was to convincingly play a character convicted for child molestation and project the turmoil experienced by a man that is repeatedly demonised in popular culture. For Knightley, the risk is in physically going 'too far' in depicting the sexual hysteric so the representation is not taken seriously. 'In doing research, I don't think we went as far as [hysteria] actually went', Knightley reflected. 'I don't think people would have bought it if we had actually went as far as some of things I read'.[41]

Bacon and Knightley's provocative performances underscore their privileged position as actors to test and transgress physical, cultural and symbolic boundaries. John Harrop acknowledges this phenomenological divide when he states: 'The actor in many ways is licensed to do what many members of society have an itch to do but know the safety of society would be destroyed if they were allowed similar license'.[42] This is not to imply that their performances allow the audience to play out a desire to be a paedophile, or an hysteric, but a desire for perversion is articulated; to play with and subvert the boundaries of acceptability and normativity or to completely do away with them altogether. Still, 'like Jack-in-the-box,' Harrop notes, 'we need to know that [the actor] can be shut back into the box at any moment'.[43] The implication is that the performance is already made safer, more comfortable, through the knowledge that what we are watching is a performance, however based on real events it may be. The audience 'acclaims the actor from its safe remove', challenged and unsettled but ultimately secure in their position as fictional bystander.[44] This has obvious implications for the impact of performance on the audience. As Rory Loughnane and Edel Semple ask: 'How much of the transgressive act's subversiveness is lost because it is simulated?'.[45]

The transgressive act might be undermined in its fictionalised depiction but in both *The Woodsman* and *A Dangerous Method*, the transgressive act is not the sexual perversion but the provocative, challenging, confrontational performance of perversion that refuses to be ignored. By playing with boundaries and courting risk, the actor's performance has the power to expose that which society seeks to contain, 'to tear off the calcified mask of social lies, politeness and good taste, and to reveal the dark and dynamic underbelly of society itself'.[46] The wider narratives of both *The Woodsman* and *A Dangerous Method* reflect this strategy of containment through Walter's questionable rehabilitation and Sabina's apparent cure. Both films end with the achievement of a normative heterosexual union – Walter is moving in with Vicki, Sabina has married and is expecting their first child – but instead of providing any sense of comfort, we are left with the memory of the provocative performances that have dominated the films. The wider narratives may seek to contain the perversions and non-normative sexuality, yet the performances disrupt and challenge that attempted containment. Their performances reveal the psychological and physical struggle when negotiating the management of inappropriate desire, cultural expectations and sexual boundaries elicited by perversion.

Notes

1. Simi Horwitz, 'Face to face: Bill Pullman: questioning boundaries in *The Goat*', *Backstage: The Performing Arts Weekly* 43/12, 22–28 March 2002, p. 7.
2. Ibid.

3. Ibid., p. 45.
4. Jamie Painter, 'Dylan Baker: pursuit of *Happiness*', *Back Stage West* 5/50 (10 December 1998), p. 8.
5. 'Q&A with Stanley Tucci of *Lovely Bones*', *Atlanta Journal Constitution*, 15 January 2010.
6. Jenny Kitzinger, 'The ultimate neighbour from hell? Stranger danger and the media framing of paedophiles', in Bob Franklin (ed.), *Social Policy, the Media and Representation* (Abingdon: Routledge, 1999), p. 217.
7. Carol-Ann Hooper and Ann Kaloski, 'Rewriting "the paedophile": a feminist reading of *The Woodsman*', *Feminist Review* 83 (2006), p. 149.
8. Karin Schofield, 'Collisions of culture and crime: media commodification of child sexual abuse', in Jeff Ferrell, Keith Hayward, Wayne Morrison and Mike Presdee (eds), *Cultural Criminology Unleashed* (London: The Glasshouse Press, 2004), p. 121.
9. For an extended overview of how the act of paedophilia has been 'obfuscated' in film, see Jon Davis, 'Imagining intergenerationality: representation and rhetoric in the pedophile movie', *GLQ: A Journal of Lesbian and Gay Studies* 13/2–3 (2007), pp. 369–85.
10. In 1994, Jesse Temmendequas – who had two prior convictions for sexually assaulting young girls – was convicted by the New Jersey Supreme Court for sexually assaulting and murdering seven-year-old Megan Kanka. 'Megan's Law' was passed the same year in New Jersey and then nationally, expanding sex offender registration and making the information publicly available. In the early 2000s, state registries were made available online. In the UK in 2001, convicted paedophile Roy Whiting was the subject of a high-profile case following the abduction and murder of eight-year-old Sarah Payne the previous year. Whiting had been one of the first people in the UK to be placed on the sex offenders register when he was released back into the community in 1997 following an earlier conviction for sexually assaulting another eight-year-old girl. In 2008, 'Sarah's Law', or the Child Sex Offenders Disclosure Scheme, was developed, allowing public access to the sex offenders register.
11. Simon Cross, 'Paedophiles in the community: inter-agency conflict, news leaks and the local press', *Crime, Media, Culture* 1/3 (December 2005), p. 286.
12. Ibid.
13. See Malcolm Cowburn and Lena Dominelli, 'Masking hegemonic masculinity: reconstructing the paedophile as the dangerous stranger', *British Journal of Social Work* 31/3 (2001), pp. 399–415.
14. 'Bacon: paedophiles "are not monsters"'. *BBC News*, 28 February 2005. Available at http://news.bbc.co.uk/1/hi/entertainment/film/4276565.stm (accessed 12 October 2013).
15. Stephanie Bunbury, 'Kevin's ambiguity', *The Age*, 10 April 2005.
16. Ann-Marie McAlinden, 'Deconstructing victim and offender identities in discourses on child sexual abuse: hierarchies, blame and the good/evil dialectic', *The British Journal of Criminology* 54 (2014), p. 188.

17. Roger Ebert, *Roger Ebert's Movie Year Book* (Missouri: Andrews McMeel Publishing, 2006), p. 782.

18. See Elisabeth Bronfen's excellent re-evaluation of hysteria across psychoanalysis, feminist theory, literature, film and art in *The Knotted Subject: Hysteria and Its Discontents* (Princeton, NJ: Princeton University Press, 1998).

19. Rachel P. Maines, *The Technology of Orgasm: 'Hysteria', the Vibrator and Women's Sexual Satisfaction* (Baltimore and London: The John Hopkins University Press, 1999), p. 22.

20. Rachel Mesch, *The Hysteric's Revenge: French Women Writers at the Fin de Siècle* (Nashville: Vanderbilt University Press, 2006), p. 128.

21. Richard von Krafft-Ebing, *Psychopathia Sexualis: A Medico Forensic Study*, translated by Franklin S. Klaf (New York: Arcade Publishing, 1965), p. 330. Originally published 1886.

22. Sigmund Freud, *Three Essays on the Theory of Sexuality*, translated by James Strachey (New York: Basic Books, 1962). Originally published 1905.

23. Justin Chang, 'Review: *A Dangerous Method*', *Variety*, 2 September 2011, p. 25.

24. Jenny McCartney, '*A Dangerous Method*, Seven magazine review', 13 February 2012.

25. A.O. Scott, 'Taming unruly desires and invisible monsters', *The New York Times*, 23 November 2011, p. C1L.

26. David Gritten, 2011 'Venice Film Festival 2011: *A Dangerous Method*, review', *The Telegraph*, 2 September 2011.

27. Manohla Dargis, 'Showing it all in Toronto', *The New York Times*, 16 September 2011, p. C1L.

28. Richard Porton, 'Filming dangerously: an interview with David Cronenberg', *Cineaste* 37/1 (Winter 2011), pp. 18–22.

29. *A Dangerous Method* Press Kit, Sony Pictures Classics, 7. www.sonyclassics.com/adangerousmethod/adangerousmethod_presskit.pdf (accessed 16 May 2015).

30. Alan A. Stone, '*A Dangerous Method* (Reel Insights)', *Psychiatric Times* 29/4 (April 2012), p. 16.

31. Kristin Thompson, 'The concept of cinematic excess', *Cine-Tracts* 1/2 (Summer 1977), pp. 62–3.

32. Carole Zucker, 'The concept of "excess" in film acting: notes toward an understanding of non-naturalistic performance', *Post Script* 12/2 (1993), p. 61.

33. Jonathan Robbins, 'Alice Winocour pulls the strings in *Augustine*', *FilmLinc Daily* (Film Society Lincoln Center), 16 May 2013.

34. Porton, 'Filming dangerously', pp. 18–22.

35. Bronfen, *The Knotted Subject*, p. 382.

36. Ibid., p. 385.

37. Scott, 'Taming unruly desires', p. C1L.

38. Anne McClintock, 'Maid to order: commercial fetishism and gender power', *Social Text* 37, special issue on sex work (Fall 1993), p. 110. Original emphasis.

39. Erving Goffman, *Frame Analysis* (New York: Harper & Row, 1974), p. 510.

40. Damon Dash, 'Kevin Bacon', *Interview* 34/11 (December 2004/January 2005), p. 154.
41. Craig Hubert, 'The Knightley courageous', *Interview*, 21 November 2011.
42. John Harrop, *Acting* (London: Routledge, 1992), p. 107.
43. Ibid., p. 108.
44. Ibid., p. 110.
45. Rory Loughnane and Edel Semple (eds), *Staged Transgression in Shakespeare's England* (Basingstoke: Palgrave Macmillan, 2013), p. 7.
46. Harrop, *Acting*, p. 110.

6

Normalising Masochism: Assimilating Sexual Perversion in *Secretary*

Caroline Walters

With the global phenomenon of E.L. James's *Fifty Shades of Grey* trilogy (published between 2011 and 2012) and subsequent film adaptation (Sam Taylor-Johnson, 2015), sadomasochism (SM) went from being a non-normative marginal sexual practice to a mass-market product consumed by a widespread female audience, instigating a host of literary and cinematic parodies and even themed sex toys. Early speculation around the film adaptation focused on how Hollywood would choose to depict the central SM relationship and whether it would 'challenge the distinction between the "erotic" versus the "pornographic"' that persists in Hollywood cinema.[1] Released a decade earlier, *Secretary* (Steven Shainberg, 2002) is a coming-of-age narrative focused on Lee Holloway (Maggie Gyllenhaal), a secretary who apparently exchanges self-injury for a sadomasochistic relationship with her boss Mr E. Edward Grey (James Spader). While praised for its representation of SM on screen and certainly offering subversive potential, I want to consider here how *Secretary* assimilates the perverse potential of SM into a heteronormative narrative. Indeed, the film normalises female masochism by drawing on the codes and conventions of romantic comedy, a genre that depends on monogamous heterosexual couples and whose typical denouement is a successful and socially sanctioned approval of the relationship. In turn, the film suggests that couple-based sadomasochistic practices are superior to and healthier than individual-based practices, which are categorised in the film as self-injury. I argue that the film represents these practices using similar techniques and, in doing so, suggests that they exist on a continuum rather than as distinctly different paraphilias. Ultimately, while there are a number of what I consider to be 'radical' moments in the narrative that challenge the film's assimilationist agenda, their radical potential is outweighed by the film's pursuit of the normalisation of female masochism.

'There are more conventional ways to show your feelings': *Secretary* as Romantic Comedy

Secretary follows what Annette Kuhn refers to as the 'enigma–retardation–resolution' trajectory of romantic comedy: boy meets girl and they embark on a relationship; a crisis occurs and a test of their relationship takes place, which leads to a 'successful' conclusion that ends in heterosexual marriage.[2] In *Secretary*, Lee meets Grey and they embark on an uncertain SM relationship; Grey withdraws because he fears it is 'wrong' and fires Lee, who becomes engaged to her boyfriend Peter (Jeremy Davies); Grey tests Lee by asking her to remain at his desk without moving until he returns, resulting in her not eating or drinking for three days; with Lee's commitment to the relationship confirmed, Grey and Lee marry and live a suburban life. Tamar Jeffers McDonald argues that the ultimate aim of a romantic comedy is the primacy of the couple and, despite the various changes to the genre, few 'suggest monogamous coupledom itself is an outmoded concept'.[3] She goes on to state, 'At the heart of every romantic comedy is the implication of sex, and settled, secure, within-a-relationship sex at that'.[4] Romantic comedies privilege the monogamous, heterosexual relationship and straight sex within that context, while anything that deviates from that mode is understood to be inferior. Thus, the kinds of relationships that function in a different manner to the primarily heterosexual, same-race, similar-age model portrayed in a romantic comedy are considered non-normative.[5] *Secretary* is able to offer a seemingly transgressive model of female sexuality by positioning its depiction of SM within the normative women's genre of the romantic comedy.[6] Yet the film, and the ending in particular, reveals a normative agenda to present a 'good' SM relationship, providing it is within the context of a 'normal' couple.

Secretary ends after Grey rescues Lee from his desk when he realises she has obeyed him and suffered for him despite the potential risk to her health, all the while wearing a white wedding dress that was intended for her wedding to Peter. Grey lifts her from the desk, where she has collapsed, scoops her into his arms and carries her out while she clings to his neck. This translation of a traditional wedding ritual where the groom carries the bride across the threshold to their house is here played out in his office and then repeated on entering his house. Once she has crossed this boundary of his private world, he takes her to the pre-prepared bedroom at his house. There is a bed covered with grass, surrounded by white net curtains that mimic the wedding-night cliché. Grey resumes his caring role as he undoes the wedding dress and lays her on the bed (see Fig. 6.1), which results in Lee stating, 'for the first time in my life,

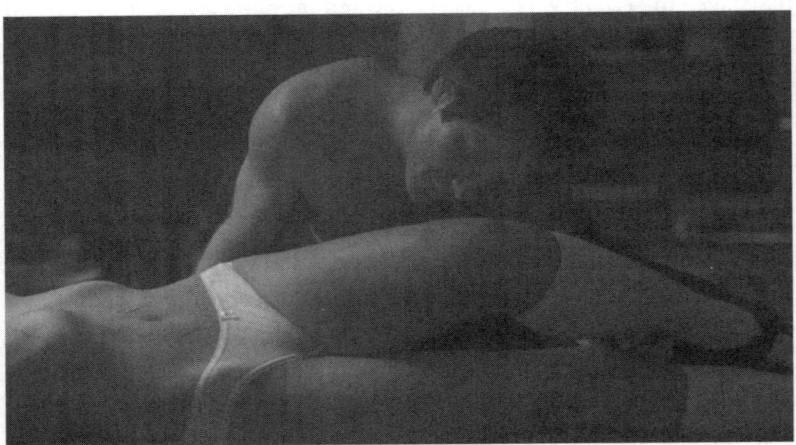

Fig. 6.1. Mr Grey (James Spader) and Lee Holloway (Maggie Gyllenhaal) in *Secretary* (Steven Shainberg, Slough Pond, 2002)

I felt beautiful. Finally part of the earth; I touched the soil and he loved me back'.

The nature imagery suggests that Grey and Lee are creating a new foundation for their life that will include their sadomasochistic relationship and that they consider this to be 'natural' too. Indeed, both of them understand the sentiment Dr Twardon (Patrick Bauchau) expresses in the film: 'who's to say that love needs to be soft and gentle?' Brenda Cossman argues that in this final sex scene 'sexual excess is, at this moment, contained within romantic love'.[7] This is indicative of the role of the heteronormative imperatives – 'the accepted singular norm against which sexual pluralism must be defended' – that inform *Secretary* and romantic comedy as a generic form.[8] In the closing section of *Secretary*, Grey is presented as the strong patriarchal man, in contrast to Lee's weak and emaciated childlike body. The couple exhibit gendered opposites, specifically active masculinity and passive femininity, which Ewan Kirkland argues is essential for the maintenance of heterosexuality within the romantic comedy.[9] For Kirkland, heterosexuality is a normative and compulsory institution within romantic comedies. Although *Secretary* features non-normative sexual practices, they occur ultimately within the sanctioned and approved context of marriage.

In a voiceover, Lee states that their SM 'activities melted into an everyday sort of life until [they] looked like any other couple you'd see'. McDonald argues that different modes of romantic comedies reflect social changes and, after the radical offerings of the 1970s, contemporary romantic comedies that she defines as 'neo-traditional' show a return to the traditional ones of the genre from the 1950s and 60s.[10] They privilege the heterosexual couple, assume there will be a long-term monogamous relationship and often conclude with marriage.[11] *Secretary* can thus be seen as a 'neo-traditional' romantic comedy because once the couple have reached their romantic conclusion – marriage – they can now continue their non-normative sexual practices within a sanctioned space. *Secretary* also diverges from the neo-traditional romantic comedy since it focuses on the sexual dynamic between the protagonists. In its relationship with romantic comedy's generic expectations, it is clear that *Secretary* both conforms to and yet also challenges the genre with the inclusion of non-normative sexuality, since female masochism is its central theme.

'In one way or another I've always suffered': Narratives of Progression and Transition

Secretary includes multiple transitional narratives in relation to its protagonist Lee: a developmental interpretation of femininity from infantilised to sexualised adult, from individual masturbation to couple-based sexual practices and from self-injury and autoerotic masochism to couple-based masochistic practices. These narratives mirror Freud's conception of female sexuality as being a progression from infantile clitoral sexuality to adult vaginal sexuality. At the beginning of the film, Lee can be read in terms of infantilised femininity, masturbation and self-injury, providing a kinky mirror of Freud's clitoral sexuality. Freud considers that the stimulation of the clitoris is a 'masculine activity' and must be eliminated as 'a necessary precondition for the development of femininity'.[12] In other words, to be feminine implies a detachment from a girl's sexual desires for self-stimulation. The logic of *Secretary*, like Freud's logic, suggests that these stages are infantile and must be replaced with their mature, adult forms. In turn, Freud's successful developmental narrative concludes with a woman attaining pleasure through vaginal sexuality, which *Secretary* mirrors when Lee becomes a sexualised adult who engages in mature couple-based masochistic practices (and, indeed, intercourse). This narrative of progression reflects the privileging of the couple, while autoerotic sexual practices are arguably considered a violation to the sanctity of the couple and a sign of immaturity.

Secretary's screenwriter Erin Cressida Wilson deployed this logic slightly differently when adapting Mary Gaitskill's short story 'Bad Behaviour'.[13] Wilson's adaptation alters the role of power from an abusive context in the short story to that of an erotic power-play dynamic in the screenplay and film. In Gaitskill's story the protagonist Debby does not self-injure; nor does she have masochistic desires or a relationship with her boss Grey. Instead, Debby chooses to leave her job because she has become disillusioned with the power difference and has become a victim of sexual harassment.[14] Wilson outlines her reason for changing the emphasis of *Secretary*'s narrative in the screenplay's introduction:

> I didn't want to create yet another drama about a woman recovering from her problems or perversions. Then I thought:

What if this were a coming-out film for a submissive? What if she were to stop fighting it – and instead – she embraced it, defined it, and then became empowered? What if her real problem was not her submissive behavior with her lawyer? What if I added a visually upsetting self-destructive activity for her in the first act? So, I gave her a painful situation to come out of – self-cutting – and worked from there.[15]

Wilson's argument posits a seemingly unproblematic coming-out narrative, yet the film's depiction of this normative transitional narrative from immaturity to maturity is problematic. Although it could seem that these narratives are identical, Wilson positions self-injurious practices as being the antithesis of masochistic ones, whereas in the film they exist as part of a continuum and the logic that seeks to separate them is based on value judgments.

In line with the typical transition narrative, Lee undergoes an 'ugly duckling' to 'swan' transformation. This happens at Grey's insistence as he considers her attire to be 'disgusting'. Before meeting Grey, Lee is seen pulling up sagging knee-high socks that are reminiscent of both a schoolchild and a poorly dressed old woman. In turn, her self-injurious practices and masturbation first occur in Lee's bedroom in the family home that seems to belong to a hyperfeminine child. It is decorated in pale pinks with a white-canopied bed and her cutting implement is a figurine of a ballerina en pointe. This conflation of the childlike and feminine with self-injury implies Lee's immaturity and her infantilisation within the narrative. Her transformation to a sensual adult woman occurs once she has made the decision to embark on an SM relationship with Grey. Her frumpy sagging socks and brown cardigans are replaced with pussy-bow blouses, figure-hugging pencil skirts and stilettos. The film's narrative suggests that in order for Lee to be an adult she must conform to the heterosexual male fantasy of the sexy secretary.

In one pivotal scene where Grey calls Lee into his office to counsel her, several key themes emerge: Grey transgresses the professional boundary and adopts a parental role, he treats Lee like a child and there is an implicit erotic power-exchange dynamic used to seek consent for the explicit introduction of a dominant and submissive relationship. He opens the dialogue aware that he is transgressing their 'prescribed relationship' because he wants to know Lee on a personal level, not just as his employee. As in Gaitskill's short story, this could be abusive, yet here Lee seems happy to follow his cues. He has prepared for their encounter because he offers her some hot chocolate that he has already made and hidden behind the sofa. His choice of drink, with its sweet taste, positions Lee in the role of a child. Later in the exchange he tells her that she should start walking home from work because she is 'a big girl, a grown woman' who needs to learn her independence and not be picked up by her mother. The rite of passage that many children undergo when they are given their first taste of independence and are allowed to walk home from school alone is translated as enforced maturity.

Grey asks Lee if she knows why she self-injures. When she quietly states that she 'doesn't know' he speaks to her paternally and provides his own interpretation of her actions. He asks her if 'sometimes the pain inside has to come to the surface and when you see evidence of the pain inside, you finally know you're really here? Then when you watch the wound heal it's comforting, isn't it?' Grey's interpretation suggests that her self-injury provides a therapeutic role by addressing her hurt with a self-prescribed method of healing. In turn, Grey's interpretation of her experiences is a form of silencing; he does not give her the room or language to capture her own experiences and instead adopts the role of the mature and experienced parent. In speaking for Lee, Grey situates her in a submissive position, indicated through the many pauses, his leading questions and her brief answers. He uses this dominant position to inform Lee that she will 'never, ever, cut [herself] again'. Grey's role alters from employer to a dominant figure that engages with Lee as a submissive. Although consent is never made explicit in the film, Lee implies it when she responds to his command with 'No, sir' in a coquettish slow manner while maintaining eye contact with him. Significantly, while her choice of the moniker 'sir' connotes authority and is used to indicate the superiority of the male to whom it is addressed, it is often used within the SM community for dominant and submissive relationships to explicitly acknowledge the power difference at play.[16] While submissives can use their limits to control the interaction and the dominant's behaviour, this is not explicitly explored in *Secretary*. This dialogue is a pivotal point in the film because it marks Lee's transition from self-injurious, autoerotic masochistic practices to couple-based SM practices. The first spanking sequence occurs shortly after and the exchange suggests Grey is testing whether or not Lee is willing to play his sexual game of domination and submission.

The understanding that self-injurious autoerotic masochistic practices and couple-based practices exist on a continuum depends on the relationship between the signification of wounds, the intentions and the power dynamics involved. In their work on 'the erotics of wounding', Viv Burr and Jeff Hearn unpack the different roles and functions of wounds, categorising them as 'the wounder; the wounded; the wound(s) produced; and the wound(s) healed'.[17] The wounder inflicts the wound upon the wounded. This then produces a wound, which can have one interpretation but take on a different significance when it becomes the healed wound. In self-injurious and autoerotic masochistic practices, the wounder and the wounded are the same person, meaning that the power circulates within a single individual. By contrast, in couple-based masochistic practices, the wounder and wounded are different people, so power is exchanged between them. *Secretary* depicts Lee's transition from the first of these two positions to the second. Although the film depicts Lee as self-injuring, the visual representation of her reaction to the self-injurious practice mirrors her reaction to the masochistic practices in which she engages. In a voiceover during the film's final love sequence, Lee recalls: 'Each cut, each scar, each burn, a different mood or time. I told him what the first one was, told where the second one came from. I remembered them all'. Describing her journey, she draws attention to the blurred boundaries between her self-injury and her couple-based SM and acknowledges a trajectory from one to the other, which Burr and Hearn would describe as a shift from the 'sexually negative' to the 'sexually positive'.[18]

Early in the film, in response to witnessing her father beat her mother in an alcohol-fuelled rage, Lee holds a boiling kettle to her inner thigh. She experiences a transgressive state of release; she gasps, her face relaxes and she moans, she is tearful yet reaches a sense of calm. Later, as Grey spanks Lee for the first time, her facial expressions mirror the moment of self-injury, shifting from pain to euphoria. The sense of relief marked on Lee's face is virtually identical in both sequences, depicting erotic satisfaction, calm and relief at externalising emotion. Indeed, Ani Ritchie argues that, for many, self-injury offers 'a private expression of relief',[19] which is what distinguishes these two scenes in *Secretary*. In the first, Lee is able to demonstrate her needed relief privately, while in the second she needs to wait until she is alone in the toilet cubicle looking at her bruised bottom after the spanking to experience comparable relief. The shift from self-injury to shared sadomasochistic experiences perpetuates the normative agenda of the romantic comedy since it reinforces the power of the couple.

'It's comforting, isn't it?' *Secretary*'s Therapeutic Narrative

Within romantic comedy's normalising imperatives, *Secretary* represents some ways that SM can have a positive effect upon its practitioners, leading to a sense of fulfilment or a therapeutic effect. Representing masochism as a form of therapy by replacing Lee's self-injuring practices with couple-based SM practices, the film's representation intersects with the medical understanding of these practices, which is one of the key discourses concerning masochism since its conception by the sexologist Richard von Krafft-Ebing in the 1880s. This mirrors a move within the theoretical literature concerning SM that seeks to examine the ways in which it can be distanced from pathology.[20] At the same time, the depiction of SM as therapeutic challenges its position within the *Diagnostic and Statistical Manual of Mental Disorders-IV*, one of the standard texts for mental health diagnoses. The *DSM-IV* pathologises masochism, considering it a diagnosable condition and a paraphilia.[21] This therapeutic narrative suggests it is possible to resituate and re-appropriate trauma so that it no longer has the same traumatic resonances.

Meg Barker, Camelia Gupta and Alessandra Iantaffi suggest that it is possible to construct SM as a safe space, a fantasy that is constructed as separate from reality.[22] Indeed, this narrative involves a deliberate engagement with the discourse of health and harm that is a principal element of the pathologising narrative put forward in medical discourses. However, both the endorsement of the healing narrative and the community rhetoric that SM must be 'safe, sane and consensual' creates an artificial categorisation between 'good' and acceptable SM practices on the one hand, and those that fall outside this remit on the other. Indeed, there is a concern that:

healing narratives could be in danger of constructing a 'good BDSMer' who, like the 'good gay citizen', sits at the top of a new hierarchy above all relationships and practices which do not fit this image, pressurising people to assimilate this rather than embracing a variety of different identities.[23]

Secretary manifests this concern through its juxtaposition of Lee and Grey's 'good' SM and the 'bad' SM Lee discovers while she is temporarily separated from Grey. These other 'bad' SMers are constructed as socially awkward men who have fetishes that she considers bizarre: 'There was one who tried to grab and pinch my nipples before we even made it to his car. [...] Another guy kept ordering me to pee on his patio [...] Then there was the one who liked being tied to a gas stove while the burners were on full blast and I had to throw tomatoes at him'. The film denounces these male characters and their SM practices by the brief amount of time given to them and the fact that Lee's encounters result in her deciding to 'stop trying' engaging in masochistic encounters. This repositions Lee's relationship with Grey as the 'good' type of SM because it focuses upon the practices within a normative heterosexual romantic couple.

A principal problem with examining the 'SM as therapy' narrative is that 'by encouraging a story of SM as healing we may also be serving to support the continuing notion of SM as pathological, rooted in trauma'.[24] This concern is one that is difficult to ignore and yet there are few ways to move away from this narrative. In 'Silencing Accounts of Silenced Sexualities', Meg Barker and Darren Langdridge adopt divergent positions in an alternating dialogue regarding the function of the discourse of SM as therapy. Barker states: 'It's like there's a kind of loop with people drawing on dominant discourses and putting stories back out there which reinforce them'.[25] Although the therapeutic narrative is appealing because of its representation in films such as *Secretary*, it offers many problems that, rather than enabling a non-pathologised interpretation of SM, can instead further pathologise these practices. Langdridge's concern that the concept of healing contains the related concept of curing is an important concern and one that is suggested by the developmental narrative in *Secretary*. Although the film engages with the normative, pathologising discourse of the Western medical model in this instance, it also challenges these norms through a 'radical' reappraisal of SM demonstrated by several rupturing moments in the film's narrative.

'Who's to say that love needs to be soft and gentle?' The Radical Potential of *Secretary*

The radical potential of SM exists in its potential to position itself outside the ubiquitous imperative for health, which dominates both medical and therapeutic narratives. In his later years, Michel Foucault gave many interviews in which he discussed the ways that SM could offer the radical potential to reconfigure existing sexual power dynamics. He considered that SM offered 'the real creation of new possibilities of pleasure' that challenged the 'norm' of genitally-focused heterosex and its reproductive imperative.[26] Instead, SM enabled a process of 'the eroticization of the body', focused on 'the desexualization of pleasure'.[27] This interpretation diverges from the discussions of SM as therapeutic, healing or part of a 'bonding' exercise. As Lisa Downing has argued in relation to autoerotic asphyxiation, practices that use the whole body or non-genital bodily regions can be understood, through a Foucauldian framework, as offering a chance to attain what Bataille referred to as 'limit experiences', that is, 'extreme experiences that push us to the limits of consciousness and shatter rationality'.[28] Foucault argued that the limit experiences accessible through some forms of SM could provide a chance to reinvent the relationship with the self from a focus upon identity to a relationship 'of differentiation, of creation, of innovation'.[29] This kind of re-evaluation of SM as 'radical' and enabling limit experiences seeks to move beyond the discourses of SM as pathological by rejecting the concepts of health and harm.

Although *Secretary* attempts to normalise and assimilate SM into the romantic comedy, there are several instances where the desexualisation and radical potential of SM's limit experiences are explored. When Lee makes a decision to obey Grey's instruction to remain seated at his desk with her hands on the table, she pushes herself to the limits of consciousness, not moving for three days, even to use the toilet. A close-up reveals urine dripping down the side of the chair from her wedding dress. The visibility of the urine could incite feelings of disgust because it is bodily waste that is often hidden, avoided or disposed of in a toilet. The urine becomes the abject object that is neither inside nor outside the body, which disrupts the romantic comedy narrative.[30] In an essay on female masochism, Alex Dymock borrows from Lacanian-inspired concepts of *jouissance* and anti-utilitarian sexuality to argue that: 'pleasure is sought through the act of suffering [...] so that pleasure and pain become indistinguishable'.[31] This provides a useful framework within which Lee's act can be viewed, as it suggests that she derives her 'pleasure' from a desire to suffer by being obedient to Grey. Towards the end of the film, in reference to this experience, Lee comments on her relationship with suffering:

> In one way or another I've always suffered. I don't know why exactly, but I do know that I'm not so scared of suffering now. I feel more than I've ever felt, and I've found someone to feel with, to play with, to love in a way that feels right for me. I hope he knows that I can see he suffers too and I want to love him.

Although they adopt some of the trappings of the normative couple (marriage, monogamy and heterosexuality), the suggestion is that both, and particularly Lee, seek 'pleasure' beyond social norms.[32] Although this scene departs from the film's assimilationist and normalising agenda, it soon returns it to this paradigm by concluding with Grey caring for Lee until she regains her full health. This suggests that masochism may itself be understood as a radical moment that can rupture an otherwise normative narrative.

Underlying these different SM narratives is the social construction of gender roles, which in turn impacts on discourses of sexuality. Broadly speaking, the therapeutic narratives may be seen as traditionally 'feminine' in that they focus on caring and nurturing, while the radical narrative that rejects the health and harm binary embodies what Staci Newmahr considers to be the stereotypically 'masculine' qualities of risk and a disavowal of the future.[33] Newmahr argues that SM should challenge this relationship between gender and risk, yet *Secretary* and the therapeutic discourses reaffirm a normative relationship with these concepts. However, there are several instances where Lee courts risk out of a desire to demonstrate to Grey that she wants to suffer for her love for him. When Grey abruptly terminates their relationship, she sends him a letter that contains a dead worm, signifying a typographical error. At this point their

SM relationship lacks definition; Lee does not know what will result from this attempt to provoke him, yet it does result in punishment and him re-instigating their dominant/submissive dynamic.

Another instance of courting risk is evident when Lee deposits a dead cockroach onto the just-made bed, waiting for Grey to find it when he returns from work to their suburban home. *Secretary*'s play with a veneer of normality is reminiscent of the opening sequences of David's Lynch film *Blue Velvet* (1986), in which the suburbs are juxtaposed with the discovery of a severed ear in the grass. Both the cockroach and the severed ear offer an anomaly, a disruption and a threat to the 'straight' and safe suburban environment. Rather than the sinister connotations of the severed ear, the cockroach is a playful subversion and serves as another invitation to engage in their illicit non-normative sexual practices. Lee is content playing the dutiful housewife but also wants her fun; she enjoys provoking Mr Grey, deliberately flirting with risk in order to receive punishment and sexual gratification.

In risking her health as a result of following Grey's orders to not move from the desk in the wedding dress scene, the conventional gendered relationship between risk and danger is disrupted with the possibility of dehydration, malnutrition and unconsciousness. A disruption is also evident when her urine soils the dress, subverting traditional femininity at the same time. The film ends with a close-up of Lee's face staring straight into the camera. There is no smile. Her expression is flat. Finishing the film with just her expression in the frame indicates that her narrative has reached fruition because now she no longer has to hide or share the frame. She has learnt to perform the masquerade required for assimilation into normative society. Although *Secretary* does normalise SM, these episodes attempt to rupture the otherwise assimilationist narrative by nodding to the 'masculine' radical SM narrative and perhaps suggesting that the designation of risk as 'masculine' is itself a conservative and misogynistic social fiction. Ultimately, however, the film's radical potential does not materialise. These attempts to rupture are not strong enough.

This chapter offers a re-conceptualisation of the discourses around masochism and self-injury, constructing them as discrete categories. Instead, the film considers them as part of a continuum. Although *Secretary* implies that masochistic practices are preferable to autoerotic ones, it positions female masochism as 'good' by re-enforcing an existing binary of healthy and unhealthy, acceptable and unacceptable, that practices should and can be divided into. *Secretary* attempts to normalise SM through its use of the romantic comedy genre that relies upon certain socially conservative expectations. In this sense it would not be able to acknowledge or explore radical and transgressive SM but can only hint at it and provide moments that amount to little more than playful quirks in an SM love story. The film is an assimilationist example of SM that encourages a liberal expansion of the category of healthy and normal practices and acknowledges that SM does not need to be pathological. Although *Secretary* includes some moments where it is possible to consider a more radical desexualised potential in its depiction of sadomasochism, these moments sit within a wider framework that seeks to normalise it. This is evident in its trajectory from harm to healing that outweighs the film's radical potential since it is a heteronormative romantic comedy that wants to appeal to a wide audience. The film's poster tagline – 'assume the position' – takes on a dual meaning in the context of my argument; for all the film's attempts to offer something more subversive and challenging, *Secretary* ultimately 'assumes the position' of heteronormativity.

Notes

1. Sarah Harman, Bethan Jones and Ruth Deller, 'Reading the *Fifty Shades* phenomenon', *Litro*, 28 February 2013. Available at http://www.litro.co.uk/2013/02/reading-fifty-shades/ (accessed 1 March 2013); Feona Attwood and Caroline Walters, '*Fifty Shades* and the law: regulating sex and sex media in the UK', *Sexualities* 16/8 (2013), pp. 975–9.
2. Annette Kuhn, 'Women's genres', in E. Ann Kaplan (ed.), *Feminism and Film* (Oxford: Oxford University Press, 2000), pp. 437–50.
3. Tamar Jeffers McDonald, *Romantic Comedy: Boy Meets Girl Meets Genre* (London: Wallflower, 2007), p. 13.
4. Ibid.
5. Ummni Khan has gone so far as to argue that the white hegemony in *Secretary* leads to the film becoming 'non-raced'. Ummni Khan, 'A woman's right to be spanked: testing the limits of tolerance of S/M in the socio-legal imaginary', *The Journal of Sexuality and the Law* 18 (2009), pp. 79–119.
6. See Kuhn, 'Women's genres', pp. 437–50.
7. Brenda Cossman, 'Sexuality, queer theory and "feminism after": reading and re-reading the sexual subject', *McGill Law Journal* 49/4 (2004), p. 870.

8. Stevi Jackson, 'Heterosexuality and feminist theory', in Diane Richardson (ed.), *Theorising Heterosexuality* (Buckingham: Open University Press, 1996), p. 29.
9. Ewan Kirkland, 'Romantic comedy and the construction of heterosexuality', *Scope* 9 (2007) Available at http://www.scope.nottingham.ac.uk/article.php? issue=9&id=957 (accessed 12 February 2013).
10. McDonald, *Romantic Comedy*, pp. 85–105.
11. Ibid., p. 86.
12. Sigmund Freud, 'Some psychical consequences of the anatomical distinction between the sexes' in *The Ego and the Id, and Other Works* (London: Hogarth Press, 1961), p. 255.
13. Mary Gaitskill, 'Secretary' in *Bad Behaviour* (New York: Poseidon, 1988).
14. There are parallels with this narrative in *Fifty Shades of Grey*, as Anastasia chooses to leave her Mr Grey due to similar disillusionment and the realisation that she cannot change him.
15. Erin Cressida Wilson, *Secretary: A Screenplay* (New York: Soft Skull Press, 2003), p. vi.
16. Dossie Easton and Janet Hardy, *The New Topping Book* (Oakland, CA: Greenery Press, 2003) p. 161. For more on consent and BDSM see Meg Barker, 'Consent is a grey area? A comparison of understandings of consent in *Fifty Shades of Grey* and on the BDSM blogosphere', *Sexualities* 16/8 (2013), pp. 896–14.
17. Viv Burr and Jeff Hearn, 'Introducing the erotics of wounding', in Viv Burr and Jeff Hearn (eds), *Sex, Violence and the Body: The Erotics of Wounding* (Basingstoke: Palgrave Macmillan, 2008), p. 4.
18. Ibid.
19. Ani Ritchie, 'Harming or healing? The meanings of wounding among sadomasochists who also self-injure', in Burr and Hearn (eds), *Sex, Violence and the Body*, p. 86.
20. See Meg Barker and Darren Langdridge, 'Silencing accounts of silenced sexualities', in Róisín Ryan-Flood and Rosalind Gill (eds), *Secrecy and Silence in the Research Process: Feminist Reflections* (Abingdon: Routledge, 2009), pp. 67–81; Meg Barker, Camelia Gupta and Alessandra Iantaffi, 'The power of play: the potentials and pitfalls in healing narratives of BDSM', in Meg Barker and Darren Langdridge (eds), *Safe, Sane and Consensual: Contemporary Perspectives on Sadomasochism* (Basingstoke: Palgrave Macmillan, 2007), pp. 197–216.
21. See Peggy Kleinplatz and Charles Moser, 'Is SM pathological?' in Barker and Langdridge (eds), *Safe, Sane and Consensual*, pp. 55–62.
22. Barker, Gupta and Iantaffi, 'The power of play', pp. 197–216.
23. Ibid., pp. 205–206.
24. Barker and Langdridge, 'Silencing accounts of silenced sexualities', p. 73.
25. Ibid., p. 74.
26. Michel Foucault, 'Sex, power and the politics of identity', in Sylvére Lotringer (ed.), *Foucault Live: Collected Interviews, 1961–1984*, second revised edition (New York: Semiotext(e), 1996), p. 284.

27. Ibid.

28. Lisa Downing, 'Beyond safety: erotic asphyxiation and the limits of S/M discourse', in Langdridge and Barker (eds), *Safe, Sane and Consensual*, p. 127.

29. Foucault, 'Sex, power and the politics of identity', p. 385.

30. Julia Kristeva, *Powers of Horror: An Essay on Abjection* (New York: Columbia University Press, 1982), p. 3.

31. Alex Dymock, 'But femsub is broken too!: On the normalisation of BDSM and the problem of pleasure', *Psychology and Sexuality* 3/1 (2012), p. 63.

32. Ibid., p. 64.

33. Staci Newmahr, *Playing on the Edge: Sadomasochism, Risk, and Intimacy* (Bloomington, IN: Indiana University Press, 2011), p. 118.

7

Smutty Swedes: Sex Films, Pornography and 'Good Sex'

Susanna Paasonen

Swedish Erotica (circa 1977–2008) is probably the most successful pornographic film series of all time. Starting out with short Super 8 loops in the late 1970s and moving into VHS and DVD production during the following decades, the *Swedish Erotica* series spans over 130 titles (in addition to the more than 600 loops produced before 1985).[1] Despite its name, the series was, from the very beginning, produced in the United States by Caballero (currently Caballero Home Video), a company established in 1974. Its producers, directors and performers – including stars such as Seka and John Holmes – had little connection to Sweden.

In what follows, I explore the articulations of Sweden, film, sex and porn. My primary interest is not *Swedish Erotica* but the international reputation of Swedish sexuality that the series both taps into and builds. First, I explore the genealogy of 'Swedish sin', as coined in journalism and film since the 1950s, with particular attention to its underlying dynamics of cleanliness and perversion. Second, I move from the histories of Scandinavian sex film to those of porn in the aim of further

charting the international reverberations of the notion of Swedish sin –
fantasies concerning Sweden as a land of sexual freedom that have been
underpinned by notions of naturalness, wholesomeness and healthiness
but also by depravity and perversion. In the final parts of the chapter I
address distinctions drawn between Nordic sexualities, with particular
attention to Finnish articulations of Swedish sin as homosexuality, in
order to investigate the contingencies of the figure of Swedish sexuality.

Swedish Sin, Swedish Perversion

The concept of Swedish sin drew from the 1950s and 1960s. It built on
the international reputation of Swedish films (such as Arne Mattson's
One Summer of Happiness/Hon dansade en sommar (1951) and Ingmar
Bergman's *Summer with Monika/Sommaren med Monika* (1953), with
their scenes of nude swimming and sex) and international reports
concerning Sweden's liberalism towards sexuality.[2] Sweden was the first
country to introduce compulsory public sex education in schools in 1955
and, according to Carl Gustaf Boëthius, a myth was soon established, in
the United States in particular, of Sweden as 'peopled by healthy, sexually
athletic blondes' assumedly educated in the clinical details of sex since
kindergarten.[3] This reputation owed largely to a sensationalist 1955 *Time*
magazine article – 'Sin in Sweden' – that labelled Sweden a promiscuous
secular nation lacking in moral fibre, even as something akin to a
'moral cesspool'.[4]

Before the 1970s and the so-called golden era of 35mm pornography,
North American theatres screened a range of titles labelled as sex
films, ranging from educational films to more or less documentary
ones, sexploitation features and imported foreign art house films
showing varying degrees of nudity.[5] Since hardcore pornography could
not be publicly shown, sex films tested and pushed the boundaries
of the permissible, the appropriate and the acceptable. Imported
films were screened with subtitles that, according to Justin Wyatt,
lent them 'an aura of sophistication'.[6] In this cultural situation, European
films arguably connoted sex to American viewers to the degree that
the term 'art film' itself became packed with licentious meaning.[7]
Swedish and Danish films were extensively featured and enjoyed

Fig. 7.1. Topless yoga in *I Am Curious (Yellow)* (Vilgot Sjöman, Sandrews, 1967)

considerable popularity due to their frequent displays of nudity and sexual action.

'Swedish films' ranged from Bergman's stylised *The Silence/Tystnaden* (1963), addressing death and corporeality, to Vilgot Sjöman's experimental *I Am Curious (Yellow)/Jag är nyfiken: en film i gult* (1967), exploring themes such as the Swedish class society, socialism and prison reform, and Torgny Wickman's educational *Language of Love/Ur kärlekens språk* (1969). These films were shown in both art house and grindhouse theatres; in the latter, both dubbed and edited versions were screened. For example, a cut version of Bergman's *Summer with Monika* was famously given a new music score, dubbed in English and advertised as suggestively titled *Monika, the Story of a Bad Girl.*[8] *I Am Curious (Yellow)* (see Fig. 7.1) was particularly successful due to the publicity it received when confiscated at US customs. The ensuing court cases, continuing for two years, guaranteed high visibility and audience interest. Once released, the film grossed 4 million dollars within six months and *Variety* magazine listed it as the highest grossing film of 1969. This is rather astonishing given that *I Am Curious (Yellow)* is largely about the shortcomings of the Swedish welfare state.[9] In addition to scenes of nude swimming, topless meditation and yoga in the great outdoors, the film features simulated sex scenes. A scene where the socially active and sexually curious Lena (Lena Nyman) kisses her lover's now-flaccid penis after an outdoor sex act gained particular scrutiny.[10]

The films had considerable export appeal in Europe as well as in North America and by the early 1960s critics were already pointing out that shots of summer nights and nude swimming scenes were becoming something of a cliché due to their thematic repetition.[11] As queer theorist Don Kulick points out, the sex shown in Swedish films was 'never decadent or perverse':

> On the contrary, such films most commonly represented sex by lingering on clean, fresh, svelte women who without hesitation or guilt had intercourse with their clean, fresh, svelte boyfriends. The 'Swedish sin' was healthy, natural, good sex'.[12]

The films helped to establish the notion of Swedish sin as a co-articulation of sexuality with cleanliness. In 1964, German weekly news magazine *Der Spiegel* defined the formula of these films as consisting of 'nude swimming plus social critique'.[13] While such sin might not seem like sin at all, the tensions involved in the term should not be underestimated. The notion encompasses both repetitive depictions of clean, 'good' sex and notions of perverted moral turpitude – of shockingly licentious detachment from moral conventions, fantasies of sexual liberalism and female sexual accessibility – and is, to a degree, defined by their mutual tension.[14] The accumulating international reputation of Swedish films was such that, in Germany for example, the term 'Schwedenfilm' became synonymous with porn.[15] In the United States, the reputation of Swedish sin was even more apparent. This is illustrated in Martin Scorsese's *Taxi Driver* (1975): when Travis Bickle (Robert de Niro) takes his love interest Betsy (Cybill Shepherd) to see a film titled *Swedish Marriage Manual* (often inaccurately identified as *Language of Love*), she is immediately able to recognise it as a dirty movie.[16]

Although 'Swedish film' connoted sex film, this genealogy does not fully account for phenomena such as *Swedish Erotica* as a particular branding strategy for hardcore pornography. The development of sex films was parallel to, and entwined with, transformations in the cultural and legal status of pornography. In 1964, the Danish Ministry of Justice established a committee to evaluate the legal status of John Cleland's classic porn novel *Fanny Hill* (1748), due to the controversy its translation had caused. The committee consulted a panel of experts consisting of criminologists, psychiatrists, psychologists and educational scientists and, in 1967, the Danish parliament repealed the laws on literary pornography. Two years later, the ban on obscene images, objects and performances was lifted.[17] This made Denmark the first European country to legalise audiovisual porn and Sweden followed suit two years later in 1971. The two countries became important producers and exporters of porn. Their practically hegemonic status in legal porn production supported the popular image of sexually permissible, liberated and, for some, perverted Scandinavia, as formed during the 1950s and 1960s.[18] US documentary films exploring Danish developments – such as *Sexual Freedom in Denmark* (M.C. von Hellen, 1970) and *Pornography in Denmark: A New Approach* (Alex de Renzy, 1970) – were the first to show hardcore porn in US theatres under the legitimisation of social interest and, in doing so, they further solidified the associations drawn between Scandinavia, sexual liberation and potential perversion.[19]

Despite Denmark's newly found status as the porn capital of the world, Sweden had enjoyed a longer history in porn production that greatly contributed to international notions of Swedish sin. Sweden had not participated in the League of Nations pact on the suppression of the circulation and traffic of obscene publications that was developed during the 1910s and 1920s, and while pornography was considered an illegal, dirty enterprise, it was an issue of domestic legislation only.[20] In 1965, Swedish pornographer and businessman Berth Milton began to publish *Private*, the first porn magazine printed in full colour, and the company grew since grown into one of the largest adult entertainment companies in Europe. Swedish porn film and video production has been influential, particularly on the Nordic market.[21] In 2009, *Dirty Diaries*, a collection of short feminist porn films directed by Mia Engberg, gained international attention due to the public funding it received. The media attention around the film worked to rearticulate the view of Sweden as a land of porn, whereas the film itself aimed at reworking the aesthetics and gender politics of porn.[22]

Lasse Braun: The King of Super 8

Once adorned with titles such as 'King of Porn', 'Emperor of Sex' and 'Father of Modern Pornography' by the press, and author of an estimated 80 films, Lasse Braun has been largely forgotten in a porn historiography that has overwhelmingly focused on American films, directors, producers, performers, trials and jurisdictions.[23] These texts tend to say very little of Europe, historical accounts of literary pornography being an obvious exception.[24] If mentioned, Braun tends to figure through his collaboration with the US porn distributor Reuben Sturman, whereas his films, their production or reception remain unstudied.[25] At the same time, popular cinematic porn historiography – addressing films such as *Boogie Nights* (Paul Thomas Anderson, 1997), *Rated X* (Emilio Estevez, 2000) and *Inside Deep Throat* (Fenton Bailey and Randy Barbato, 2005) – has focused on 1970s US porn directors and producers in explicitly auteurist tones.[26]

Considered in a historical perspective, Braun's career is particularly central in terms of North America's perception of Swedish pornography. Born Alberto Ferro, son of an Italian diplomat, Braun began his career in porn by producing novels and magazines in the early 1960s and started making films after moving to northern Europe. Braun was a self-proclaimed 'sex revolutionary' and advocate for anti-censorship who directly influenced Danish porn legislation. Indeed, he saw the distribution of his pornography across Europe as done in the name of sexual freedom.[27] In 1966, Braun set up Stockholm-based production company AB Beta Film and began producing porn loops. Instead of the black and white 8mm film used in the stag films produced up to this point, Braun invested in colour. Shot on the higher quality format of 16mm, the films were transferred onto Super 8 (a format only launched the previous year) and sold through newspaper and magazine advertisements. According to Braun, the number of European customers grew to 50,000 by 1969 and Beta Film set up a film laboratory of their own. Since their activities

Fig. 7.2. Bondage and domination on display in Lasse Braun's Super 8 film *Perversion* (Lasse Braun Productions, 1971)

were still illegal, Ferro changed his name to Braun, a name allegedly purchased from a Swedish carpenter who had been present as the police arrived at the Stockholm office.[28] While based in Stockholm, Braun was a markedly translocal operator who shot his films in Sweden and Denmark, Netherlands, France, Spain, UK and the Caribbean alike, aiming to profile the productions as quality pornography with some narrative framing.

Braun's film series contributed to the increasingly mythic status of Swedish sin, offering films that ranged from those abiding by the rhetoric of healthy, 'good' Swedish sex, as in *Love in Scandinavia* (Sweden, 1971), to ones explicitly detached from it, such as *Perversion* (Denmark, 1971, see Fig. 7.2), *Shocking* (Netherlands, 1972), *Bondage* (Netherlands, 1972) and *Deep Arse* (Netherlands, 1973). All in all, the films marked a clear departure from the by now well-established notion of Swedish film; while occasionally shot outdoors during summer, they had little resemblance to the educational, clean and socially concerned tone of their more mainstream contemporaries. Exploring anal sex, double penetration, fetishes, bondage, domination and urination in close-up, the films were not confined to given notions of sexual normalcy but were in fact branded and marketed as deviations from it.

With notable exceptions such as *I Am Curious (Yellow)*, the audience for Swedish films, sex films included, was generally small. Again, Braun's Super 8 films were not shown in cinemas as they were targeted for private use, although his 1975 feature film, *Sensations*, did gain theatrical release. Mass markets nevertheless became available in the United States when Reuben Sturman – one of the wealthiest and most influential pornographers in North America at the time – distributed Braun's films across his (illegal) peep-show parlours in 1971. Mainly set in sex shops, peep show machines included a coin-operated Super 8 projector and a booth with a lock. Sturman developed the distribution and exhibition method and received divvies from tens of thousands of peep show machines across the United States, with the profits being an estimated two billion dollars in the 1970s alone. In the early 1980s, the US Department of Justice estimated Sturman to be the largest distributor of hardcore pornography in the country.[29] This scale of the operation had an obvious impact on the distribution of Beta Film's porn, as well as on the company's productivity and the reputation of Swedish porn before the beginning of the video era at the end of the 1970s. The furtive means of distribution and exhibition added to the imagery of Swedish sin as potentially seedy and perverted.

Braun's close-to-forgotten status may have to do with film format and methods of distribution: Super 8 versus 35mm, home and peep show consumption versus theatre screenings. Loops often fall off the film history map. I nevertheless argue that, along with the long-standing reputation of Swedish film, the peep show distribution of Braun's films contributed to the co-articulation of Sweden and pornography in North America. The title of Caballero's *Swedish Erotica* series can most likely be explained by its loops competing over the same peep show markets in which Braun had made a name for himself during the 1970s. Since Super 8 loop production was strongly associated with all things Swedish, the regional referent functioned as shorthand for hardcore pornography. While *Swedish Erotica* films gained broader fame in the course of video production, the initial title owes to the appeal and market value of Swedish pornography at the

1970s loop market. Braun's films helped to further associate Sweden with pornography and to strengthen the perverted undertones of the concept of Swedish sin.

The Perverted North

The image of Scandinavia as a hub of pornography grew during the 1970s and, although US production began to dominate international markets of video porn during the following decade, the reputation remained. After joining the anti-porn feminist cause, Linda Lovelace, the star of Gerard Damiano's *Deep Throat* (1972), grew worried about her lecture trip to Sweden and Norway, since she knew Scandinavia to be the 'porn capital of the world'.[30] Writing from a Norwegian perspective, Anne G. Sabo notes that, in the United States, Scandinavia tends to be seen as a promised land of sexuality and pornography despite the considerable differences within the national legislation within the region.[31] Contrary to Danish and Swedish liberal legislation, Norway, Iceland and Finland had in fact rather strict legislation concerning obscenity. In other words, the interchangeability of Sweden and Scandinavia in the North American imagination owes to defective knowledge of the regional contexts.

Yet, the question still remains as to why Sweden, rather than Denmark – a country with a more liberal legislation and abundant export of both porn and sexploitation films[32] – was established as *the* land of free sex and porn? Additionally, how did this reputation persist in a country like Germany? Indeed, why has Germany not been similarly figured as a land of sexual freedom, given its long tradition of nudism, free-body culture (*Freikörperkultur*) and diverse porn industry?[33] Public sex education was already widespread in Germany in the 1920s and porn legislation was liberalised in West Germany as early as 1976.[34] German films exploring sexuality in a 'moral' framework appeared in the 1910s and 1920s. The 1950s and 1960s witnessed a swell of sex films (*Deutscher Sex-Film*) ranging from educational to documentary and softcore sexploitation, such as Erich F. Bender's *Helga* (1967) and Fransz Joseph Gottlieb's *Das Wunder der Liebe* (1968).[35] German porn production grew since the late 1970s and the country soon became one of the hubs of Europorn.

Despite the frisky nudism and popularity of Hans Billian's Bavarian sex comedies of the 1960s and 70s, with their Dirndls, Lederhosen and Alps, German sexuality has not been associated with cleanliness or health. Quite the contrary: since World War II, depictions of German sexuality have tended to focus on themes such as sadomasochism, barbarism and sexual perversion.[36] This is particularly the case with characters associated with Nazism in films as different as Lucino Visconti's art house classic *The Damned/La caduta degli gei* (1969) and Nazi sexploitation films such as *Ilsa, She Wolf of the SS* (Don Edmonds, 1975). In spite of the range of porn production carried out in country, the international reputation of German porn often impinges on the scatological subgenre of Scheißeporn, especially in North America.

According to Stephan Schröder, Sweden is associated with sexual freedom in Germany since it is understood as *the* prototypical Nordic welfare state and a prototypical Scandinavian country.[37] Swedish sexuality has similarly come to represent Scandinavian sexuality and the figure of the emancipated Swedish woman has come to stand for Nordic femininity in general. Female emancipation, then, takes the shape of activity, initiative and availability alike. Sabo further points out that the imagery of free Scandinavian sexuality is associated with the tradition of social democracy and policies advancing gender equality.[38] The association of free porn with gender equality may strike some as strange, given that Nordic gender equality discourse has tended to be characteristically anti-porn. Examining some of these frictions in the Swedish context, Kulick argues that feminists actively began to address and critique commercial sex in the 1970s, after which North American anti-porn feminism gained a somewhat hegemonic role.[39] For Kulick, the discourse of Swedish sexuality is a paradoxical assemblage of associations of freedom, legal constraints and normative framings productive of a national model of healthy and morally responsible sexuality: of 'good sex'. Good sex, then, involves:

> socially approved, mutually satisfying sexual relations between two (and only two) consenting adults or young adults who are more or less sociological equals. It must not involve money or overt domination, even as role-playing. It should occur only in the context of an established social relationship.[40]

That which does not meet these criteria (the commercial, the kinky and the promiscuous) is defined as less wholesome, or perverted.

Kulick's argument draws on Gayle Rubin's overview of divisions drawn between good and bad sex. According to Rubin, good – 'normal, natural, healthy, and holy' – vanilla sex is practiced by married heterosexual people of the same generation in a monogamous relationship, preferably marriage, at their home for reproductive and non-commercial purposes, without the aid of pornography, fetish objects, sex toys or role-playing. That which falls outside these parameters – sex practiced by, or with, transvestites, transsexuals, fetishists and sadomasochists, sex for money or in cross-generational assemblages – becomes labelled as bad sex: 'abnormal, unnatural, sick, sinful, "way out"'.[41]

The Swedish, and more broadly Nordic, ethos of 'good sex' is based on the premise of sexual health; it is liberal, heavily influenced by psychotherapy and emphasises 'personal autonomy, socially responsible sexual conduct and equality'.[42] Contrary to the ideal of sexual abstinence advanced in North America, the Nordic ethos frames sexuality as a form of self-expression that is crucial to physical and mental wellbeing. It also frames 'false interpretations', 'myths' and 'slanted attitudes' towards sex as risks and problems to be avoided and overcome.[43] Inherently normative, the model of good sex can be easily mapped onto Swedish sex films but far less so to pornography and Braun's oeuvre. Pornography tends to fall categorically outside the parameters of good sex as representative of 'false interpretations' and 'slanted attitudes' towards sexuality.

While similarly linked to the notion of uninhibited sexuality, Swedish sin involves strong undertones of risk and perversion. In Sweden's neighbouring country of Finland, the myth of Swedish sin has been drawn somewhat differently than in the United States or Germany. Finland was never an important exporter of sexploitation films, although films such T.J. Särkkä's *The Milkmaid/Hilja maitotyttö* (1953) and *Preludes to Ecstasy/ Kuu on vaarallinen* (1961) owed their racy reputation to scenes of nude swimming and sexual encounters in the countryside very similar to their Swedish counterparts. At the same time it can be argued that Finnish film history has involved an explicit differentiation from Swedish sexuality.

Between the 1950s and 1970s, Swedish sexuality became co-articulated with homosexuality by the Finnish media. This association was reiterated amply enough to give rise to the stereotype that 'all Swedish men are gay', which remains popular to date. Examining the originating context of the stereotype, queer scholar Tuula Juvonen traces it to postwar media scandals. Homosexuality was legalised in Sweden in 1944, whereas in Finland its decriminalisation did not occur until 1971. While homosexuality was legal, Swedish media scandals concerning male prostitutions were recurrent and Finnish media covered these with gusto.[44] In the course of the scandal coverage, homosexuality was identified as a 'Swedish disease' and 'the Swedish' gradually became synonymous to the homosexual.[45] Film culture played an active part in this, framing Sweden, and Stockholm in particular, as decadent and morally depraved. Finnish films such as *Finnish Girls in Stockholm/Suomalaistyttöjä Tukholmassa* (Roland af Hällström, 1952) and *Road of Temptations/Viettelysten tie* (Kaarlo Nuorvala, 1955), for example, depicted Swedish men as depraved stalkers of both young Finnish men and women.

During the course of the 1950s, homosexuality was associated with feminine Swedish men in one arena after another.[46] Identifying male homosexuality as a particularly Swedish quality enabled the articulation of Finnish masculinity as agrarian, healthy and heterosexual at the very moment when migration from Finland to Sweden began to boom. In *Finnish Girls in Stockholm*, young Kirsti (Eija Inkeri) arrives in Stockholm looking for work, only to be sexually harassed. She becomes an erotic artist's model, mistress and a prostitute before committing suicide. For his part, medical student Olavi (Esko Saha) witnesses a suspicious all-male party where men sip cocktails, dance together, wear make-up and sport jewellery. Once male-on-male contact gets too much, Olavi punches the host, cursing, and simultaneously draws a clear boundary between Swedish and Finnish masculinity. Critiqued for its anti-Swedish depiction of Stockholm as a lair of criminals, pimps, prostitutes, nude models and homophiles,[47] the film inspired a sequel, *Road of Temptations*, with its share of gay Swedish men, prostitution and drugs, and a Finnish male protagonist striking down a Swedish male homosexual artist for his sexual advances. In these films, young Finnish women were threatened by commercial sex, whereas for young Finnish men the threat was homosexuality.

The Finnish image of Swedish sexuality has also been tied to pornography. As Finnish legislation concerning audiovisual porn was considerably strict until the 2000s, books, 8mm films and later videos were bought from Sweden and ordered from Swedish mail-order companies. In addition to being the land of homosexuality in popular imagination, Sweden was also the land of porn.[48] Finland was marked apart from its assumedly sexually excessive and perverted neighbour. While drastically different, these articulations of Swedish sexuality shared and revolved around the familiar notion of sexual liberation, seen as both a risk and a possibility and as leading to both good and bad sex.

The Evasive Perversion

Defined as turning away from the right, proper and good, as debasement, distortion, corruption and misuse, the term perversity is connected to the evasive notion of normality. In a lecture on the abnormal in 1975, Michel Foucault referred to perversity as an historically unstable set of notions linked with the sexual, encompassing both intentional malice and psychiatric notions of abnormality, noting that 'the weaker it is epistemologically, the better it functions'.[49] Given the malleability of the term, it takes little analytical effort then to note that the instability of Swedish sin and Swedish sexuality presents them as exemplary examples of boundary work between the normal and the abnormal, the acceptable and the perverse that speak of their contexts of creation more than they do of Sweden or the Swedes. Just as the 1955 *Time* magazine article told of certain North American norms and conceptions concerning sexuality, matrimony, socialism and religion at the time, Finnish figures of gay Swedish men speak of the fantasy of Finnish men as their opposite: as regular and straight. Constructions of Swedish sin in Europe and North America have varied in their local articulations and emphases. United through their differences, these contingent figures redraw the boundaries between good and bad sex, perversity and normality in terms of national boundaries, politics, religion and moral norms, yet these boundaries are elastic, leaky and ephemeral.

Contrary to the figures of dark and gloomy perversity associated with Germany, Swedish perversion – 'the Swedish sin' – has been invested with transgressive potentiality and promise as that which, by deviating from the norm, points to different possibilities of being and doing. In other words, while entailing an element of risk and danger, it also titillates in a more positive register. Swedish sin has been knowingly used as a branding and marketing strategy, as with 1960s sex films and hardcore pornography. By naming their film series *Swedish Erotica*, Caballero tapped into the already established reputation of Lasse Braun's Swedish porn loops in the US peep show market and their added value of international flair while detaching this all from the physical location of Sweden. This exemplifies the uses of Swedish sexuality as a floating signifier that traverses national boundaries without necessarily being recognisable to the Swedes themselves.[50]

Conceptions of Swedish sex emerge as values, judgements, fantasies and fears that are attached to it, and as they layer and conflict with one another, they change form and take new shape. Swedish sin is contingent, contradictory and anachronistic, carrying echoes of the sexual mores of the 1950s and the early years of commercial legal porn production. It is open for appropriation and celebration (as in the theme of Stockholm's 2008 EuroPride: 'Swedish Sin – Breaking Borders') while offering a longstanding challenge for those desiring to brand the nation in more wholesome terms. As a figure of fantasy, Swedish sin is likely to circulate as long as it manages to evoke even the faintest aroma of perversion.

Notes

1. See http://adultloopdb.nl/category/swedish-erotica/for a database of the films.
2. See Frederick Hale, 'Time for sex in Sweden: enhancing the myth of the "Swedish sin" during the 1950s', *Scandinavian Studies* 75/3 (2003), pp. 351–74; Elisabet Björklund, 'This is a dirty movie': *Taxi Driver* and "Swedish sin"', *Journal of Scandinavian Cinema* 1/2 (2011), pp. 163–76.
3. Carl Gustaf Boëthius, 'Sex education in Swedish schools: the facts and the fiction', *Family Planning Perspectives* 17/6 (1985), p. 276.
4. Jack Stevenson, *Scandinavian Blue: The Erotic Cinema of Sweden and Denmark in the 1960s and 1970s* (Jefferson: McFarland, 2010), pp. 17–8; see also Hale, 'Time for sex in Sweden', pp. 351–74.
5. See Linda Williams, *Hard Core: Pornography and the 'Frenzy of the Visible* (Berkeley, CA: University of California Press, 1989), p. 96; Justin Wyatt, 'Selling "atrocious sexual behavior": revisiting sexualities in the marketplace for adult films in the 1960s', in Hilary Radner and Moya Luckett (eds), *Swinging Single: Representing Sexuality in the 1960s* (Minneapolis: Minnesota University Press, 1999), pp. 105–31.
6. Wyatt, 'Selling "atrocious sexual behavior"', p. 114.

7. Stevenson, *Scandinavian Blue*, pp. 64, 66.
8. Eric Schaefer, *'Bold! Daring! Shocking! True!' A History of Exploitation Films, 1919–1959* (Durham: Duke University Press, 1999), pp. 335–7; Stevenson *Scandinavian Blue*, p. 16.
9. See Wyatt, 'Selling "atrocious sexual behavior"', pp. 114, 116.
10. Stevenson, *Scandinavian Blue*, p. 93.
11. See Stevenson, *Scandinavian Blue*, p. 21.
12. Don Kulick, 'Four hundred thousand Swedish perverts', *GLQ: A Journal of Lesbian and Gay Studies* 11/2 (2005), p. 210; see also Björklund, 'This is a dirty movie', p. 166.
13. Stephan Michael Schröder, 'More fun with Swedish girls? Functions of a German heterostereotype', *Ethnologia Scandinavica* 27 (1997), pp. 124, 128.
14. Björklund, 'This is a dirty movie', pp. 164–5.
15. Stevenson, *Scandinavian Blue*, p. 159.
16. See Björklund, 'This is a dirty movie', p. 163–76.
17. Berl Kutchinsky, 'Pornography, sex crime, and public policy', in Sally-Anne Gerull and Bornia Halstead (eds), *Sex Industry and Public Policy: Proceedings of a Conference Held 6–8 May 1991* (Canberra: Australian Institute of Criminology, 1992), p. 43. Available at http://aic.gov.au/media_library/publications/proceedings/14/kutchinsky.pdf (accessed March 2013).
18. See Clarissa Smith, 'A perfectly British business: stagnation continuities and change on the top shelf', in Lisa Z. Sigel (ed.), *International Exposures: Perspectives on Modern European Pornography 1800–2000* (New Brunswick, NJ: Rutgers University Press, 2005), p. 151; Stevenson, *Scandinavian Blue*.
19. See Williams, *Hard Core*, pp. 97–8; Chuck Kleinhans, 'Pornography and documentary: narrating the alibi', in Jeffrey Sconce (ed.), *Sleaze Artists: Cinema at the Margins of Taste, Style, and Politics* (Durham: Duke University Press, 2007), pp. 108–9; Stevenson, *Scandinavian Blue*, pp. 154–7.
20. Stevenson, *Scandinavian Blue*, p. 131.
21. MAX's Video was a central Nordic porn distributor in the 1990s and 2000s and Demotikos AB (est. 1985, producer of the brands Scandinavian Erotic Video Production and Blue Hotel) remains active to date.
22. See Ingrid Ryberg, *Imagining Safe Space: The Politics of Queer, Feminist and Lesbian Pornography* (Stockholm: Stockholm University, 2012).
23. For example: Williams, *Hard Core*; Walter Kendrick, *The Secret Museum: Pornography in Modern Culture* (Berkeley, CA: University of California Press, 1996); David Jennings, *Skinflicks: The Inside Story of the X-Rated Video Industry* (Bloomington, IN: 1st Books, 2000); Frederic S. Lane, *Obscene Profits: The Entrepreneurs of Pornography in the Cyber Age* (New York: Routledge, 2000); Legs McNeil and Jennifer Osborne, *The Other Hollywood: The Uncensored Oral History of the Porn Film Industry* (New York: Regan Books, 2005). The authorised Lasse Braun biography, available at www.lasse-braun.com, also features press clippings on Braun and his films.

24. See Steven Marcus, *The Other Victorians: A Study of Sexuality and Pornography in Mid-Nineteenth Century England* (New York: Basic Books, 1966); Lynn Hunt, *The Invention of Pornography: Obscenity and the Origins of Modernity 1500–1800* (New York: Zone Books, 1993); Kendrick, *The Secret Museum*.

25. With the early exception of Al Di Lauro and Gerard Rabkin, *Dirty Movies: An Illustrated History of the Stag Film 1915–1970* (New York: Chelsea House, 1976).

26. Such porn nostalgia has been relatively absent in Europe, perhaps partly since the 'porn wars' – public political debates on the cultural meaning and role of, and regulation concerning pornography – have been less sharp than in North America. See Susanna Paasonen Susanna and Laura Saarenmaa, 'The golden age of porn: nostalgia and history in cinema', in Susanna Paasonen, Kaarina Nikunen and Laura Saarenmaa (eds), *Pornification: Sex and Sexuality in Media Culture* (Oxford: Berg, 2007), pp. 23–32.

27. See www.lasse-braun.com.

28. Ibid.

29. See McNeil and Osborne, *The Other Hollywood*, pp. 104–105; Lane, *Obscene Profits*, pp. 48–9.

30. Linda Lovelace and Mike McGrady, *Out of Bondage* (Secaucus, NJ: Lyle Stuart, 1986), p. 171.

31. Anne G. Sabo, 'The status of sexuality, pornography and morality in Norway today: are the critics ready for Bjørneboe's joyful inversion or Mykle's guilt trip?' *Nora – Nordic Journal of Women's Studies* 13/1 (2005), p. 37.

32. 32 Kutchinsky, 'Pornography, sex crime, and public policy', p. 45; Kulick, 'Four hundred thousand Swedish perverts', p. 209; Stevenson, *Scandinavian Blue*.

33. See Chad Ross, *Naked Germany: Health, Race and the Nation* (Oxford: Berg, 2005).

34. See Heather MacRae, 'Morality, censorship and discrimination: reframing the pornography debate in Germany and Europe', *Social Politics* 10/3 (2003), pp. 314–45.

35. Dagmar Herzog, *Sex after Fascism: Memory and Morality in Twentieth-Century Germany* (Princeton: Princeton University Press, 2005), pp. 143–4. Germans have been known as eager consumers of porn. In 1971 alone, an estimated 50 million marks were spent in West Germany on imported, mainly Danish and Swedish pornography, and 125 million on locally produced, albeit not entirely legal, porn. Former Luftwaffe pilot Beate Uhse established one of the world's first sex shops in 1962, creating an international empire. Ibid., p. 145.

36. Carolyn Dean, 'The Great War, pornography, and the transformation of modern male subjectivity', *Modernism/Modernity* 3/2, pp. 62–5; Herzog, *Sex after Fascism*, pp 11–19.

37. Schröder, 'More fun with Swedish girls?' p. 130.

38. Sabo, 'The status of sexuality', p. 37.

39. Kulick, 'Four hundred thousand Swedish perverts', p. 211–13.

40. Ibid., p. 208.

41. Gayle Rubin, 'Thinking sex (1984)', in Carole S. Vance (ed.), *Pleasure and Danger: Exploring Female Sexuality* (London: Pandora, 1989), pp. 280–2. See also Kath Albury, *Yes Means Yes: Getting Explicit About Heterosex* (Crows Nest: Allen & Unwin, 2002), pp. 67–8.

42. Ilpo Helén and Katja Yesilova, 'Shepherding desire: sexual health promotion in Finland from the 1940s to the 1990s', *Acta Sociologica* 49/3 (2006), p. 258.

43. Ibid., p. 267.

44. Tuula Juvonen, *Varjoelämää ja julkisia salaisuuksia* (Tampere: Vastapaino, 2002), p. 86.

45. Ibid., pp. 98, 103–4.

46. Ibid., p. 141.

47. Kari Uusitalo (ed.), *SK: Suomen kansallisfilmografia 4* (Helsinki: SEA, 1992), pp. 469–71.

48. See Susanna Paasonen, 'Homespun: Finnporn and the meanings of the local', in Darren Kerr and Claire Hines (eds), *Hard To Swallow: Reading Pornography On Screen* (London and New York: Wallflower Press, 2010), pp. 177–93.

49. Michel Foucault, *Abnormal: Lectures at the Collège de France, 1974–1975*, Valerio Marchetti and Antonella Salomoni (eds), Graham Burchell (trans.) (New York: Picador, 2003), p. 33.

50. See Björklund, 'This is a dirty movie', pp. 163–76.

8

'Does this look sexual to you?' Neoliberal Culture and Everyday Perversion in Recent Cinema

Martin Fradley

There is nothing spontaneous, nothing natural about human desires. Our desires are artificial. We have to be *taught* to desire. Cinema is the ultimate pervert art: it doesn't give you what you desire; it *tells* you how to desire.[1]

Introduction: Neoliberal Culture and the Sexual Subject

A father and son converse in a banal domestic setting. A smartly dressed woman goes to work in Manhattan. A child sits on a sofa, absently gazing at a television screen. A woman wearing a wedding gown sits at a desk. A group of college students discuss a short story written by one of their peers. These scenes could appear in any number of mainstream films. But something is missing in this account. The young boy in *Happiness* (Todd Solondz, 1998) earnestly discusses his father's predilection for child rape.

The confident female professional in *The Girlfriend Experience* (Steven Soderbergh, 2009) is an upscale sex worker *en route* to an appointment with an 'erotic connoisseur'. The child in *A Serbian Film* (Srđan Spasojević, 2010) gazes vacantly at images of his father having sex in a pornographic film. In a gesture of amorous devotion, the runaway bride in *Secretary* (Steven Shainberg, 2002) sits for days in a urine-soaked wedding dress. The students in *Storytelling* (Todd Solondz, 2001) listen to an autobiographical account of a brutal and humiliating sexual encounter between the author and her college professor. In different ways these scenes bespeak a contemporary cinematic fascination with sexual transgression. What particularly interests me, however, is recent cinema's critical engagements with socio-sexual conditioning under the *hegemonic norms* of neoliberal culture. As Yael D. Sherman explains, neoliberalism 'is both a social policy based on extending the logic of the market to every sphere and a corresponding norm for how individuals behave and govern themselves'.[2] This commitment to the primacy of the free market has given rise to the concept of *homo economicus*: an abstract human subject characterised by personal autonomy, competitive individualism and rational self-interest.[3] Under a neoliberal regime devoted to consumer sovereignty, individuals are encouraged to realise themselves in the pursuit of pleasure that, as Hilary Radner points out, 'is first and foremost sexual – with individual gratification being the final expression the citizen's inalienable right to the pursuit of happiness'.[4]

The widespread commodification of sexuality – exemplified by the omnipresence and broad cultural influence of pornography – is symptomatic of the cultural logic of advanced capitalism. The ramifications of the commercial sexualisation of contemporary culture – variously dubbed 'pornotopia',[5] 'striptease culture',[6] 'pornification'[7] and 'the sexualisation of Western culture'[8] – has inspired much critical debate. Sex and sexuality are now widely understood as culturally constructed and historically contingent discursive formations. Following Freud's assertion that any sexual activity engaged in for non-procreative purposes is perverse, it is now broadly accepted that the vast majority of human sexual behaviour is perverse to varying degrees.[9] This de-essentialising of sexuality has, in turn, manifested itself in popular culture that has increasingly mobilised the conceptual precepts of queer theory in its representation of sexual behaviour and identity as a broad spectrum of varied perversions.[10]

For Brian McNair, the sexualisation of culture has led to 'a democratization and diversification of sexual discourse' and 'a break with many of the most restrictive and patronising [sexual] stereotypes of the past'.[11] McNair's welcoming of contemporary sexual culture's democratic potential nevertheless elides what Linda Williams describes as 'the two-edged swords of liberation and further disciplinary control'.[12] At the heart of this debate are the fundamental contradictions of neoliberalism. If the free market empowers the sexual autonomy of neoliberal subjects, how does this 'freedom' tally with a growing reliance upon popular media to regulate, shape and normalise sexual practices and identities?

Following Slavoj Žižek's argument that cinema teaches neoliberal citizens how to desire, Williams astutely notes that moving images 'are surely the most powerful sex education most of us will ever receive'.[13] Here I discuss films that express – whether explicitly or more obliquely – critical ambivalence towards a sexual regime driven by the logics of neoliberal culture. First, I analyse the relationship between sex and work in *Secretary* and *The Girlfriend Experience* before examining the continuum between sexual dysfunction and the failings of the broader neoliberal culture in the films of left-field American director Todd Solondz. Finally, the chapter discusses the convergence of these themes in the controversial extremism of *A Serbian Film*. Taken together, these analyses offer a tentative critical overview of contemporary responses to the sexualisation of contemporary culture in the wake of the neoliberal turn.

'For everybody who's ever been tied up at work': Sex/Work in *Secretary* and *The Girlfriend Experience*

Ostensibly a romantic comedy about the burgeoning relationship between the timid Lee (Maggie Gyllenhaal) and her authoritarian boss E. Edward Grey (James Spader), *Secretary*'s open valorisation of BDSM practices and desires remains rare in mainstream cinematic representation. Indeed, *Secretary* is self-consciously 'queer' in its thematic emphasis on the everyday perversity of heteronormativity and the self-abnegating dynamics of traditional romance. Rather than simply celebrating sexual alterity, however, *Secretary* asks provocative questions about the inextricable bind between sociality and sexuality: the psychosocial interpellations of work and familial obligation; the regulatory processes of socio-sexual normalcy; and the structuring queerness of social relations. As such, the film intelligently explores the parameters of sexual normalcy. Lee and Edward's sexual dissent ultimately forms a nurturing romantic bind of mutuality and tenderness, which stands in stark contrast to the banality and dysfunction of their social surroundings.

In *Secretary*, key institutions – family, marriage, work – are unambiguously depicted as perverse in their strictures, conventions and oppressive demands upon the self. It is precisely the humiliations of the social everyday – exploitation, sublimation, aggressive self-regulation – that Lee and Edward adapt to their own self-affirming ends. In the film's sly coda, Lee and Edward set up home in an idyllic suburban street. 'All our activities melted into an everyday sort of life', muses Lee, provocatively placing a dead cockroach on their freshly starched bed sheets for Edward to discover on his return from a day at the office. *Secretary*'s parody of middle-class normativity reaffirms the film's critical emphasis on everyday imbalances of social–sexual power relations.

More importantly, it is Lee's persistent eroticisation of labour and the dialectic of transgression and punishment that serves to transform the workplace into a *mise-en-scène* of mutually sustaining desire. By infusing the daily rituals of the workplace with erotic affect, Lee's wholesale sublimation of her self to mundane secretarial labour both sexualises and critiques the deadening norms of careerism. Licking envelopes, photocopying and typing banal formal letters become infused with polymorphous pleasure. In one early scene, Lee types with furious proficiency during a mundane secretarial exam. When Edward sternly warns her that the job is boring, Lee sensually avows her fetishistic investment in the negative affect of menial labour: 'I *want* to be bored. I *like* dull work'. Lee's erotic investment in submissive positioning is underscored by her absolute devotion to the hierarchies of the workplace: her pleasure in obeying Edward's punitive commands ('put your elbows on the desk and bend over'), her evident delight in being chastised for secretarial errors ('straighten yourself up and go type it again!') and the joyous erotic revelation at being spanked by her boss. 'I'm *your* secretary!' she later avows with self-subjugating rapture.

Secretary mobilises sexual perversion in order to satirise the neurotic investments of normative psychosexual development via BDSM practices. As an attorney, Edward is a symbolic register for the nexus of law, social regulation and prohibition. While Lee's investment in Edward arguably functions as a substitute for her relationship with her alcoholic father, the role-play at the heart of Lee and Edward's mutually sustaining relationship ensures that the film avoids reiterating the strictures of patriarchy. Moreover, Lee's psychosexual investment in subverting these strictures is perhaps most obvious in her deliberate secretarial errors. In the film's most gloriously erotic scene, Lee locks herself in a toilet cubicle and masturbates over a letter filled with typing errors marked in red pen by Edward. Lee's onanistic rapture is fuelled by fantasies about banal transgressions (neglecting to order mayonnaise for Edward's sandwiches) and delirious vocalisations of taboo language ('Cock! Put your prick in my mouth! Screw me!'). The BDSM relationship between Lee and Edward thus re-stages the dominant/submissive hierarchical relationships and sanctioned humiliation of the workplace for their own erotic ends.

Mirroring the way she appropriates traditional signifiers of femininity (most obviously in the coveted pink figurine she uses to ritualistically self-harm), Lee adopts normative modes of behaviour – professional decorum, the prohibitions of collegiate relationships – and imbues them with libidinal verve. *Secretary* underscores the interwoven matrices of neoliberal professionalism and contemporary sexual identity in a scene featuring Edward's domineering ex-wife, a card-carrying stereotype of the careerist *femme castratrice*. Conversely, Lee's erotic self-abasement ridicules the imperatives of self-improving individualism, a form of role-play that finds its counterpart in Edward's neurotic, authoritarian-disciplinarian persona. If the eroticisation of both the workplace and traditional gender norms functions for both characters as a coping mechanism, it is nevertheless the everyday paraphilias, polymorphous perversities and tender co-dependence of their relationship that *Secretary* most fully endorses.

Whereas Lee and Edward eroticise the strictures and limitations of the social contract in the workplace, Steven Soderbergh's *The Girlfriend*

Experience offers an indivisible view of sex/work. Set during the early stages of the 2008 economic meltdown and shot with sober documentary-style realism, the film features adult film star Sasha Grey as Chelsea, an upscale female escort working in Manhattan. Her unique service offers busy clients the 'girlfriend experience': for $2000, Chelsea provides empathetic conversation and romantic dinner dates alongside sexual services. In many ways, the film illustrates Eva Illouz's concept of emotional capitalism, a neoliberal symptom in which economic relationships are invested with profound affect. While the 'cold intimacy' of personal relationships are shaped and informed by 'market-based cultural repertoires':

> Emotional capitalism is a culture in which emotional economic discourses and practices mutually shape each other, thus producing [...] a broad, sweeping movement in which affect is made an essential aspect of economic behaviour and in which emotional life – especially that of the middle-classes – follows the logic of economic relations and exchange.[14]

This new form of sociability is at the epicentre of *The Girlfriend Experience*: the film's central conceit is that Chelsea's relationship with boyfriend Chris (Chris Santos) is practically indistinguishable from the professional service she provides to her client base.

The resonance of Grey's celebrity intertext is far from insignificant. Indeed, Grey has earned a well-deserved reputation for both her preternatural business acumen – she made her pornographic debut on her 18th birthday – and the physical extremity of her on-screen labour. Successful, professionally autonomous and sexually confident, Grey's enterprising career trajectory and economic success exemplifies the way in which femininity is transformed under the conditions of the 'new economy', a contemporary gender regime described by Sherman as 'neoliberal femininity':

> While traditional femininity connotes 'sex object', neoliberal femininity connotes competent subject; while traditional femininity implies dependence, neoliberal femininity implies independence; while traditional femininity is associated with the sin of vanity, neoliberal femininity implies that one is actively self-responsible.[15]

With Grey ultimately playing a version of herself, *The Girlfriend Experience* repeatedly underscores the ephemeral nature of commodified identity. Chelsea's real name – Christine – echoes Sasha Grey's status as a successfully marketed brand. ("Grey's" real name is Marina Ann Hantzis). With its upscale Manhattan milieu, solipsistic business district workers and hyper-affluent *mise-en-scène*, *The Girlfriend Experience* shares the same cultural logic and rarefied setting of Brett Easton Ellis's 1991 novel *American Psycho*. However, *The Girlfriend Experience's* depiction of the debased ideological wasteland sustaining this affectless post-industrial world are arguably even more unnerving than Ellis's controversial novel. The 'self' in *The Girlfriend Experience* is entirely sublimated into erotic-commodity form. Like the over-determined formal rhetoric of sexual presence and corporeal excess that sustains Grey's pornographic films, Chelsea's service offers her clients the reified *simulacrum* of emotional and physical intimacy. Sexual exchange in *The Girlfriend Experience* is indistinguishable from any other commercial transaction, a point underscored when Chelsea is brutally 'reviewed' online by a client:

> With her smoky eyes, dark straight hair and perky little body, Chelsea would appear to have the potential to satisfy in the goth or girl-next-door modes. Alas [...] with her flat affect, lack of culture and utter refusal to engage, Chelsea couldn't dazzle Forrest fucking Gump [...] Just as her perky little tits seemed to literally shrink at my touch, so too did the connoisseur's cock fail to launch at the clammy touch of her hand and the lukewarm and loose embrace of her mouth.

Where *Secretary* circumnavigates the neoliberal abyss through appropriation and affective investment, *The Girlfriend Experience's* critique is as applicable to the dehumanising concept of professionalism as it is to the commodified illusions of the sex industry. This world of cold intimacy is synopsised by one of Chelsea's co-workers: 'I think that feeling you get when you connect with a client is the *best* feeling in the world.' When Chelsea's boyfriend tells her 'you are the *best* at everything you do' – emotional capitalism's bland accolade *par excellence* – the slender gap between their relationship and the commercialised simulations she provides collapses entirely. In the film's final scene, one of Chelsea's regular clients – an obese, fully-clothed jeweller – offers her financial advice before ejaculating prematurely. The intertwined negative affect of sex and the economy is encapsulated in a Wall Street broker's plaintive wail: 'the economy is *fucked*'!

'Are you a pervert?' Todd Solondz and Erotic Dystopia

Like the ideologically torpid world of *The Girlfriend Experience*, the bleak socio-sexual imaginary of director Todd Solondz is best described as erotically dystopic. Solondz's emphasis on dysfunctional sexual mores and their inextricable relationship to socioeconomic regulation is forthright in expression. Rather than avowing 'arch-emotional nihilism',[16] the taboo-crossing of Solondz's films is best understood as a rejection of the commercial interpellations of democratic sexual culture. In this way, Solondz's middle-class sexual delinquents are positioned as the inevitable human detritus of neoliberal consensus.

Often accused of misanthropy, Solondz's films are instead acute diagnoses of the contradictions of a brutally individualist sexual culture. Ostensibly a teen movie, *Welcome to the Dollhouse* (1995) is wholly instructive in this respect. Documenting the socio-sexual initiation of Dawn 'Wiener Dog' Wiener (Heather Matarazzo) in an anonymous Junior High School, the film underscores the relentless sexual aggression that infuses a culture rife with bullying. Dawn's induction into the daily humiliations of a microcosmic United States is staged in a series of cruel Social Darwinist rituals. The film presents the normative socialisation rites of neoliberal culture as a nightmare of interpellative brutality and unending socio-sexual tyranny. Sexually taunted by homophobic peers ('lesbo!!'), Dawn's bespectacled outsider is persistently harassed in a hyper-competitive milieu where vulnerability signifies social death. The rituals of adolescent dating are illustrated through tales of 'finger-fucking' and threats of rape serve as veiled expressions of affection. In one scene, Dawn is forced to defecate while a soporifically sadistic classmate looks on. Dawn's older brother Mark (Matthew Faber), is rejected by an unseen girlfriend after his online efforts to coerce her into sex are rebuffed. The scene is prescient, foretelling the emotional, physical and ontological disconnections of the digital epoch. At the start of *Palindromes* (2004), Solondz's loose sequel to *Welcome to the Dollhouse*, Dawn has committed suicide after becoming pregnant following a date rape. Mark (Faber) returns as an adult, having been formally accused of molesting his niece. 'People never change', he sadly muses.

The remark underscores the counter-hegemonic philosophy of Solondz's world. As his self-commentary suggests, Solondz's films function as a deliberate counterpoint to the individual self-improvement demanded by neoliberal culture: 'Some may find the idea that we never change a bleak and deterministic way of thinking. And yet the inability to change is in many ways freeing, freeing from, amongst other things, the imperative to change'.[17] This 'imperative to change' is, of course, key to the interpellative rhetoric of consumer culture, wherein 'continual change and self-improvement [is] a sign of individual agency'.[18] Perversion for Solondz, then, is a manifestation of the aggressive competitiveness that infuses all interpersonal relations. In an atomised and socially fragmented culture, self-worth is largely determined by the individualist drive towards success. This in turn flattens and subsumes all relationships to the debilitating and dehumanising logics of the market. Solondz's symptomatically depressed characters are consumed by their endless sense of failure as citizens: at work; in relationships; as parents; in their sex lives. His characters' flaws turn these imperatives inward, exposing them as always already perverse; 'If only I had been raped as a child', yearns novelist Helen (Lara Flynn Boyle) in *Happiness*, 'then I would *know* authenticity'. The flattening of moral and ethical values underscores the logics of commodity culture, the traumatic reality of child abuse refigured as fashionably marketable. Correspondingly, in *Life During Wartime* (2009) sexual abuse becomes a game of competitive one-upmanship. 'Your molestation has been, like, *so* done', mocks one college student to her dorm-mate. 'It was just fingers anyway – *get over it!*'

Happiness typifies Solondz's thematic concern with the inevitable flipside of McNair's 'democratization of desire': an entropic social order underpinned by the schizophrenic demands of neoliberal ideology. While the film was controversial for its humanised representation of incest and child rape, *Happiness* is emblematic in its portrayal of social stasis and sexual dysfunction. Bill Maplewood's (Dylan Baker) paedophilia is thrown into relief by both his sexless marriage and his encounter with a homophobic father who ponders aloud whether he ought to procure a prostitute in order to 'cure' his pubescent son, whom he suspects to be gay. Allen's (Phillip Seymour Hoffman) lurid rape fantasies echo the banal and repetitive lexicon of the pornography he consumes:

> I wanna undress her and tie her up. And I wanna pump her. Pump pump pump 'til she screams bloody murder. And then I wanna flip her ass over and pump her even more, so hard that my dick shoots right through her and my cum squirts out of her mouth.

The pursuit of happiness is unveiled as a self-defeating trap: Allen's obscene phone call only makes his crushing insecurity and loneliness more manifest; Helen's emotionally cold professionalism and affectless promiscuity render her incapable of the empathy she craves; while Joy's (Jane Adams) romantic idealism serves only to expose her to casual sexual exploitation. *Happiness* concludes with Bill's son Billy (Rufus Read) masturbating while gazing at a half-naked woman sunbathing on the roof of an adjacent building. Like Allen, the adolescent's longing for normalcy is expressed through an atomised and tragicomic act of voyeuristic objectification. His brief orgasmic spasm serves not as the affirmation of the heteronormativity he craves in order to distinguish himself from his father's pederasty, but – as Billy proudly announces his ejaculatory debut to his bemused family – as only another dysfunctional manifestation of a sexually entropic culture.

In *Storytelling*, Scoobie's (Mark Webber) nonchalant attitude towards his homosexuality is undermined when erotic reveries take the form of fantasies about immolating his parents and achieving success as a popular chat-show host. In *Life During Wartime*, Bill (Ciaran Hinds) and Jacqueline (Charlotte Rampling) both seek an affirmation of self in a casual sexual encounter. Their functional coupling in a generic hotel room reconfirms only the inescapability of negative affect. Solondz repeatedly uses familiar televisual personae to similar ends. Michael Kenneth Williams – best known as streetwise survivalists Omar Little in *The Wire* (2002–2008) and Chalky White in *Boardwalk Empire* (2010–2014) – is re-cast as compulsive sex-pest Allen in *Life During Wartime*. Paul Reubens – popular child entertainer 'Pee Wee Herman', whose career was destroyed after being caught masturbating in a porn theatre – appears in the same film as the ghostly Andy. Reubens' presence underscores the schizophrenia of a neoliberal culture where the omnipresence of pornography is shorthand for sexual liberalism but the inappropriate use of sexually explicit materials is morally condemned. In *Palindromes*, teenager Aviva's pathological longing to conceive is coupled with erotophobia. After being forced into an abortion by her would-be liberal parents, Aviva's maternal desires are thwarted by her pro-life lover's insistence upon anal sex as an effective form of birth control. The use of sex as simply another weapon in the individualist armoury of the everyday is reiterated in *Storytelling*. Asked by an inquisitive child to explain 'rape', Consuelo (Lupe Ontiveros) is blunt in her reply: 'It's when you love someone and they don't love you', the housemaid states, 'and you do something about it'.

The campus-set 'Fiction' section of *Storytelling* is arguably Solondz's most precise distillation of the crushing limitations of 'politically correct' sexual liberalism. Echoing *Welcome to the Dollhouse* in portraying a liberal arts system rife with competitive aggression and self-seeking individualism, 'Fiction' is based around a sexual encounter between creative writing student Vi (Selma Blair) and her African-American professor Mr Scott (Robert Wisdom). The film opens with Vi having sex with Marcus (Leo Fitzpatrick), an undergraduate with cerebral palsy. This serves as a coercive prelude to Marcus's attempt to read Vi the revised ending to his latest short story. Vi's obvious disinterest leaves Marcus complaining that 'the kinkiness has gone' from their relationship. In the next scene, classmates offer facile compliments about Marcus's work ('It reminded me a little of Faulkner. But East Coast. And disabled') before Mr Scott savagely critiques his prose, calling it 'a piece of shit'. Afterwards, Marcus's distress and obvious insecurity is manifested in a crude denunciation of Vi's failure to defend him from Mr Scott's criticisms: 'You just want to fuck him [...] *like every other white cunt on campus!*' A frustrated Vi later encounters Mr Scott in a local bar. After an awkward verbal exchange, Mr Scott caresses Vi's hand, appreciatively murmuring 'you have beautiful skin', while a close-up highlights the stark contrast between the dark tone of his hand and Vi's porcelain complexion.

As Linda Williams argues, the successful marketing of interracial sex in contemporary pornography exposes the mythologies of a 'post-racial' epoch. The selfsame taboos that once served to prohibit miscegenation and culturally outlaw cross-race desire now function to powerfully eroticise transgressions of the racial border:

> [I]n a culture now so determined to be officially blind to racial difference that it has created a new kind of taboo around their very mention, it can seem excitingly risqué to notice differences of skin tone, ass or lip shape.[19]

Like Vi's sexual attraction to the disabled Marcus, Vi and Mr Scott's mutual attraction is predicated on precisely the 'risqué' *frisson* to which Williams refers. By cutting to the image of their entwined hands, Solondz draws attention to this racialised erotic connection. Retiring to Mr Scott's apartment, Vi visits the bathroom, where she discovers a pile of explicit photographs. The images are exclusively of young naked white women – some instantly recognisable as Vi's classmates – in a variety of lurid and submissively pornographic poses. Prohibitively censoring herself ('don't be racist, don't be racist'), Vi returns to the bedroom where Mr Scott coolly instructs her to remove her clothes. Mr Scott's gaze and authoritative voice collude in the objectification of Vi. Mr Scott rises from the bed; looming over Vi, the film offers an ideologically loaded tableau of interracial sex (see Fig. 8.1). Dwarfed by Mr Scott, Vi's sylphlike figure appears barely pubescent, the provocative two-shot deliberately evoking the inflammatory semiotics of *The Birth of a Nation* (D.W. Griffith, 1915) and *King Kong* (Merian C. Cooper, 1933). Ordering Vi to face away from him, Mr Scott unbuttons his trousers. As he begins to thrust, Mr Scott instructs Vi to acknowledge racial difference in the most sexually transparent terms: 'Say, "nigger, fuck me". Say, "nigger, *fuck me hard!*"'.

'The excitement of interracial lust – for both blacks and whites', argues Williams, 'depends on a basic knowledge of the white racist scenario of white virgin/black beast'.[20] A product of 'indiewood',[21] *Storytelling*'s provocative jabs at the liberalism of its (white, middle-class, university educated) target demographic become more pronounced. Although initially uncomfortable and intimidated, as the sex becomes more frenetic Vi's recital of the sexually-charged racial epithets become more

Fig. 8.1. Vi (Selma Blair) is dwarfed by Mr Scott (Robert Wisdom) in *Storytelling* (Todd Solondz, New Line Cinema, 2001)

enthusiastic. In fetishising taboo, in other words, racial and sexual transgression becomes erotically reified. Subsequently transposing the evening's events into a confessional short story, Vi's experience becomes both a form of 'authentic' emotional capital and a passive-aggressive expose of Mr Scott's sexual predilections.

Inevitably, the university campus is no sanctuary from the commercial colonisation of erotic selfhood. The illusory open forum of the seminar mirrors the virtual public sphere of the internet or reality TV where – as ever in Solondz's films – there is no real catharsis, nothing outside the neoliberal text. Mr Scott's Pulitzer Prize-winning novelist is as thoroughly interpellated by the erotics of interracial lust as Vi and her liberal white peers. It is strongly implied that the writing career of another student, Catherine (Aleksa Palladino), is being given a boost due to her sexual liaisons with the professor. Led by Catherine, classmates inevitably denounce the racist clichés of Vi's first-person account. In an echo of the self-serving ethical capital Vi seeks to gain in her relationship with Marcus – she is significantly 'on top' in the film's opening sexual tableau – literary criticism is unveiled as yet another competitive tool used for inflicting cruelty. Mr Scott's truth-teller teaches Vi a key lesson in neoliberal *realpolitik*. The supposedly nurturing and egalitarian world of the liberal arts education system is unveiled as simply an extension of neoliberal culture: self-seeking, exploitative and aggressively individualist.

'Start with the little one': Sexual Apocalypse in *A Serbian Film*

As Diane Negra has argued, popular films have formed part of a recent cultural trend serving to de-stigmatise pornography and ideologically normalise sex work. Films such as *Closer* (Mike Nichols, 2004) and *The Girl Next Door* (Luke Greenfield, 2005) 'demonstrate that mainstream sexual culture is so suffused with pornographic codes and concepts that pornography itself can no longer be seen to constitute any degree of difference'.[22] In this way, sexual exchange becomes subordinated to, and regulated by, the commercial imperatives of neoliberalism. To this end, heated critical attention paid to the so-called 'torture porn' cycle – best illustrated by films such as *Captivity* (Roland Joffé, 2007) and the *Hostel* (Various, 2005–2011) and *Saw* (Various, 2004–2017) franchises – emphasised their Sadean imagery and affective appeal.[23] Owing an obvious debt to this production trend, *A Serbian Film* is arguably the most notorious feature film of the early twenty-first century. Featuring scenes of paedophilia, oral rape and necrophilia, *A Serbian Film* registers its violently pornographic transgressions through the hyperbolic emotional and psychological register of the horror film. As Soderbergh's subdued use of gothic metaphors in *The Girlfriend Experience* attest, intimations of sexual deviance are key to unlocking cultural critique in a genre in which psychosexual dementia, sadism, incest and other paraphilias are practically generic norms.[24]

Too easily dismissed as a crude exploitation shocker, *A Serbian Film* mobilises pornographic labour as an emblematic metaphor through which to critique the dehumanising logics of late capitalism. Director Srđan Spasojević self-consciously framed the film as an expressionist allegory of the exploitative logic of the neoliberal labour market. The pornographic locale of *A Serbian Film* is, he suggests, primarily metaphorical:

A naked metaphor; standing for every kind of job you can have in our society and be viciously exploited by your boss, your ruler of your destiny. When you go to your regular job, it's like you're whoring yourself non-stop. That's what the pornographic nature of the film is; it's every indecent job you've ever had. Eastern Europe is famous for its porn industry anyway, so it fitted perfectly.[25]

The film's plot is sparse. Famed porn star Miloš (Srđan Todorović) is enticed out of retirement by a lucrative opportunity to perform in an avant-garde 'art' film directed by Vukmir (Sergej Trifunović), a charismatically Sadean ideologue. *A Serbian Film* persistently conflates the psychosocial investments of individual labour with the logics of the pornographic imagination. Although Miloš is outwardly dismissive of his former career, he nevertheless compulsively re-views his video portfolio and admits that he 'miss[es] the money'. Embarking upon a punishing training regime in preparation for his new job, Milo's overdetermined investment in his professional ego-ideal becomes increasingly transparent. In one scene, Miloš's wife playfully asks him to 'fuck me like the girls in your films'. Thus hailed, Miloš aggressively reprises his hardcore persona, the subsequent sexual 'performance' is a disturbingly pornographic approximation of domestic rape. The film repeatedly cuts between the couple's rough sex and the pornographic images flickering on a television screen; both characters are apparently aroused by their mimetic intercourse. This state of mimesis is echoed in a later scene where Miloš's brother Marko (Slobodan Beštić) watches Miloš's films in bed with a prostitute. Marko's impotence leaves the woman masturbating while gazing vacantly at the screen; their sexual encounter is displaced by the potency of the images. Both scenes bleakly fulfil Baudrillardian prophecy as the pornographic map precedes – and, ultimately supersedes – the sexual Real.

The obscenities continue unabated: Vukmir forces Miloš to have violent sex with an abused woman while a school-age girl watches. Later, Milos is coerced into raping a woman before beheading her mid-coitus. Phallic brutality is repeatedly underscored: erections are wielded as crude weapons to suffocate women and gouge eye sockets; people are filmed being raped while unconscious. The most notorious scene in *A Serbian Film* features a pornographic film-within-the-film depicting the rape of a newly delivered infant by an 'obstetrician' while the child's mother looks on with a melancholy postpartum smile. 'This is a new genre, Miloš', states a triumphant Vukmir, '*Newborn porn!*' The film's central conceit is that Vukmir's amoral egomania is ultimately only an exaggerated gothicised mirror of Miloš's successful pornographic ego-ideal and legendary phallic prowess.

A Serbian Film's critique of the dehumanising coercions of contractual obligation in the workplace is made manifest in its re-imagining of the sexual contract as a callously demeaning form of manual labour. The tone of amoral phallocentrism reaches its nadir when Miloš and his brother – both drugged – are filmed pneumatically fucking two anonymous and unconscious bodies that, it transpires, belong to Miloš's son and wife. *A Serbian Film* concludes with the suicide of Miloš and his traumatised family. Following a brief ellipsis, a film crew arrive at the family home. Upon discovering the fresh corpses, a man begins to disrobe and the director coolly instructs him to begin his necrophile labour: 'Start with the little one'. *A Serbian Film*'s metaphors are barely subtle – the neoliberal marketplace treats human beings as exploitable resources from birth through to death – but the film's savage critique of hyper-reification cannot help but resonate in an age of ongoing economic crisis.

Conclusion: 'The economy is fucked!'

Neither prudish nor reactionary, the films discussed here offer ambivalent critiques of contemporary sexual culture. Aesthetically, generically and ideologically there is considerable remove between *Secretary*'s playfully queer romantic comedy and the neo-Marxist tract of *The Girlfriend Experience* or between the derogated humanism of Todd Solondz's output and the moral and ethical wasteland of *A Serbian Film*. The films may not offer coherent or consistent answers to the multivalent questions they pose, but this is only appropriate. In an accelerated sexual culture whose commercial outlines and ideological trajectory we are only just beginning to distinguish, it is important to critically re-evaluate how we define and interpret 'perversion'. As *A Serbian Film* in particular makes clear, the theoretical end-point of neoliberal sexual ideology is aligned to the individual's *perverse* pursuit of pleasure, a self-actualising trajectory ultimately predicated upon the wholesale elision of empathy or solidarity with other human beings.[26] Yet these disparate films all interrogate what constitutes normative and perverse sexual practices under the conditions of late capitalism. Neoliberal ideologies of consumer freedom and choice increasingly form a porous interface with the enigmatic intimacies of contemporary sexual subjectivity. What ultimately unites these diverse texts, then, is the way they critically probe the commercial sexualisation of culture and the concomitant extension of free market logic into the most intimate areas of our lives.[27]

Notes

1. Slavoj Žižek, *The Pervert's Guide to Cinema*, Directed by Sophie Fiennes, UK/Australia/Netherlands, 2006.
2. Yael D. Sherman, 'Neoliberal femininity and *Miss Congeniality* (2000)', in Hilary Radner and Rebecca Stringer (eds), *Feminism at the Movies: Understanding Gender in Contemporary Popular Cinema* (Abingdon: Routledge, 2011), p. 82.
3. See Michael A. Peters, *Poststructuralism, Marxism and Neoliberalism: Between Theory and Politics* (Oxford: Rowman and Littlefield, 2001).
4. Hilary Radner, *Neo-Feminist Cinema: Girly Films, Chick Flicks and Consumer Culture* (London: Routledge, 2011), p. 12.
5. Laurence O'Toole, *Pornocopia: Porn, Sex, Technology and Desire* (London: Serpent's Tale, 1998).
6. Brian McNair, *Striptease Culture: Sex, Media & the Democratisation of Desire* (London: Routledge, 2002).
7. Susanna Paasonen, Kaarina Nikunen and Laura Saarenmaa (eds), *Pornification: Sex and Sexuality in Media Culture* (Oxford: Berg, 2007).
8. Feona Attwood (ed.), *Mainstreaming Sex: The Sexualisation of Western Culture* (London: I.B.Tauris, 2009).
9. See Bruce Fink, 'Perversion', in Molly Anne Rothenberg, Dennis A. Foster and Slavoj Žižek (eds), *Perversion and the Social Relation* (Durham, NC: Duke University Press, 2003), pp. 38–67.
10. See Nikki Sullivan, *A Critical Introduction to Queer Theory* (Edinburgh: Edinburgh University Press, 2003); Martin Fradley, ' "Why doesn't your compass work?": *Pirates of the Caribbean*, fantasy blockbusters and contemporary queer theory', in Karen Ross (ed.), *Handbook of Gender, Sexualities and the Media* (London: Wiley–Blackwell, 2012), pp. 294–312.
11. McNair, *Striptease Culture*, pp. 205–206.
12. Linda Williams, *Screening Sex* (Durham, NC: Duke University Press, 2008), p. 13.
13. Ibid., p. 6.

14. Eva Illouz, *Cold Intimacies: The Making of Emotional Capitalism* (Cambridge: Polity Press, 2007), p. 5.
15. Sherman, 'Neoliberal femininity and *Miss Congeniality* (2000)', pp. 82–3.
16. Jeffrey Sconce, 'Smart cinema', in Mike Hammond and Linda Ruth Williams (eds), *Contemporary American Cinema* (Maidenhead: Open University Press, 2006), p. 429.
17. Todd Solondz, 'Director's Notes', *Palindromes* (DVD), Tartan Video, 2004.
18. Radner, *Neo-Feminist Cinema*, p. 7.
19. Linda Williams, 'Skin flicks on the racial border: pornography, exploitation and interracial lust', in Linda Williams (ed.) *Porn Studies* (Durham, NC: Duke University Press, 2004), p. 276.
20. Ibid., p. 302.
21. Geoff King, *Indiewood, USA: Where Hollywood Meets Independent Cinema* (London: I.B. Tauris, 2009).
22. Diane Negra, *What a Girl Wants? Fantasizing the Reclamation of Self in Postfeminism* (London: Routledge, 2009), p. 101.
23. See Pamela Craig and Martin Fradley, 'Teenage traumata: youth, affective politics and the contemporary American horror film', in Steffen Hantke (ed.), *American Horror Film: The Genre at the Turn of the Millennium* (Jackson, MS: University Press of Mississippi, 2010), pp. 77–102.
24. Harry M. Benshoff, *Monsters in the Closet: Homosexuality and the Horror Film* (Manchester: Manchester University Press, 1997).
25. Cited in Alan Jones, 'The nightmare of truth', DVD sleeve notes, *A Serbian Film* (DVD), Revolver Entertainment, 2010.
26. See Rebecca Whisnant, 'From Jekyll to Hyde: The grooming of male pornography consumers', in Karen Boyle (ed.), *Everyday Pornography* (Abingdon: Routledge, 2010).
27. I would like to thank Natasha Copeland for clarifying many of the issues raised in this essay.

III

Coming of Age:
Generational Encounters
and Dangerous Liaisons

9

Larry Clark's Sex Education: Adolescent Sexuality and the Denial of Denial

Sarah Arnold

In 2010, the photography of Larry Clark was exhibited at the Paris Museum of Modern Art. The *Kiss the Past Hello* exhibition featured over 200 photographs and film of previously unpublished work from the days of his *Tulsa* and *Teenage Lust* photographic series.[1] The subject matter was the marginalised, taboo world of subcultures and adolescents engaging in sex, drug use, and other illegal and subversive behaviours including, among others, a photograph of a young male injecting drugs in a bath, another of a young male posing with a gun and a naked couple in a dirty bath. The aesthetic mode of the Clark's photographs often evokes that of his films. The camera, frequently situated in close relation to the subjects, suggests an intimate connection to those photographed. Yet this intimacy and closeness to the subjects is often compromised by the voyeuristic nature and composition of the shot. In the cover image of *Teenage Lust*, for example, in which a young male and female kiss while she masturbates him, sexual intimacy between them is negated by their forward facing position within the frame. Their sexual activity is directed towards the camera. Thus, the image suggests both the intimacy of sexual contact as well as the pornographic exhibition of sex. While the vérité style of the photographs suggest a moment captured spontaneously, the subjects' relation to the camera points towards the photographer's staging of the scene.

The Paris exhibition of these photographs caused some controversy that led to calls for censorship and restricted access, igniting debates about the relationship between art and pornography. The age of the subjects caused the most concern; a trend with Clark's work more generally. As Amy Adler has noted, 'one of the most disturbing and well-known art photographers, Larry Clark, who documents the lives of drug-addicted and violent teenagers, takes photographs that, one could argue, easily meet the definition of child pornography'.[2] In the case of the Paris exhibition, a decision was made by the Mayor to ban access for those younger than 18 years old. This move enraged Clark, who claimed that this, in effect, banned the intended audience of the photographs. In an interview with French newspaper *Le Monde*, he argued that this represented an attack on youth and a denial of the right for them to 'see themselves'.[3] Here, he said that this ban was 'an attack by the older generation on teenagers' and was similar to 'sending a teenager to his room'. He claimed instead that adults should be prohibited from attending the exhibition. This event reveals the anxieties produced by Clark's work that concerns the representation of teenagers as sexually active.

Similar controversy surrounded his film *Ken Park* (2002), which was never submitted to the Motion Picture Association of America for certification and, due to music copyright issues, remains unreleased in the US.[4] Scenes showing young people having group sex, as well as a scene in which a teenager engages in autoerotic asphyxiation, later murdering his grandparents, ensured that the film would be difficult to distribute regardless. Notably, Clark refused to remove any scenes from the film. In Australia, where the film was banned, the police raided a screening held by Free Cinema and confiscated the print. Australia's Office of Film and Literature Classification stated afterwards that the film contained images of 'child sex abuse, actual sex by people depicted as minors and sexualised violence' and that the images 'offend against the standards of morality, decency and propriety generally accepted by reasonable adults'.[5]

The call for the regulation and policing of adolescent sexuality, while emerging at a time of moral crisis with regard to sexuality, also represents the production of a discourse of sexuality that seeks to contain and render invisible the sexuality of youth. Michel Foucault, speaking of childhood sexuality in the eighteenth century, considered the sexuality of children and adolescents a contested terrain subject to discursive strategies:

> It may well be true that adults and children themselves were deprived of a certain way of speaking about sex, a mode that was disallowed as being too direct, crude, or coarse. But this was only the counterpart of other discourses, and perhaps the condition necessary in order for them to function, discourses that were interlocking, hierarchized, and all highly articulated around a cluster of power relations.[6]

In the case of Clark's work and the censorship of it, the strategy is that of denial and prohibition, where adolescent sexuality is considered vulnerable and in need of protection and where exhibitions and films are banned or censored in order to safeguard their young subjects.

In this way, Clark's films produce a denial of the ways in which adolescent sexuality has been denied. The denial of an adolescent sexuality is repudiated by the overt focus on youth and sex. Thus, where discourses of sexuality depend upon the disavowal of adolescent sexuality, films such as *Kids* (1995) and *Ken Park* make explicit that which is typically denied. Thus, regimes of sexuality are upset. This chapter will consider the issue of adolescent sexuality in respect of both teens themselves as well as intergenerational sexuality between youths and adults. It examines the controversy surrounding the film *Kids* and suggests that Clark's work bears the weight of wider right- and left-wing political discourses, primarily with regard to the regulation of adolescent sexuality. It then accounts for the ways in which *Ken Park* attempts to engage with the taboo subject of adult/child sexual encounters, primarily and ironically through the reinstatement of traditional gender roles. Ultimately, this chapter suggests that the films plant themselves firmly within a contested and morally ambiguous terrain and offer no consistent politics of representation. The films refuse and deny the denial of adolescent sexuality, but neither can they, nor do they care to, posit what adolescent sexuality should be, outside of patriarchal and conservative norms.

Clark, Youth and Sexual Morality

Where normative social and sexual morality depends upon a clear polarisation between adult and child sexuality, Clark's films expose the slipperiness of such age categorisations and the illusory correlation between age and maturity. Clark's youthful characters occupy a liminal space between childhood and adulthood, as do the childish adults who populate his films. If terms and identificatory strategies such as 'child', 'adolescent', 'youth' and 'minor' operate, as Foucault suggests, as a means of producing adult-centred discourses of power, then Clark's use of liminality disrupts this hierarchy. Indeed, the issues central to Clark's films echo the approaches to youth culture taken by those in the Birmingham School, such as Paul Willis and Dick Hebdige, who drew attention to the material and economic conditions that produced and facilitated cultures of youth.[7] The Birmingham School critics considered how youth culture could be understood in terms of resistance to or subversion of dominant hegemonic norms. However, where the Birmingham School academics acknowledged the means by which youth culture tended to appropriate the values it initially resisted, so too might we understand Clark's films as reinstating the conservative sexuality morality that he seeks to critique.

While it may be tempting to categorise Clark's films as transgressive or subversive in their representation of adolescent sexuality, I would prefer to focus on the particular mode of representation within his films *Kids* and *Ken Park* that problematises such notions, as they can be considered both complicit in and oppositional to traditional and conservative discourses of adolescent sexuality. Of particular interest here are those films that frame adolescent sexuality and encounters from the perspective and narrative point of view of youth. These films centralise the sexual awakening or development of youths without silencing or making invisible the repercussions and consequences of their essentially adult experiences (at least within typical film narratives). The controversy surrounding Clark's films and subsequent censorship is perhaps not surprising given the particular historical moment in which his films were released, a moment governed by anxiety about adolescent sexuality, paedophilia and the increasing media attention on both. American cinema has become embroiled in these issues.

In his discussion of childhood sexuality and motion pictures, James Bristol notes that childhood sexuality has only recently emerged as a taboo subject.[8] Historically, there are moments where the expression of sexuality in children and young teens was normalised and not repressed.[9] Bristol notes the proliferation of artistic imagery of young boys in particular, which was often coded as sexual and not considered exploitative. At certain periods within Greek and Roman culture, young boys and girls were sexually inducted at young ages (and more likely with an adult). In their highly controversial interview on 'the danger of child sexuality', Michel Foucault, Jean Danet and Guy Hocquenghem outline some of the contemporary debates about the meaning and expression of sexuality in minors.[10] The interview was a response to the proposed changes to the French Penal Code in 1979 that stemmed from a petition supporting the release of a number of people charged with statutory rape. While some of the authors' claims remain unsettling, they demonstrate the tensions apparent today in representing such sexual explicitness in children. For example, Danet notes the tendency within psychiatry to present all sexual activity between an adult and a minor as damaging for the latter. He goes on to note that psychiatrists in this respect take on the role of author, determining how the child must understand their sexual encounter. While this is certainly controversial, these same issues present themselves in cinematic constructions of childhood sexuality. Childhood sexuality on screen is mostly authored by adult culture and so we are often presented with a particular ideological and cultural framework one in which childhood sexuality is non-existent (as in the case of abuse) or deviant (in which the child 'does wrong' and is punished for his or her transgressions). This has been the typical trend of mainstream cinema.

As Bristol notes in the early years of cinema, images of naked children were not deemed problematic or offensive. However, following the increasing calls for censorship from vocal lobbyists and moral guardians, the first official and regulatory document on moral behaviour was produced. The Motion Picture Producers and Distributors of America's (MPPDA) 1927 list of 'Don'ts and Be Carefuls' clearly demonstrated a concern about children and their association with sexuality. The depiction of 'children's sexual organs' was among the 'Don'ts', while the 'Be Carefuls' included 'apparent cruelty to children' and the 'deliberate seduction of girls' (and the term girls rather than women was specified). In the 1930 Motion Picture Production Code there is again a deep concern with the expression of sexuality more generally and the stipulation that 'children's sex organs are never to be exposed'.[11] While the Code did not elaborate on childhood sexuality to nearly the same degree as adult sexuality, it is notable that such a concern with the exposure of children indicated that absolute censorship was called for. Therefore, the first efforts to deny childhood sexuality, and indeed deny the sexual identity of children at all, are evident. As such, children are not permitted, within film at least, to be associated with sexuality. However, it is not simply the case that childhood sexuality is silenced. To deny entails a process of encounter and re-articulation. In fact, one might say that the film industry and censors were preoccupied with childhood sexuality, given the amount of regulation it required. Within US cinema more broadly, such contradictions were also evident with the contrast between mainstream representations of 'contained' sexuality and peripheral representations of deviancy and transgression evident within B-movies, exploitation films, art house and independent films, as well as pornography. Speaking about regulatory institutions such as schools, Foucault argues that they were in a perpetual state of articulation, organisation and monitoring (of childhood sexuality). He notes that 'what one might call the internal discourse of the institution [...] was largely based on the assumption that this sexuality existed, that it was precocious, active and ever present'.[12] The same case might be made for boards of censorship.

Childhood sexuality thus necessitated a system of regulation that would both articulate childhood sexuality (in terms of innocence or lack) and ensure its repression:

> This sexuality of the child is a territory with its own geography that the adult must not enter. It is virgin territory, sexual territory, of course, but territory that must preserve its virginity.

The adult will therefore intervene as guarantor of that specificity of child sexuality in order to protect it.[13]

Yet, as Foucault adds, the psychiatrist, as part of an institution that regulates, also imposes their own reading on the child. The psychiatrist tells the child that their desires must be contained and regulated, that their sexual experiences may be traumatic. Again, we can see the practice of this in film, even in those films acknowledging childhood sexuality. Hence, where the years following the demise of the Production Code saw a liberalisation of the representation of adult sexuality, representations of childhood or adolescent sexuality have become, perhaps because of this, more restricted. The child may express sexual desire, but this is often within the context of a traumatic event and rarely a positive experience.

Here lies the moral tension produced by Clark's films; they exhibit explicit childhood sexuality as already existing, already developed and, often, as mature. Sexual exploration is thus framed within a distinctly adult sexuality and, in so doing, these films could be read as highly subversive. They represent one of the ultimate social taboos. The clear articulation of the voice of youth is apparent within the filmic space of *Ken Park*, *Bully* (2001) and *Kids*. These films, therefore, seem to fulfil the Foucauldian objective of finding the expression of the child within the act. Foucault calls for the adult (be it legislators, the public) to listen, to allow the child to determine their experience, even if they are not yet fully capable of doing so. He observes, 'to assume that a child is incapable of explaining what happened and was incapable of giving his consent are two abuses that are intolerable, quite unacceptable'.[14] The films present a response to these issues and construct subjective positions from which youths can speak and be heard. In terms of sexual desire, these films allow for the expression of a sexuality that is not determined exclusively through the adult. In other words, the adult does not make the child a sexual being; the child is already exploring their sexual identity prior to the sexual encounter. Clark's films do not guard teenagers from sexuality. Rather, they undermine the denial of it. In his films, adolescent sexuality is passionate, inquisitive, naïve and, indeed, vulnerable. Thus, the films not only make visible that which is ordinarily denied in cinematic representation but also call into question the regulatory mechanisms that produce discourses of sexuality.

Adolescent Sexuality as Social Problem

Clark has been chastised for his fascination with the young male body, with some questioning the extent to which his films offer a subjective space for adolescent expression or whether they are exploitative, if not paedophilic.[15] In other words, in representing adolescent sexuality, Clark is considered to have an ulterior motive, objectifying rather than 'subjectifying' youth. Henry Giroux notes of Clark's films:

> Young people are primarily identified with their bodies, especially their sexual drives. Stripped of any critical capacities, youth are defined primarily by a sexuality that is viewed as unmanageable and in need of control, surveillance, legal constraint, and other forms of disciplinary power.[16]

Such conflicting criticism, in which Clark is posited as both pervert and conservative moralist, might say more about adult repression than it does about adolescent sexuality. Although Giroux's comments about the destructive sexuality of Clark's teenage characters might be evidenced within his films, it is much more problematic to view this as a call for disciplinary power. On the contrary, the films suggest it is precisely these same forms of disciplinary power, with their regulation and denial of adolescent sexuality, which produce its excess in teenagers.

While Clark's films have polarised critics and audiences, the films arguably negotiate both conservative and progressive moral debates about adolescent sexuality. Clark's films both oppose and are complicit in the regulation of adolescent sexuality. They exist as part of a discourse that constructs adolescent sexuality as a social problem but also frames this as a problem stemming not from teenagers themselves but from a legacy of adult deviancy, anxiety, irresponsibility and corruption. The films engage in a discourse of power in which adolescent sexuality is spoken by (adults) and not spoken by (teenagers). This tension is evident in the way that the film texts claim to speak from a position of youth. The films are often presented from the perspectives of a range of sexually active and experienced youths. Yet this youth perspective is constructed by an adult filmmaker who ultimately organises adolescent sexuality in the representational terms of the 'outsider'. Thus, it is not youths who organise and represent their own subjective experiences, perspective and morality – rather, it is assumed. As Giroux notes of teenage sexuality:

> Youth as a complex, shifting, and contradictory category is rarely narrated in the dominant public sphere through the diverse voices of the young. Prohibited from speaking as moral and political agents, youth become an empty category inhabited by the desires, fantasies, and interests of the adult world.[17]

This sense of youth being inhabited by and reflective of adult interests is certainly evident in Clark's films. After all, much of the debate concerning his films centres upon his fascination with teenagers and particularly their sexuality. This debate stems from the anxiety of representing that which adults are supposed to deny. There is a tension here once again. Where adult articulations of adolescent sexuality and culture are projected onto the body of youth, the films are also conscious and reflective of this. In *Ken Park* and *Teenage Caveman* (2002), for example, the corrupting force of the adult shapes and disturbs adolescent sexuality. In the latter film, the adult male leader of a group of apocalypse survivors speaks of chastity and sexual morality while secretly raping teenage girls to satisfy his own sexual desires. Thus, while Clark's status as director might situate him as the authorial and regulatory voice, he also acknowledges within the films the means by which adults regulate and control adolescent sexuality. Similarly, *Kids* was, in fact, scripted by the 18-year-old Harmony Korine. Such a collaboration undermines the adult authorial role of Clark and suggests that the film's scenarios, at least, originated from the perspective of a youth. My point is not that Clark's films are either wholly conservative or progressive, rather that they demonstrate ambiguity about how to represent adolescent sexuality, an ambiguity that is typically denied within mainstream representation.

Writing about *Kids*, bell hooks argues that the film can be understood as complicit 'with those cultural forces that view the dilemmas in teenage life as solely a function of the absence of coercive control and authority'.[18] However, this is problematised by the film's treatment of AIDS, a disease that is not the product of these teenagers, but a legacy of an older generation. The naivety of the 'kids' is demonstrated in one young virgin's fear of getting pregnant; much less of a concern for her is contracting HIV from her first sexual partner. In Clark's later film *Ken Park*, it is precisely those parents who embody patriarchal and heteronormative values that are most corrupting of youth. Teenage dilemmas are manifested where coercive control and authority are present. Evident in the work of both Giroux and hooks is the question of responsible representation. These authors are associated with critical pedagogy that seeks to advocate and encourage the participation of young people within the political and cultural sphere. Both authors propose that social action should be encouraged in youths and that youths should be empowered through their relationships with figures of guidance. It is perhaps unsurprising, then, that both authors criticise *Kids* for its lack of moral perspective or political voice. Clark is taken to task for his lack of historical and social contextualisation, in which issues relating to class, race and gender are rendered invisible. Undoubtedly, the film shows little concern for exploring these contexts and the broader debates centred upon teenage behaviour, such as the rejection of adult goal-oriented culture. Where theorists such as Bill Osgerby seek to identify the factors productive of teenage behaviour, such as rebellion, subversion and delinquency, Clark's films avoid such explorations.[19] Similarly, Giroux notes that:

> Clark's narrative about youth plays on dominant fears about the loss of moral authority while reinforcing images of demonization and sexual license through which adults can blame youth for existing social problems, and be titillated at the same time.[20]

For Giroux, the images of teenage sexual deviancy and exploration deny 'any political understanding of the relationship between sex and violence'.[21] Similarly, hooks critiques the film's lack of constructive representation or politics. She argues that, in light of the continued racial and sexual discrimination and disempowerment and the renewed right-wing attack on personal liberties, 'there is certainly a need for films that offer constructive insights, progressive alternatives. *Kids* is not that film'.[22]

The point of *Kids* is that that it offers no constructive insights nor progressive alternatives. In fact, the film insists on this. *Kids* is, to counter Giroux's point, quite frank about the relationship between sex and violence. Additionally, the film lacks a political goal because there is no sufficient political voice that would or might address the issues raised by the film. There is a notable absence of adult figures that would act as moral guardians for the teenagers. Thus, while the teenagers are at once left to their own devices, they also, at times, appear lonely. Jenny (Chloë Sevigny) cannot reach her mother on the phone following her HIV diagnosis and relies upon the support of other teenagers. Where adults are present they seem disinterested and indifferent to the behaviour of youth. Telly's (Leo Fitzpatrick) mother leaves him largely unregulated. Her questions about his whereabouts seem a matter of routine rather than genuine interest or concern. At the medical clinic where Jenny and Ruby (Rosario Dawson) are tested, there are allusions to regulation, medical guidance and prohibitions: the walls are covered in posters and signs encouraging safer sex; the doctors ask probing questions regarding the girls' sexual activity; and Ruby's doctor encourages her to read pamphlets in order to be more careful in her sexual behaviour. All of this is represented as a tired exercise, more 'going through the motions' than an assertive effort to limit the spread of HIV. The political vacuum lies more within the diegesis than without. The film laments the indifference of teenagers and attitudes towards them, seeing little political or social effort that seeks to address the problems of youth. *Kids* denies the usual strategy of offering solutions that would, in effect, equally deny or negate the problems themselves.

Similarly, *Kids* is overtly conscious of the gendering of adolescent sexuality. Contrary to Giroux, I would suggest that the film is explicit about the way in which adolescent sexuality is governed by the same sexual hierarchies as typical patriarchal adult sexuality. Women are positioned as victims and men as sexual villains. While this undoubtedly perpetuates a conservative and heteronormative vision of sexuality more generally, it does so for the purposes of critique rather than complicity. The film is bookended by two scenes in which Telly has sex with a virgin. In the first, Telly's sexual partner, a young teenage girl, raises concerns about pregnancy. In the final scene, in which Telly has sex with Darcy (Yakira Peguero), it has already been revealed that he is HIV-positive and will, mostly likely, pass this on to Darcy. This mirroring of sex scenes turns the 'ordinary' positioning of male/active and female/passive, typical of most cinematic representation, into something far more sinister, not only for Darcy but also for Telly, who is unaware of his HIV status. The shot in which Telly and Darcy are curled up together, asleep, reiterates this and presses the fact that these are, ultimately, youths facing adult issues; they exist in a liminal space in terms of their social status as children and their biological status as sexual beings. Likewise, the middle section of the film is framed through the juxtaposition of male and female characters as they navigate the city in search of sex (in the case of the boys) or responsibility (in the case of the girls).

Thus, the criticism of Clark's film as a 'surface exploration of a typical twenty four hours in the lives of some drug and sex-crazed, morally rudderless adolescents'[23] neglects the role of Jenny and the other girls within the narrative. Both Giroux and hooks infer that *Kids* might appeal to the conservative right, since the film seems to confirm moral panics regarding delinquent youth and the consequences of the lack of regulation and prohibition. While the film might allow for this reading, it equally problematises it. After all, Telly, Casper (Justin Pierce) and their other male friends embody all the characteristics that would be understood as conventionally masculine; they are sexually assertive, confident and dominant. The film is also vocal about the extent to which women suffer the consequences of this and are left to take responsibility for both male and female sexuality. It is, after all, the women who get tested for HIV and not the men. This point is reinforced towards the end of the film when a drunk and high Casper rapes the passed-out Jenny. Like the shot of Telly and Darcy sleeping, here again neither Casper nor Jenny are fully aware of the implications of this (or in Jenny's case even the action itself). While the film might be a surface exploration of adolescent sexuality to the extent of its lack of implicit social contextualisation, it nonetheless keeps at this surface the very gendered categories that need to be addressed and examined in wider culture.

The debates that *Kids* has provoked seem less concerned with the extent to which youth issues and problems are addressed. That the film refers less to the wider socio-political factors that produce such youth cultures and more to youth behaviour and its consequences has led to accusations of moral conservatism. *Kids'* representation of the sexual habits of teenagers certainly emphasises its destructive qualities. Giroux and hooks are critical of the film's lack of constructive insights that might offer more liberal or progressive solutions to the problems of adolescent sexuality. Clark's later films further explore the issues of regulation and management of adolescent sexuality. Interestingly, these films – *Ken Park*, *Teenage Caveman* and *Bully* – seem sceptical of the roles that adults play in organising and regulating adolescent sexuality. These later films, much more so than *Kids*, construct adults not as productive moral forces, but as damaged and corrupt. In particular, adult investment in adolescent sexuality is represented as perverse itself. If the debates about *Kids* related to Clark's lack of explicit commentary about adolescent sexuality, *Ken Park* responds by problematising such authoring and regulatory measures. For Clark, adults are in no position to regulate as their sexuality is just as debased, if not more so, than adolescent sexuality.

Intergenerationality and Gendered Sexual Discourse

Ken Park evokes Foucault's proposal to allow the child to articulate their sexual experience with an adult:

> Listening to a child, hearing him speak, hearing him explain what his relations actually were with someone, adult or not, provided one listens with enough sympathy, must allow one to establish more or less what degree of violence if any was used or what degree of consent was given.[24]

Ken Park insists on this articulation of the experience of adolescent sexuality. It also tests the boundaries of intergenerational sexual relationships in other, perhaps more provocative, ways. In the film, an adolescent forms a mutually satisfying sexual bond with an adult. Departing from a clear binary of adult/child, the teenagers in this film traverse the borderline between young adolescent and young adult. While the film at times problematises intergenerationality, it also proposes that there is scope for pleasure on the part of the youth. *Ken Park* refuses to take up a coherent position on the subject of adult/youth sexual encounters. For the most part, youths are constructed as more sexually normative than their adult counterparts. Yet, at the same time, they are coded as distinctly child-like.

Shawn (James Bullard) bullies and teases his younger brother in a highly infantile manner. This contradiction functions to challenge the typical association of youths and children with sexual immaturity.

In fact, the regulatory capacity of adults and parents in terms of childhood sexuality is called into question. The fathers of two characters act as strict monitors of their children's sexuality. Yet, later, their sexuality is structured as perverse and deviant. Thus, the film refuses to allocate any normative sexuality to any one type of person. Sexual inexperience and promiscuity are equally shared among adults and children alike. Claude's father (Wade Williams) teases his son (Stephen Jasso) with accusations of homosexuality, testing him on his sexual prowess and asking him how many girls he has 'fucked'. He responds positively to his son's claims that he has many girlfriends yet, in the same breath, he tells Claude he is ashamed of him and that his mother thinks he is a 'fairy'. Such contradictory behaviour is later explained by his father's own closet homosexuality and incestuous desires for his son. He later creeps into Claude's room and attempts to perform oral sex on him, before being pushed away by Claude. His father's hypermasculinity, emphasised for him in his weight training, is revealed as a mask, an attempt to 'wear' heterosexual masculinity. Claude, in contrast, has a secure sense of sexual desire. Despite his dysfunctional family situation, he has what is, in the film's terms at least, a mature sexual encounter with a male and female friend: one defined by consent and presented as intimate and emotionally satisfying for all.

Other intergenerational romances in the film are constructed in equally ambiguous terms. The representation of Shawn's affair with his girlfriend's mother (Maeve Quinlan) clearly demonstrates a visual age gap between both. The mother guides Shawn during oral sex and asks Shawn questions about her daughter (see Fig. 9.1). In the two scenes depicting the sexual encounter and the moments following, the mother dominates the screen. She refers to Shawn as a 'good boy' during sex and talks him through the actions. He is coded as an adolescent throughout. His body is soft and hairless, his underwear resembles a diaper and in later scenes he is framed in the background, making him look smaller in comparison to her obviously adult body. At the same time this relationship is not marked as problematic. There are no repercussions for them. Neither is traumatised or remorseful. Peaches' (Tiffany Limos) sexuality is shown in

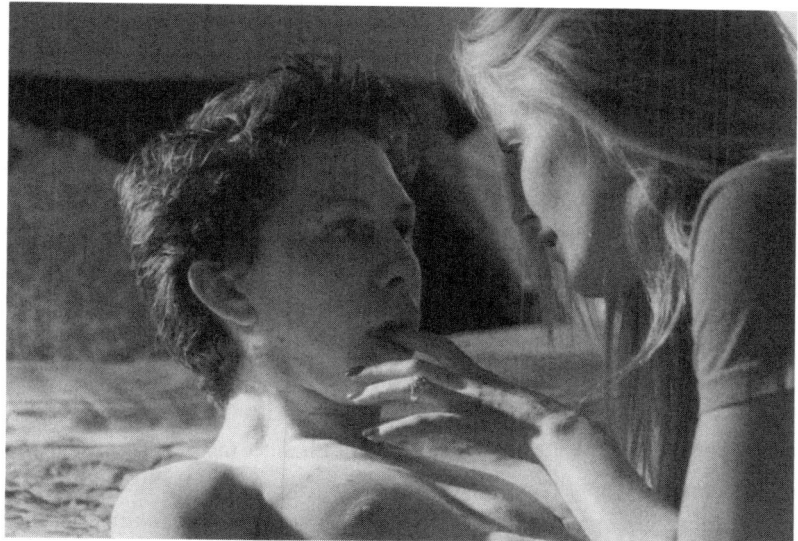

Fig. 9.1. Shawn (James Bullard) is guided by his girlfriend's mother (Maeve Quinlan) in *Ken Park* (Larry Clark, Cinéa, 2002)

similarly mature terms. While her father goes to great pains to ensure she does not reach sexual maturity, she nonetheless demonstrates that she is sexually aware and comfortable when engaged in sexual activity with her friends. Again, adolescent sexuality is not a problem in and of itself. In Peaches' case it is her father who introduces perversion into her 'sexual geography', to use Foucault's term. Once he discovers that she is sexually active, he imposes his repressive Christian morality on her body. In order to protect her from what he deems morally deviant, he dresses her in her dead mother's virginal wedding gown and acts out a marriage between them. As with Claude's father, parents do not act as sexual regulators but as sexual deviants.

Here, internal contradictions are at play. The film opens up the possibilities of dialogue about childhood sexuality and assigns a certain amount of sexual agency to the youths. However, this agency and voicing of sexual desire is often structured along conservative gender lines. In comparison to the fathers who are defined as sexually aggressive, the sexuality of the adult female is constructed as non-threatening. The mother is not so much an 'abuser' as she is a mentor, a figure who comforts and guides the young Shawn. Likewise, Peaches, although sexually desiring to some extent, is constructed as the object of desire for other men. Early on in the film, Tate's voiceover describes how Peaches would let the other boys watch her undress. Later, we see her father mould her into the image of a virginal bride before taking her as his wife. Peaches' initiation into sexual practice is framed in distinctly objectified terms, whereby she is acted upon. This makes her vulnerable, as we see with her father's abuse of her. This is the opposite of Shawn's experience, whereby his sexual encounter with a woman is represented as a liberating and enlightening rite of passage. Hence, any radical potential offered by the film (in terms of challenging the repression of childhood sexuality) is problematised by the film's insistence on perpetuating patriarchal norms of active male and passive female sexuality.

Within these explorations of childhood sexuality, then, some forms of power are challenged (like that of speaking for the child, speaking their experience) but also reproduced through conventional gender terms. Sexual abuse is coded as masculine, whereby the most threatening of sexualities is adult male desire. The experience of such abuse is negated if the subject of abuse is coded in equally similar masculine terms. In other words, where the abused is male, the abuse is not represented in terms of victimisation (Shawn) and where the abused is female, she is victimised (Peaches). Likewise, the abuser is constructed as infantile themselves. In *Ken Park,* Claude's father is drunk, unsteady and highly emotional during his attempted abuse. Femininity, on the other hand, is subject to little enquiry in these films. It retains its cultural association with receptivity and passivity. The codification of femininity operates as an indicator of sexual commodification. Femininity connotes not only 'to-be-looked-at-ness', to borrow Laura Mulvey's phrase, but 'to-be-abused' as well, given the extent of Peaches' abuse.[25] Telling signs of the limits of any potential rethinking of childhood sexuality can be found. In Foucault's reference to the issue of consent and desire on the part of the child, he says 'it is a quite different thing when we are dealing with the likelihood of a child being believed when, speaking of *his* sexual relations, *his* affections, *his* tender feelings, or *his* contacts [...] a child's ability to explain what *his* feelings are'.[26] This is what is at stake in the representation of childhood sexuality.

Ken Park is subversive but only within the parameters of conformist patriarchal gender norms. The film opens up a space for the expression of childhood desire, but only so long as that desire is firmly embedded within a masculine subjectivity.

Through the denial of denial, both *Kids* and *Ken Park*, as well as Clark's other films, produce youth-centric discursive spaces in which sexuality can be represented, discussed, explored and questioned. Countering a tradition of non-representation and relative silence on the issue of adolescent sexuality, Clark's films assertively call for an acknowledgement of its existence and its acceptance. The denial of denial takes place as the films challenge the prevailing morality, which renders youth as sexually invisible. It also does so without an overt political project that would seek to reframe adolescent sexuality. *Kids* does not produce a politics of youth because this is a politics largely born of adult regulatory mechanisms. Yet, lacking such a politics, the film traverses the border between liberal and conservative concepts of adolescent sexuality. Thus, the films struggle to produce wholly progressive images of youth culture. However, given Clark's traditions of representation within both photography and film, this appears to be his agenda. For Clark, simply opening up a discourse about adolescent sexuality is enough. As he says of the motivation for his work, 'when I was a young kid everything was hidden. No one talked about drugs or child abuse or any of those issues. In America it just wasn't supposed to be happening. But I saw kids come into school with black eyes and their parents had beat them up.'[27] His work is not about producing a political context, rather it makes visible that which is 'not supposed to be happening'. For Clark, denial itself (of adolescent sexuality, drug use, violence) is far more destructive than the acknowledgment of it. Yet, his refusal of critique and commentary alienates him. His work is not only oppositional and controversial to the moral Right, who have repressed adolescent sexuality, but also the liberal Left, who call for more progressive modes of gendered representation. Thus, Clark's films, as much as the young characters of his films, occupy a similarly liminal space. Just as Clark's adolescents are content with the liminality of their sexuality, caught as it is between childhood and adulthood, so too for Clark's politics, which find him caught between a set of political viewpoints. The films facilitate the voice of youth and open up spaces for youth representation, yet what is seen and heard still exists within a set of power relations, whether moral conservatives, or liberal progressives, that seek to organise adolescent sexuality. In any case, it is ultimately more important to admit than to deny.

Notes

1. Larry Clark, *Tusla* (New York: Lustrum Press, 1971) and *Teenage Lust* (New York: Self-published, 1987).
2. Amy Adler, 'The perverse law of child pornography', *The Columbia Law Review* 101/2 (March 2001), p. 154.
3. *AFP*, 'Photographer Larry Clark attacks age limit on his Paris show', *AFP Agence France-Presse*, 2 October 2010. Available at http://www.expatica.com/fr/news/ Photographer-Larry-Clark-attacks-age-limit-on-his-Paris-show_210804.html (accessed 2 January 2013).
4. Michael Martin, 'The Nerve Interview: Larry Clark', *The Nerve*, 6 September 2006. Available at http://www.nerve.com/content/the-nerve-interview-larry-clark (accessed 9 March 2013).
5. Robert Cettl, *Offensive to a Reasonable Adult: Film Censorship and Classification in 'Secular' Australia* (Adelaide: Wider Screenings, 2011), pp. 168–70. As of March 2013, the film remains banned in Singapore and Malaysia and is unrated in the US. It is currently unavailable in the UK after it was pulled from the 2002 London Film Festival due to a fist-fight Clark had with Hamish McAlpine, the owner of the film's intended UK distributor Metro Tartan.
6. Michel Foucault, *History of Sexuality. Volume 1: An Introduction*, translated by Robert Hurley (New York: Pantheon Books, 1978), p. 30.
7. Dick Hebdige, *Subculture: The Meaning of Style* (London: Methuen, 1979); Paul Willis, *Learning to Labour: How Working Class Kids Get Working Class Jobs* (London: Saxon House, 1977).
8. James E. Bristol, 'Free expression and a satisfied society: what child pornography laws really protect', *bepress Legal Series*, working paper 1870 (8 November 2006). Available at http://law.bepress.com/expresso/eps/1870 (accessed 2 January 2013).
9. See Robert Darnton, *The Great Cat Massacre and Other Episodes in French Cultural History* (London: Allen Lane, 1984).
10. Michel Foucault, Jean Danet and Guy Hocquenghem, 'The danger of child sexuality', *Semiotext(e) Magazine* 40-4, summer issue, translated by Daniel Moshenberg (1980).
11. Reproduced in Jon Lewis, *Hollywood v. Hard Core: How the Struggle Over Censorship Created the Modern Film Industry* (New York and London: New York University, 2002), pp. 302–7.
12. Foucault, *History of Sexuality*, p. 28.
13. Foucault, Danet and Hocquenghem, 'The danger of child sexuality', p. 44.

14. Ibid.
15. See Todd McCarthy, 'Kids', *Variety* (31 December 1994). Available at http://www. variety.com/review/VE1117792292/?refcatid=31 (accessed 20 March 2012); Rita Kempley, 'Kids', *The Washington Post* (25 August 1995). Available at http://www. washingtonpost.com/wp-srv/style/longterm/movies/videos/kidsnrkempley_c029f5. htm (accessed 20 March 2012).
16. Henry Giroux, 'Teenage sexuality, body politics, and the pedagogy of display', in Jonathon S. Epstein (ed.), *Youth Culture: Identity in a Postmodern World* (Oxford: Blackwell, 1998), p. 45.
17. Ibid., p. 24.
18. bell hooks, *Reel to Real: Race, Sex, and Class at the Movies* (London and New York: Routledge, 1996), p. 67.
19. Bill Osgerby, *Youth in Britain Since 1945* (Oxford: Blackwell, 1998).
20. Giroux, 'Teenage sexuality', p. 42.
21. Ibid., p. 44.
22. hooks, *Reel to Real*, p. 67.
23. Giroux, 'Teenage sexuality', p. 44.
24. Foucault, Danet and Hocquenghem, 'The danger of child sexuality', p. 44.
25. Laura Mulvey, 'Visual pleasure and narrative cinema', *Screen* 16/3 (Autumn 1975), pp. 6–18.
26. Foucault, Danet and Hocquenghem, 'The danger of child sexuality', p. 44.
27. 'Larry Clark: "Why can't you show everything?"' *The Talks* (28 March 2012). Available at http://the-talks.com/interviews/larry-clark (accessed 2 January 2013).

10

The Age of Perversion: *L'ennui*, Erotic Combat and Intergenerational Existentialism

Beth Johnson

She bores me. We have no contact. Or rather only physical contact. You can't imagine how basic she is. She has no conversation. When she speaks she sounds silent. Her only means of expression is sexual. Sometimes when she's laying there, legs apart, I find her cunt more expressive than her mouth. Yet, oddly, she's not sensual; she's only frenetic and avid. When she kisses, her lips are flaccid, cold, inert, but her cunt is hard-hitting, domineering. When we make love her belly moves powerfully, rhythmically, like a machine. She is unstoppable. She goes at me, goes at herself, to make me come, make herself come, to the last spasm. After orgasm then, her face is calm, expressionless. She smiles like she doesn't see me. It's not coldness, not detachment, it's something else [...] Sometimes she seems vacuous and opaque like an object. I bring her to life by making her suffer, by tormenting her [...] because she bores me.

The above speech is made by a middle-aged philosophy professor, Martin (Charles Berling), about Cécilia (Sophie Guillemin), a teenage girl with whom he embarks upon a sexually perverse relationship in Cédric Kahn's French film *L'ennui/Boredom* (1998). The term 'perverse' is to be understood in the following chapter as double-horned. On the one hand, perversion will be considered as a psychic structure, a structure that Molly Anne Rothenberg and Dennis Foster describe as 'a specific relation to the paternal function'.[1] On the other hand, perversion is to be conceived as a description of behaviours based on the conflation of intergenerational sexual desires, boredom and absurd violence. Kahn's film is the second film adaptation of Alberto Moravia's 1960 political novel *La noia/The Empty Canvas*.[2] It tells the story of the troubled sexual relationship between Dino, a rich but bored middle-aged painter striving to find sense in his life and Cécilia, a teenage girl who soon becomes his sexual obsession and muse. Moravia's text focuses on the concept of 1950s 'boredom' as a state of disconnection with the real or, as novelist Umberto Eco recalls of a meeting with Moravia, 'the crisis of the relationship with reality'.[3] In Kahn's contemporary film adaptation of the novel, he changes Dino's name to Martin, makes Martin an obsessive philosophy professor rather than a painter and sets the narrative in 1990s France rather than 1960s Italy.

Thematically, *L'ennui* highlights the theme of 'existentialist ennui' via consciously making visible and perversely playing out critical models of thought: specifically philosophical, psychoanalytic, existentialist and deconstructivist theories. Again, at the centre of the narrative remains a deformed tale of love, obsession and disconnection. Yet, while in Moravia's text such tainted love is understood as a crisis of the real, in Kahn's film adaptation, the notion of tainted love is predominantly understood through the contemporary dissatisfying prism of sexual excess. In this chapter I will argue that while Moravia's novel functions as a social critique of existentialist ennui in the 1960s, an ennui leading to violence and destruction, Kahn's film adaptation of this text conveys contemporary ennui and civil discontent through the prism of perversion in the form of 1990s relentless sexual excess.

Boredom and Brutal Intimacy

Perverse age-gap relations are politicised and psychologised by Moravia and Kahn, expressed as obsessive, dangerous, violent, humiliating and utterly mysterious. As Dominique Mainon and James Ursini argue in their discussion of 'love gone wrong in the movies', 'Obsession is a different form of love, if it is indeed love at all. It seems more like psychological fetishism of the very act and emotion of love itself [...] It is edgier, perverse and far more intense'.[4] In Kahn's adaptation of Moravia's tale, the edginess, extremity and what Tim Palmer might refer to as the 'brutal intimacy' of dysfunctional sexual relations can be read in line with a trend in French cinema, from the 1990s onwards, to produce cinematic works that pair sexual excesses with characterisations of both boredom and explosive action.[5] Indeed, as Palmer argues in more detail:

> While actual acts of violence and sex are represented as intrusive and alarming, even nondescript events and settings manifest a brooding, unspecified malaise. In part this builds from measured narrative pacing, an insidious form of storytelling, with plots pared down to the point of simplicity, attenuated to relentlessness. The most shocking and unflinching of sexual interactions are situated, in effect, within narratives that oscillate between experiential extremes: drawn-out sequences of passive meditation, inscrutable character interactions, even, at times, an abiding sense of boredom, and contrasting bursts of sudden, overwhelmingly abrupt movement and action.[6]

The characteristics of brutally intimate cinema as described by Palmer above can be mapped onto L'ennui in various ways. Martin's behaviour, for example, is precisely made up of this type of rhythm of extremes; oscillation between lingering, boring meditation and explosive abrupt sexual action. The suggestion of restlessness in particular belies symmetry in Martin's moments of frenzy and absurd behaviour such as his attempts to stalk Cécilia, sabotage her other relationships and finally strangle her. Indeed, as Victoria Best and Martin Crowley note in *The New Pornographies: Explicit Sex in Recent French Fiction and Film*, Martin's 'behaviour is remarkable for its edgy, pent-up quality, perpetually on the point of explosion in crazy driving, or lengthy, searching interrogations of Cécilia or intense sexual activity'.[7] Accordingly, the brutal intimacy of Martin's actions can be understood through Palmer's frame as a social critique on the dysfunction of contemporary intimacies; the film shows the disintegration, failure and the tainting of intimate ideals through an 'explicit dissection of the body and its sexual behaviours'.[8]

Kahn's L'ennui is set nearly 40 years after Moravia's story, which is significant in terms of recognising the ways obscenity and boredom operate differently both through time and in the distinct media of literature and film. Philosophically, Moravia's novel explicitly posits the 1950s as a moment of 'existentialist ennui', a crisis in Marxism (or the state Marxism embodied by Stalinist Russia and the eastern bloc and symbolised by the Soviet Union's violent crushing of Hungarian independence). This crisis notably coincided with a certain existentialist ennui and 'apocalyptic tone' in culture and philosophy, symbolised by Moravia's characters. That is, these are characters who express a prominent or paralysing disillusionment with the mechanised world that surrounds them, the type of paralysis that means that Dino's art canvas remains blank. As such, Moravia (in line with his contemporaries Albert Camus, Jean-Paul Sartre and Simone de Beauvoir) can be seen to explicitly address existentialist themes marked out, according to Steven Crowell, by 'dread, boredom, alienation, the absurd, freedom, commitment [and] nothingness'.[9] Similarly, Kahn's adaptation reconsiders the crisis of civil discontent in the 1990s as a philosophical moment of déjà vu in line with Francis Fukuyama's 'end of history'.[10] In opposition to the intellectual projects of the 1950s, the 1990s adopts boredom as a theme by way of its alignment with the existentialist movement, Generation X and modern-day sexual excess. Jacques Derrida talks of a strong feeling of déjà vu when speaking in response to Fukuyama's declaration that the fall of the Berlin Wall signified the defeat of communism and Marxism as well as the definitive victory of liberal democracy. He writes:

> Many young people today probably no longer sufficiently realize it: the eschatological themes of the 'end of history', of the 'end of Marxism', of the 'end of philosophy', of the 'ends of man', of the 'last man' and so forth were, in the '50s, that is, forty years ago, our daily bread. We had this bread of apocalypse in our mouths naturally, already, just as naturally as that which I nicknamed after the fact, in 1980, the 'apocalyptic tone in philosophy'.[11]

This link between a 1990s philosophical 'boredom boom' and the analysis of such ennui is explored by Kahn by means of the erotic combat through which Martin attempts to counter his nothingness. The absurdity of Martin's behaviour (an irrationality that increases as his relationship with Cécilia, his young, 'care-free' sex 'partner' becomes more established in line with his demand) can again be placed in a philosophical context. The order Martin attempts to instil in, and on Cécilia, and the structured relationship he demands (via an incessant and increased renegotiation of meetings, demands for her to justify her feelings for him and her moral attitude towards sex) can be read in line with Camus's notion of 'absurdity'. For Camus, absurdity occurs 'when an individual "consciousness", longing for order, collides with "the other's" lack of order'.[12] The absurdity of the human relationship (absurdity, here, seen as disturbing and crazed; beyond the rational and thus symbolised by the act of sex) is utilised by Kahn and Moravia to demonstrate the serious nature of misconnection and alienation amid the world of others. The relationships in Kahn's film are, in fact, indexed by this type of absurd behaviour, in that the increasingly violent intergenerational sexual relations that litter the text signify Martin's out-dated attempt to enact some sort of excessive anarchy. The relationship between violence, generational difference and sex is clearly a complex one and can be understood as perverse in the sense that Kahn frames the suffering of Martin as part of a masculine world textured by madness. Indifference quickly becomes obsession and obsession becomes violent, self-destructive and absurd. Haunted by the supposed pleasures of the past, Martin fails to enjoy the present, violently losing control of his mind and body. In contrast, Cécilia's mechanised response to Martin's increasingly desperate and violent sexual demands is other-worldly. She is not afraid of Martin but is instead focused upon a new feminine world of meaning marked out in the 1990s by an 'embrace of fatal risk'.[13]

Notably, the crisis of meaning in the 1980s and 1990s as portrayed through film is most evident in the 'serial killer' film (in which killing is apparently an unmotivated or sexually motivated act and signifies the exhaustion of rational/political thought). Countless examples, such as *Henry: Portrait of a Serial Killer* (John McNaughton, 1986), *The Silence of the Lambs* (Jonathan Demme, 1991), *Sombre* (Philippe Grandrieux, 1998) and Kahn's *Roberto Succo* (2001), unveil the links between the mechanics of sexuality, the irrationality of desire/love and the death drive. What is most significant about Kahn's portrayal of Succo (Stefano Cassetti), based on a real-life French serial killer, is the way in which Kahn presents him as a perverse and powerful figure in terms of defining 1990s anarchy in response to the boredom and alienation of the age. This film is disturbing not because of the theme – murder – but because it brings to light the perversity of Succo's ability to love: oscillating between normative and transgressive subject positions. This is demonstrated by a relationship between Succo and Léa (Isild Le Besco), a teenage girl, that defies notions of serial killers as inhuman and incapable of empathy. Interestingly, it is scenes marking out the failure of this romantic relationship, rather than the spectacular nature of Succo's sadistic acts, that function as both the most penetrating and anxiety-causing moments in the film.

In contrast, the real crisis of the 1940s and 1950s (both militaristic and philosophical) is made visible by Moravia's Marxism. This Marxism (or the cultural exhaustion of it) posits a meticulous middle-class paralysis – concerned with the ego – in the face of 1950s political and cultural disconnection. Interestingly, Moravia's account of this simultaneous frenzied boredom is explored by way of erotic transgression and trauma and, as such, his text exists as a metaphor for a 1950s cultural apocalypse. Moravia's elevation of irrational desire over rational thought, of 'feeling' over 'rational thinking' is significant in that the concept of the body as an irrational machine operates as a metaphor for the events of the time (specifically the nuclear stand-off and the Cuban Missile Crisis). The body in crisis is thus symbolic of man's increasingly automated desire to both display and dispel excess, even in acts of intimacy.

Patterns of Disorder: Excess, Eroticism and the Denial of Pornographic Pleasure

Both Moravia and Kahn utilise a model and aesthetic of repetition (a model commonly used to order depictions of sexual relations) to produce texts that dominantly foreground sexual alienation and erotic combat. In short, such sexual displeasure is represented in order to distort and trouble traditional schemas of representation and thus represent the breaking-down of established order on a formal as well as thematic level. By way of clarification, the definition of eroticism that I employ here stems from the writings of Georges Bataille, who argues that 'eroticism always entails a breaking down of established patterns, the patterns of the regulated social order'.[14]

As both *La noia* and *L'ennui* feature, at their core, explicit sexual relations between a 17-year-old girl and a middle-aged man, I would like to situate this erotic partnership amid a larger literary and filmic history of pornographic aesthetics. Pornography as a genre, whether in literature or shown on screen, employs specific aesthetics, aesthetics frequently dominated by what Linda Williams refers to as the 'hyper-visibility of genitals, the hydraulics of sex, the pleasure of the male orgasm and the repetition of sexual acts'.[15] Indeed, it is, among other things, the insistence of pushing such scenes front-and-centre that differentiates porn from other genres. Like other erotic representations, the sexual relations presented in *La noia* and *L'ennui* do not exist in a vacuum; they are socially and culturally informed by generic and narrative conventions. Moravia and Kahn both employ pornographic tropes such as genital description/visibility, frequent scenes of sexual hydraulics and, the perverse age-gap coda (so often seen in pornography) in their aforementioned texts, however, they do so purely to demonstrate the different ways in which established patterns of reading and seeing can be broken down, perverted and adapted, even while they are seemingly repeated. As Jonathan Light argues in *The Art of Porn*, 'Sexual repetition is not, of course, true repetition. It's repetition with subtle variations'.[16] Following this trajectory, Moravia and Kahn's texts can be situated not as works that merely repeat the pornographic tropes that they employ, but as texts that offer subtle variations. More specifically, adaptations of the modalities of porn achieve a new type of erotic aesthetic by way of telling or showing a disturbance in the pornographic 'patterns of the regulated social order'.[17] Thus, *La noia* and *L'ennui* appropriate pornographic strategies in order to subvert and pervert them.

As Kath Albury notes in 'Reading porn reparatively', 'Sexual moralities [...] assist in distinguishing acceptable sexual practices and partnerships from those that are unacceptable'.[18] In *La noia*, Moravia employs a narrative strategy of repetition to clearly imply the morally transgressive nature of intergenerational sex partnerships and attempt to articulate their erotic frisson. Foregrounding the structure of repetition, Moravia situates Dino as a middle-aged, hyper-anxious artist. Living in an Italian apartment opposite another more commercially successful and older male painter, Balestrieri, Dino repeatedly watches young female models entering his home, presumably for sex. On Balestrieri's sudden death, Dino is informed that the painter suffered a heart attack while making love to a teenage model, Cécilia. Entering the empty apartment, Dino is confronted by countless explicit paintings of female nudes, nudes he designates as displaying an aesthetic of 'the hideous perfection that belongs essentially to pornography'.[19] While viewing the paintings, Dino is disturbed by Cécilia herself, who has arrived at the apartment to collect her belongings. Questioning Cécilia about her relationship to Balestrieri, Dino clearly articulates his view that the partnership was perverse, presenting Balestrieri as a man 'old enough to have been [her] father's father'. Cécilia's response to Dino's questioning regarding 'why' the relationship occurred is disarmingly erotic: 'I felt very strongly attracted to him. Oh well, I'll tell you. Balestrieri was a little like my father, and when I was younger I had a real passion for my father [...] I used to dream about him at nights'. Cécilia's clear confession of incestuous desire serves to point to a clear loss of order; a dysfunction of authority, if the normative family unit is understood to be the basis of social structure. Rather than responding with horror to Cécilia's confession, Dino appears to be unwittingly and perversely attracted by it, almost immediately asking Cécilia to visit his own studio. On her arrival, however, Dino is suddenly overcome with disgust, recognising the strategy of perverse repetition that he is enacting.

Dino's acknowledgement of the strategy of repetition does not prevent imminent sexual relations with Cécilia, but instead works to provide a moral limit or boundary that he desires to transgress. Dino engages in sex with Cécilia, yet is clearly infatuated by her previous age-gap relationship. Because of this very obsession, the sexual relationship between Dino and Cécilia is figured as perverse. Rather than focusing on the physical pleasure of their coupling, Dino repetitively either reflects on the disassociation between their minds when having sex or absurdly disturbs or defers their coupling to interrogate Cécilia about her former relationship with Balestrieri. In doing so, he alienates himself.

In Kahn's film, differing aesthetic strategies are employed in order to foreground the modern malaise of alienation. Specifically, Kahn's film opens with a blurred vision of a French highway/town where the blazing headlights of endless cars and blinding streetlights denote the primacy of contemporary consumer capitalism in the 1990s. Latin tango music plays relentlessly for the duration of this introductory scene, illuminating the passionate 'dance of life' of the city and making way for an image of Martin seated in his car, watching people frequent the sex-trade venues in Paris. In this scene the illicit is clearly rendered explicit. Surrounded by neon signs advertising 'porno shops' and sex shows, the city is clearly depicted as a pornographic culture built upon an imperative to enjoy. Yet, as the unsmiling faces of prostitutes, punters and Martin alike indicate, something is clearly 'out of place' here. This is not a utopian world of freedom and excess but a world where sex is figured as pedestrian, ordinary and everyday. As Fred Botting and Scott Wilson argue, in pornographic cultures 'sex becomes the same dull daily grind as work: a banal, repetitive, mundane event absorbed in the pleasure principle of the productive and consumptive economy'.[20] In other words, sex becomes boring and mechanical. Speaking of his sexual relations with Cécilia, Martin notes that he is bored by her physicality, which he describes as 'frenetic, avid and rhythmical – boring like a machine'.

Formally invoking the mechanical rhythm of Martin's sexual experiences, Kahn employs, via his own machine, the camera, differing registers of performance by way of two recurring shot patterns that dominate the film. The first recurring shot pattern employed by Kahn consists of a disorientating swish-pan followed by rapidly edited and fragmented close-up shots designed to carry what Linda Williams refers to as 'maximum genital visibility'.[21] A strong example of this pornographic aesthetic is visible in the sequence when Martin first comes across the nude images of Cécilia painted by his recently deceased neighbour Meyers (Robert Kramer), Kahn's adaptation of Moravia's Balestrieri character. On entering Meyers' apartment, Martin is confronted by a large painting of a naked young woman on her hands and knees in front of a mirror. The voyeurism invited by the painting is soon echoed by Martin himself as a reverse shot shows Martin's eyes rapidly darting around the room. A swish-pan then reveals precisely what Martin's gaze is following: a succession of painted images of young women with their legs apart, the last of which sees the female masturbating. Kahn's conscious employment of rapid and fragmented close-up shots in this scene clearly references hardcore pornographic codes of maximum visibility. Yet, the pornographic ideal that Cécilia represents (in that she is young, carefree, interested in sex and not in a complex committed relationship), soon disintegrates for Martin, replaced instead by a growing anxiety regarding his inability to possess, control and connect with her on any other level than the physical.

Kahn's second recurring shot pattern makes such anxiety visible by featuring long, lingering and unevenly timed shots that focus on Martin's deferral of the sex act with Cécilia. A clear example of this shot pattern can be seen slightly later in the film in a sequence in which we see Cécilia enter Martin's apartment, wordlessly undress, climb into Martin's bed and tell him to 'come quick'. While Martin undresses and climbs in to bed beside Cécilia, he defers the sex that Cécilia seems to so readily want by asking her to get up and close the curtains. Having done so, Cécilia rejoins Martin, only for him to insist that she get up a second time and close the bedroom door. On her way back to the bed, Martin then insists she should unhook the telephone, then bring him his cigarettes, then his matches, then switch off the gas in the kitchen and then put music on – but not too loud – and then get him an ashtray. Recognising Martin's clear deferral of the 'final sexual aim', Cécilia ignores his last request, instead laying her body on top of his own and kissing him passionately, thus insisting on the sex act that Martin has been so persistently deferring. Rather than revealing what Williams refers to as the 'hydraulics of sex',[22] Kahn refuses maximum visibility in the majority of the actual sex scenes between the couple. Instead, the film pushes front-and-centre Martin's perverse, repetitive and, for Cécilia as well as the audience, boring deferral of sex (see Fig. 10.1). Of course, such a deferral can also be linked back to Kahn's own aesthetic technique of appropriating and then subsequently negating pornographic tropes, deferring any real or metaphorical 'money shot'.

In repeating both shot patterns several times throughout the duration of the film, Kahn espouses then denounces the banal-yet-repetitive pornographic rhythm of contemporary culture. This rhythm is arguably reflected in the characters' patterns of speech. Whereas Martin's speech rhythms are repeatedly shown as frantic, anxious and hurried, Cécilia's rhythms of speech are predominantly calm, unhurried, monotonous and dull-sounding, thus functioning as a clear counterpoint to Martin's

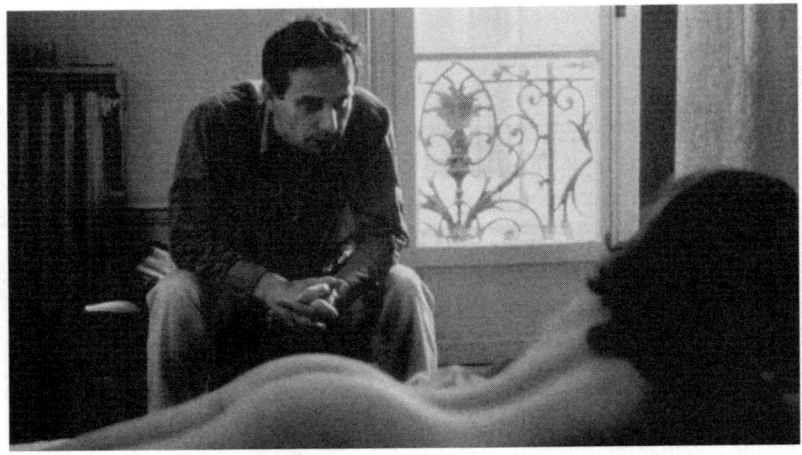

Fig. 10.1. Martin (Charles Berling) defers sex with Cécilia (Sophie Guillmin) in *L'ennui* (Cédric Kahn, Gemini Films, 1998)

increasingly frenzied thoughts and actions. The gendered and indeed intergenerational implications of such distinct rhythms point to a fundamental incompatibility. Whereas Martin represents a somewhat neurotic middle-aged 'feminine' anxiety, Cécilia's eventual dominance and insistence upon her own sexual pleasure is figured as youthful, straightforward and 'masculine'. In addition to this rhythmical and intergenerational mismatch, the couple's interactions are figured as increasingly out-of-sync. As the narrative progresses, this mode of being out-of-sync – out-of-time – can also be considered the reason Kahn repetitively employs the two aforementioned shot patterns: to erotically espouse (fast-paced, fragmented close-up shots) and then denounce (long, lingering and unevenly timed shots), a model of meaning in which sex equates to pleasure.

For Martin, sex with Cécilia does not mean pleasure or satisfaction, but rather, it is 'a true perversion in the sense of Lacan's pun of *père-version*, the father's version, where the subject denies its own excessive enjoyment, its *jouissance*, and instead makes itself into an instrument of the Other's *jouissance*'.[23] *Père-version* is introduced via Martin's desire to fill in the hole that Meyers (the late lover of Cécilia) and her dying father have vacated. As the new symbolic father, Martin gives over his pleasure to Cécilia. As such, the perverse repetitions of Martin's sexually unfulfilling encounters with Cécilia lead him further and further down a path of dark destruction towards the point of death. The sex appears to point to 'the location of sex as a scene of potential disaster',[24] an act that opens up, for Martin at least, a gap to reveal the true obscenity of the age. Through his violent dread and horrific alienation from his young lover (a girl who Martin is desperate to 'know'), Martin suffers a perverse predicament. The loss of meaning, loss of authority and loss of order represented through this failed sexual pairing can thus be understood as a critique of modernity, a signifier or disaster; an enactment of disastrous intergenerational civilisation and discontent.

Civilisation and Discontent in the Contemporary Age

Ironically, Kahn utilises the technology of film to occlude the vision of the spectator. Although Kahn's film depicts graphic sexual scenes, it is rather the feminine unseen – Cécilia's mind, her understanding and reasoning (or lack of it) – that remains veiled for the duration of this vision. While Cécilia can be understood as an idealistic projection of Martin's excessive middle-aged sexual desires, her lack of interest in anything other than her own sexual pleasure eventually serves to increase Martin's anxiety. It is precisely this gap between Martin's middle-aged sexual fantasy and the reality of the relation as experienced by Martin that is explicitly exposed and stripped bare by the camera. In short, Martin's misconceptions about Cécilia, his obsessive, frantic boredom and violent neuroses are revealed not to be the end result of his affair with Cécilia, but the starting point of it. Martin's desire to connect emotionally with Cécilia, to really find pleasure in her, is thus revealed to the spectator as a circular and increasingly neurotic obsession that, in psychoanalytic terms, can arguably be read as a desire circling the 'thing' (*das Ding*) in an attempt to attain an impossible *jouissance*. In other words, Martin's desire to connect with Cécilia can be understood as a means of absurdly attempting to experience the pleasure of the forbidden, a mission that he knows he can never truly succeed in but one that he believes, neurotically, will bring him closer to feeling or knowing the 'real'.

Unable to work due to his anxiety, Martin chooses to 'waste' his time in pursuit of objectless *jouissance*, which in turn serves to increase his anxiety. Embodying a quintessential psychoanalytic paradox, Martin explicitly describes his (Freudian) experience of 'civilisation and its discontents'. He states:

> I've realised I can't stand myself, I have no patience with books, films, I can't concentrate, even on music, I want to see no one, yet I can't stay alone. I can't stay at home, I can't go out, I can't sleep. I want to work but I can't, there's nothing ... except revulsion. I even thought I wanted to die [...] I'm jittery. I need my energy for my work. I have to finish my book. I have given up love [...] I need sublimation. Freud is very good at that. He says certain acts that seem unrelated to sex are motivated by sexual compulsion especially intellectual or artistic acts. A man without sublimation is pathetic, a lunatic with a tyrannical penis and a tiny brain.

Martin's use of language is, on the one hand, clearly intellectual (as shown in his knowledge of Freud) and, on the other, nonsensical, as can be seen by his reference to and admittance of 'lunacy'. The tyranny and fascism of the penis evident in Martin's clear lack of self-control over his sexual desire for Cécilia can again be understood as perverse and paradoxical, mirroring his own disjointed mental state, his anguish and his anxiety. As Antonios Vadolas argues, 'Perversion functions as the "scum" of discourse, that is to say, it becomes the main reference for any failing point in discourse that eradicated the knowledge produced within its boundaries and thereby exposes its limits'.[25] Indeed, Martin's language is perversely revealing, precisely because of what it exposes: Martin's own lack.

As works that diagnose perversion, Moravia and Kahn's texts convey a sense of dystopia that can be understood through their representations of existential despair. Interestingly however, in both texts it is the male protagonist – and the patriarchal world of knowledge-by-proxy – that is most fundamentally unhinged. Dino/Martin obsessively desire to really 'know' Cécilia, yet both fail, making visible their own lack. Marking an inversion of libidinal economies of power, Dino/Martin succumb to what Best and Crowley define as 'a kind of hystericisation, a loss of self-control that expresses a loss of cultural power and manifests itself in excessive eroticism'.[26]

The psychological matrix between the hysterical and the perverse is, according to Nitza Yarom, housed 'in the arena of the body'.[27] Situating the differentiation between the perverse and the hysterical in Freudian terms, Yarom notes: 'For the perverse, the sexual aim is primarily a defence against disintegration through differentiation, while the hysteric uses sexuality and seduction to obtain love and absolve gender vacillation'.[28] This cohabitation of the hysterical/perverse can be read in the obscene threats that Dino/Martin feel in response to their position as meaningless subjects in the world, as well as in the ways through which they try to counteract their fears through increasingly violent and uncontrolled acts of sex. One such example of Dino's hysterically perverse actions can be seen when he believes that Cécilia is cheating on him. Dino narrates:

> I do not remember ever having loved Cécilia with such violence as I did during the time when I was spying on her and suspecting that she was being unfaithful to me. I would throw myself upon her as if she had been an enemy whom I wished to tear to pieces [...] still with the illusory idea that, by having her, I could nullify her independence and her mystery. Immediately after the embrace I realised, of course, that I had not possessed her. But it was too late: Cécilia went away and I knew the whole thing would begin again the next day – the useless watching, the unattainable possession, the final disappointment.[29]

Dino's perverse and dogged pursuit of Cécilia's enigmatic core – her presumed knowledge – can be understood in Kahn's adaptation as a performance of 'ontological difference of knowledge that is intrinsic to the genders; men display a frantic demand for a knowledge of emotions that women refuse to give [...] because their approach to what might be knowable is entirely other'.[30] Yet, as Best and Crowley conclude, the fact that Cécilia remains 'at one with her existence [...] only highlights the painful division of [Martin] from himself'.[31] Martin's hysterical reaction to his own self-division can be understood as markedly and psychoanalytically perverse here. As a philosophy professor, we can infer that Martin's knowledge of psychoanalysis is strong. While Freud's definition of the perverse is not explicitly referred to in the diegesis, Martin does make reference to his Freudian knowledge when discussing sexual sublimation with his doctor.[32] Martin is driven, it seems, by a compulsion for repetitive behaviour that takes the form of both frustrated and unpleasurable sex and, secondly, boring and dissatisfying conversations between Martin and Cécilia that eventually lead to chaos, physical violence, mental combat and, for Martin, attempted suicide in a car crash. The *topos* of boredom works then to highlight the rupture of reason. Despite Martin's attempted self-annihilation, he does not die at the close of the narrative, but rather sees his relationship with Cécilia and thus with himself 'transformed into an existential principle [in that] despite the odds, Martin now has a truth to live by, even if it is one shot through with negativity'.[33] While Best and Crowley make an interesting point here, my reading of this ending identifies the crash as a meaningful point of rupture that serves to prevent Martin from continuing to spiral downward on his anxious axis. Instead, the crash introduces a point of praxis in which Martin's anxiety and boredom is recognised and diagnosed. In this sense, Kahn's camera can be understood as an instrument of diagnosis.

Conclusion

The intergenerational differences, firstly, between the respective time periods of the novel and film and, secondly, as a narrative theme in these two texts, convey boredom in the very fabric of the modern social relation, a boredom that can only be overcome through excessive violence and attempted self-destruction. Kahn's film makes visible the notion that the existentialist moment of the 1990s, while a partial repetition of 1950s alienation, is now filtered through sex, capitalism and the boredom of sexual excess. Ultimately, the ennui of both the 1950s and 1990s is encapsulated in the generational difference *between* Martin and Cécilia. Martin embodies 1950s existentialist boredom, exhaustion and a type of mid-life crisis, which drives him to look for excessive stimulation to turn him on and make him feel alive. In this way, Martin is a metaphor for a 1950s society that is exhausted and desires excessive stimulation to stave off the 'end of history'. Cécilia, in contrast, represents 1990s existentialism in that she is essentially the projection of Martin's excessive sexual desire;

a young woman who willingly and excessively abandons her body to sex and animalistic passion. Together, the generational and gender differences between the couple and the intimate disconnection they represent symbolises the social and similarly alienated conditions of these two ages. It is for this reason that the age gap is so important and so perversely revealing.

Failed attempts to regulate the excessive desires – sexual, emotional or nihilistic – of the social order are thus mined via the intergenerational legibility of Moravia and Kahn's narratives. Indeed, the emotional lodestone of *L'ennui* is exposed and disclosed through the tensions of difference that exist between Martin and Cécilia. While the intergenerational difference between the pair initially makes for a playful repeated mismatch, the irreconcilable and overt clashing of comparable registers (a clashing also reflected in Kahn's repeated shot patterns) becomes a powerful and pressing tool, forcing the intense and evolving discourse of violence and destruction to the surface.

Notes

1. Molly Anne Rothenberg and Dennis Foster, 'Introduction. Beneath the skin: perversion and social analysis', in Molly Anne Rothenberg, Dennis Foster and Slavoj Žižek (eds), *Perversion and the Social Relation* (Durham, NC: Duke University Press, 2003), p. 4.
2. The first film adaptation of *La noia* was directed by Damiano Damiani in 1963.
3. Cited in Gaither Stewart, 'Alberto Moravia: a man of his times – an interview with Umberto Eco', *Critique Magazine* (January 2001). Available at http://critiquemagazine.com/article/moravia.html (accessed 5 August 2004).
4. Dominique Mainon and James Ursini, *Cinema of Obsession: Erotic Fixation and Love Gone Wrong in the Movies* (New York: Limelight Editions, 2007), pp. xi–vii.
5. Tim Palmer, 'Style and sensation in the contemporary French cinema of the body', *Journal of Film and Video* 58/3 (2006), pp. 22–32.
6. Ibid., p. 29.
7. Victoria Best and Martin Crowley, *The New Pornographies: Explicit Sex in Recent French Fiction and Film* (Manchester and New York: Manchester University Press, 2007), p. 46.
8. Palmer, 'Style and sensation', p. 22.
9. Steven Crowell, 'Existentialism', in *Stanford Encyclopaedia of Philosophy* (2004). Available at http://plato.stanford.edu/entries/existentialism (accessed 5 February 2007).

10. Francis Fukuyama, *The End of History and the Last Man* (London and New York: Penguin Books, 1992).

11. Jacques Derrida, *Spectres of Marx*, translated by Peggy Kamuf (London: Routledge, 1994), pp. 14–15.

12. Albert Camus, *The Myth of Sisyphus: And Other Essays* (London: Vintage. 1991), p. 9.

13. Hélène Cixous in Elisabeth Bronfen, *Over Her Dead Body: Death, Femininity and the Aesthetic* (Manchester: Manchester University Press. 1992), p. 368.

14. Georges Bataille, *Erotism: Death and Sensuality* (New York: Walker and Company, 1962), p. 18.

15. Linda Williams, *Screening Sex* (Durham and London: Duke University Press, 2008), p. 5.

16. Jonathan Light, *The Art of Porn* (New York: Light Publishing, 2002), p. 11.

17. Bataille, *Erotism*, p. 18.

18. Kath Albury, 'Reading porn reparatively', *Sexualities* 12/5 (2009), p. 650.

19. Alberto Moravia, *La noia/The Empty Canvas*, translated by Angus Davidson (London and New York: Granada Publishing, 1979), p. 68. Originally published in 1960. Subsequent page references in text appear in parentheses.

20. Fred Botting and Scott Wilson, 'Sexcrash', in Jane Arthurs and Iain Grant (eds), *Crash Cultures: Modernity, Mediation and the Material* (Bristol and Portland: Intellect, 2003), pp. 79–90.

21. Williams, *Screening Sex*, p. 5.

22. Ibid.

23. Oliver Speck, 'The method of madness in the cinema of Michael Haneke', in Rebecca Thomas (ed.), *Crime and Madness in Modern Austria: Myth, Metaphor and Cultural Realities* (Newcastle: Cambridge Scholars Publishing, 2008), p. 211.

24. Botting and Wilson, 'Sexcrash', p. 86.

25. Antonios Vadolas, *Perversions of Fascism* (London: Karnac Books, 2009), p. xvi.

26. Best and Crowley, *The New Pornographies*, p. 48.

27. Nitza Yarom, *Matrix of Hysteria: Psychoanalysis of the Struggle Between the Sexes as Enacted in the Body* (London and New York: Routledge, 2005), p. 112.

28. Ibid., p. 113.

29. Moravia, *La noia/The Empty Canvas*, pp. 198–9.

30. Best and Crowley, *The New Pornographies*, pp. 47–8.

31. Ibid., p. 48.

32. Freud defines perversion as 'sexual activities which either a) extend, in an anatomical sense, beyond the regions of the body that are designed for sexual union, or b) linger over the intermediate relations to the sexual object which should normally be traversed rapidly on the path towards the final sexual aim'. Sigmund Freud, *Three Essays on the Theory of Sexuality*, translated by James Strachey, (New York: Basic Books, 1962), pp. 61–2. Originally published 1905.

33. Best and Crowley, *The New Pornographies*, p. 49.

11

A Mother's Love Cannot Be Denied:
Ma mère

Clarissa Smith

> We live in a time in which transgression has lost its sting, when
> it has become trivial, boring, and irrelevant. Bataille's giddy
> gaze into the abyss no longer inspires exhilaration or dread.[1]

Christophe Honoré's 2004 film of mother–son incest, an adaptation
of Georges Bataille's 1966 novella *Ma mère,* is an outlier example of the
French cinema James Quandt dubbed 'the New French Extremity'.[2] As
Richard Falcon has argued, such films manifest 'an aggressive desire to
confront their audiences, to render the spectator's experience problematic'.[3]
The generic term may be an uneasy fit for a film such as *Ma mère,* with
its slow-moving images and obfuscating dialogue. Although its central
theme, mother–son incest, certainly offers a disturbing viewing experience
characterised by what Asbjørn Grønstad terms a 'mischievous appetite for
the unwatchable'.[4] At the same time, he cautions that:

> To confuse this proclivity with a prosaic desire to shock
> the viewers, however, would be to miss the point entirely.

The unwatchability of the films [...] lies not so much on an experiential level as on a philosophical one [...] preoccupied with deeply humanist issues even as they at times seem disturbingly misanthropic. Rather than being stigmatised as representatives of an over-hyped 'shock cinema' [...] the films in question [can] more usefully be regarded as an antidote to the numbing complacencies and stock humanity of much mainstream cinema.[5]

Certainly the film does not include scenes of explicit nudity, nor is there any performance of sex or violence that could be understood as simply seeking to shock viewers, yet the status of *Ma mère* as an antidote to complacency is not secure. The film has variously been described as a 'psychosexual farce';[6] 'a self-mortifying, crypto-religious quest for ultimate transgression and totalized carnal abjection', which offers viewers 'an interminable back-and-forth of joyless orgasmic frenzy and postcoital vacationers' lull';[7] while for Stephen Holden the film 'is such a grim affair that after a short while, the spectacle of its aimless characters bending themselves out of shape for the sake of alleged pleasure mutates from titillating to pathetic to laughable'.[8] *Ma mère* united critics in its condemnation. A minority recognised the film's bravery, its attempts to tell a difficult tale of incest without resorting to crudity, offering transgressive acts that raise 'curiosity, with the occasional intake of breath, rather than guffaws'.[9] Other commentators regarded Honoré's attempt to bring Bataille's unfilmable narrative to the screen as queer, avoiding sentimentalism and making 'a minor point in Marxist mode about local patterns of consumption'.[10] More positively, Tina Kendall suggests *Ma mère* offered an 'aesthetic of impurity [to] conjure a mythic placelessness that seems in keeping with the idea of transcendence'.[11] Despite its flaws, 'Honoré's film seems determined to explore the limits of hedonism'.[12]

For my own part, this is a film that causes me considerable unease, having watched it numerous times – on my own, in company, on a small screen, in a cinema. Each time I have felt differently about it, ranging from bored, through infuriated, to enchanted and back again. I have found it very difficult to write about as I have yet to move beyond my unsettledness and, indeed, I may never reach a settled response to this film. On the one hand, a narrative about a woman who pursues her own path, ignoring social injunctions about 'appropriate' maternal feeling or feminine sexuality, is quite thrilling. Yet there is little comfort in its incest theme, or its contrasts between the commodified sexual hedonism of industrial tourism and the pursuit of outrageous fulfilment, whatever its philosophical underpinnings. The presence of Isabelle Huppert makes the film eminently interesting but her performance also leaves me unsettled. I find myself in agreement with Tony McKibbin that 'there is something in Huppert's roles that begs interpretation maybe more than any other actress of her generation'.[13] Finally, if I recognise my own libidinal investments, the persistent nakedness of Louis Garrel as her son Pierre – dismissed by Steven Shaviro as simply guaranteeing an adult rating for the film[14] – arouses in me a distinctly queasy kind of desire.

Bringing Bataille to the Screen

Bataille's original story is set in Paris at the beginning of the twentieth century. In its narration of Pierre's journey into debauchery it is a claustrophobic novel, with elements of religious renunciation in line with Bataille's own preoccupations with the sacred. Difficult to read and, of course, difficult to translate to the screen, *Ma mère*'s themes are of the fleshy extremes of sexual desire, involving self-loathing, fascination with the repugnant and the transgression of taboos, including death.

In the film, Pierre, an indolent and moody 17-year-old, joins his parents at their villa in the industrial tourist resort of Gran Canaria. All is not well at home; his father (Philippe Duclos) is remote and dissatisfied with the way his life has turned out and, before we are introduced to Pierre, a brief scene where the wife rejects her husband's sexual advances suggests that his parents' relationship is strained. His mother, Hélène (Huppert), is by turns coquettish and withdrawn with her son, but at least the servants, Marthe (Dominique Reymond) and Robert (Olivier Rabourdin), seem pleased to see him. Following her husband's sudden death, Hélène insists Pierre show some semblance of sorrow, at least to the hired help, but there is little sense that either feels any grief. As Pierre attempts to get closer to his mother, she confesses to being a 'bitch' and a 'slut', insisting that he understand her as 'disgusting' and love her nonetheless. Against a backdrop of hedonistic holidaymakers, their relationship takes a transgressive turn: Hélène offers her girlfriend Réa (Joana Preiss) to Pierre and watches as Réa deflowers him in public. After an orgy in which Hélène and Pierre's feelings for each other become transparent to themselves and others, Hélène leaves the villa, telling Pierre 'We went a little too far.' Pierre comforts himself during his mother's absence by hooking up with Hansi (Emma de Caunes), a girl his own age but also one of his mother's acolytes. Even as he begins to fall in love with Hansi, Pierre's thoughts turn to Hélène. Similarly, Hélène seems unable to forget her son. Finally, they act on their mutual desire in a scene of masturbation and mutilation, culminating in Hélène's off-screen suicide. The film closes with Pierre masturbating over his mother's corpse in the chapel of rest.

Ma mère's incest story is a working-through of Bataille's understandings of the human struggle between taboo and transgression, a set of ideas he put forward in his 1957 text *Erotism: Death and Sensuality*. Bataille suggests that eroticism (acts and experiences of sexual stimulation) and death are fundamental to understanding human experience, as are their links to the existential tensions between *continuity* (union with others) and *discontinuity* (individualisation). Our self-consciousness as humans, aware of our finite existence, means, according to Bataille, that we treat nature and our own selves as instruments and objects, doomed to engage in the processes of production that confirm our inability to live 'like water in water'.[15] Only through violence and debauchery do we glimpse the possibilities of the boundary-less state of Bataille's continuity. In this sense then, the transgression of taboos enables transcendence. But much of the critical response to the film has centred on Honoré's failure to retain its Bataillean bite.

Shaviro suggests that Honoré reduced 'Bataille's obsessions from the ontological to the merely physiological', producing a domesticated tragedy.[16] Likewise, Kendall argues that 'if Bataille remains, it is certainly not in the reassuring places we would expect to find him: not in the treatment of sex and violence as inherently transgressive, and not in the critically endorsed notion of transcendence through transgression.'[17] There may be particular pleasures to be enjoyed in the assessment of the film for its fidelity to the original narrative and philosophy, although I find it more fruitful to look outside of its status as adaptation to think about what it might have to say about more current concerns about incest as taboo and what is at stake in attempting to represent its transgression.

In an interview published on the film's release, Honoré acknowledged that the contemporary moment renders much of Bataille's outrage toothless:

> I transported the novel to today and tried to see what of the story's transgressive side persisted. *Ma mère* [...] came out in the 60s after Bataille's death. Since then, we have passed through the sexual revolution, all those things which changed the relationship between morality and the body.[18]

Interestingly, much as the sexual revolution may have challenged traditional morality and increased acceptance of sex outside of heteronormative and monogamous marriage, not all boundaries have been transgressed. Levi-Strauss concluded, 'the prohibition of incest can be found at the dawn of culture ... [It] is culture itself'[19] and James L. Peacock and A. Thomas Kirsch observe that 'the taboo on incest within the immediate family is one of the few known cultural universals.'[20] The incest taboo is a means to encourage exogamy – the formation and strengthening of allegiances between unrelated households through marriage – where marriage is primarily an exchange of women between two social groups. Durkheim further understood incest as deriving from man's ambivalence towards blood as a supernatural substance and women's symbolic association with it as they became 'the theatre of bloody manifestations' during menstruation.[21] The incest taboo has its roots in the 'near-religious horror' primitive man felt for the possibility of sexual contact with the menstrual blood, which was also part of his own substance.

Like all taboos, incest arouses fear and unease but its unique revulsion lies in its location within what ought to be most sacrosanct. Incest tears apart the 'proper' fabric of our intimate relationships, threatening the very foundations of that institution of socialisation: the Family. Families are 'held together by a matrix of rights, expectations, obligations and role relationships',[22] but incest destabilises these established roles. While sexual liberation may have blown away all kinds of prohibitions for adults, it has been accompanied by a growing characterisation of childhood sexuality as absolutely different: children should be innocent, their sexuality both present biologically and absent physiologically. As R. Danielle Egan and Gail Hawkes observe, the rights of children to healthy sexual development are 'often singularly framed as the right of protection [...] rarely do these conversations turn toward the equally important right of sexual agency'.[23] This protectionism and its attendant forms of 'social quarantine' are institutionalised within the family with parents bearing the responsibility for ensuring 'the symbolic performance of "child innocence"'.[24] The family is, of course, also the site of incest but as a culture we have conveniently outsourced the threat to children's sexual innocence onto the single figure of the paedophile. The predatory stranger can be the repository for all our worst fears, thus preserving the family from critical review and establishing intimate desire for children as incomprehensible, unnatural and abusive.

The particularly modern understanding of incest as *abuse* has resonance for my discussion here. In Bataille's writings on the incest taboo, its transgression is an offence against laws of Nature, God and Family, whereas our own times have positioned incest as an offence (violent and criminal) against the child and childhood as a state of absolute innocence. A key driver of the contemporary abhorrence for incest is surely the recognition of the 'unique traumatic force' and the 'abuse of power',[25] of fathers or mothers over daughters or sons; older siblings over younger brothers or sisters; adults in positions of parental responsibility over their charges. Honoré's film opens up some of the cultural ambiguities regarding incest. The incest narrative in film is not, of course, a facsimile of actual incidences of incest. It offers ways of thinking and engaging with the moral and emotional dimensions of incest. It offers us glimpses of the motivations, experiences and endurance of victims and perpetrators in ways that are comprehensible to us and that elicit, via their interrogation of the nature of the incest, some form of moral response.

Incest has a long history in fiction, including the Greek myth of Oedipus in Freudian theory, Daniel Defoe's *Moll Flanders* (1721), William Faulkner's *Absalom, Absalom!* (1936), Stephen King's *Gerald's Game* (1992), Marilyn French's *Our Father* (1995), as well as the hundreds of autobiographical titles going under the label of 'misery-lit'. In many of these accounts incest acts, as Katie Roiphe puts it, as 'a flash of lightning illuminating the entire book'.[26] Roiphe offers a reductive but nonetheless incisive indictment of the incest narrative trope as 'Mary or Maisie or

Rose is acting kind of strange. She is fat or promiscuous or bitter or she dives headfirst into a shallow pond, and it turns out, many pages later, that Mary or Maisie or Rose was molested as a child by her father or stepfather or father figure'.[27] Similar usage of incest can be found in films as diverse as *Natural Born Killers* (Oliver Stone, 1994) and *Girl, Interrupted* (James Mangold, 1999). In such narratives, incest has been the answer to the riddle of the character, the reason why the bad girl (and it often is a girl) gets badder.

Some critics have argued that cinematic representations of incest are complicit in a wider denial of the trauma of incest by their picturing it as 'medical[ised] as a "syndrome" or "disorder" rather than a crime, and [...] being positioned in dominant discourse as a sensationalized and prurient topic'.[28] In *The War Zone* (Tim Roth, 1999) incest is graphically depicted on screen as precisely *abuse*, a crime within the family. In *Festen* (Thomas Vinterberg, 1998) confession and testimony are powerfully used to highlight the damage caused to the adults who were victims of incest as children. It is difficult to write about a film about incest. The seemingly appropriate way to do so is to weigh up whether or not it sufficiently condemns the transgression it depicts. If it does not then its ideological message is a 'recommendation' of incest, or absolution of the perpetrator.[29] Much of the work on films about incest worry about the 'right' messages being offered, in particular how faithful the representation is to current understandings of the harms done to the victim of incest, dealing with the pain and anguish felt by survivors and stressing the violence or coercion that victimise the child.[30] There is nothing wrong with this per se, although it does seek to limit particular forms of representation to a close relation to the real, where the 'real' is actually what is currently acknowledged as 'the truth about incest' and may well obscure the complexities of experiences and behaviours. The 'realism' and 'believability' of the relationship between Pierre and Hélène is not a literal one and I am not sure that it is helpful to think in terms of whether or not the film depicts the mother as the victimiser, as current thought on incest might expect.

In contrast, *Ma mère* does not show the relationship between mother and son and their sexual interactions as acts of violence or non-consensual activities; there are no clear indicators that its protagonists are deviant

Fig. 11.1. Mother Hélène (Isabelle Huppert) and son Pierre (Louis Garrel) in *Ma mère* (Christophe Honoré, Gemini Films, 2004)

or 'sick'. Its sexual scenes are, as Kendall notes, 'oddly flat, distanced and abstracted' so that they do not sensationalise.[31] Instead, its representations of desire for, and of, the child, unsettle any fixed boundary around the taboo, its transgression and the nature or obviousness of its abuses. Honoré's directorial strategies, static camerawork, close-ups on impassive faces (see Fig. 11.1) and the acting performances in this film disrupt any easy responses to the horror of the incestuous relationship as they bring to the fore larger philosophical questions: 'when and within what kind of relationship(s) are (what kinds of) eroticism and sexuality allowed and desired?'[32]

The Trouble with Mom

'We reserve our linguistic wrath for the most abhorrent act: mother–son incest', James Twitchell notes, 'The most obscene and ferocious curse in the English language is "mother-fucker", which with gnomic concision expresses both social and familial outrage at a fever pitch'.[33] The powerful rejection in that curse expresses sexual repulsion towards mother–son incest but perhaps also suggests 'the subject's fear of his very own identity sinking irretrievably into the mother'[34] and a recognition of the symbolic threat incest poses to the patriarchal order: the undermining of paternal authority. Certainly in a film like *Bad Boy Bubby* (Rolf de Heer, 1993) we can see that outrage at work. 'Mam' (Claire Benito) is a truly terrifying creature. From the lies that keep Bubby (Nicholas Hope) incarcerated in a concrete bunker, through to her demands that he service her sexually and the sight of her large body almost smothering her son, her actions surely make her Barbara Creed's 'monstrous-feminine' incarnate: 'the abyss, the monstrous vagina, the origin of all life threatening to reabsorb what it once birthed'.[35]

Yet, mother–son incest is not always represented as abhorrent. For example, in both *Murmur of the Heart* (Louis Malle, 1971) and *Spanking the Monkey* (David O. Russell, 1994), the sexual relationship between mother and son develops out of enforced periods of dependence and growing intimacy that results in consensual sex. These relationships appear to offer the possibility of some form of fulfilment, a return to a kind of unity with the ideal mother. This idea of fulfilment and of comfort in the arms of a mother figure, who will love but also instruct, is part of the cinematic tradition of sexual liaisons with an older woman, for example in *Tea and Sympathy* (Vincente Minnelli, 1956), *The Graduate* (Mike Nichols, 1967), *Harold and Maude* (Hal Ashby, 1971), *Summer of '42* (Robert Mulligan, 1971), *Luna* (Bernardo Bertolucci, 1979) and *The Reader* (Stephen Daldry, 2008).

Similarly, *Ma mère* does not offer us a mother rendered comprehensible via a monstrous pathology, but neither is it an attempt to justify a deviant relationship. Instead, it is an example of what John Orr calls the free-fall movie, 'a narrative of downward movement in which the protagonist consciously chooses or risks the pattern of descent'.[36] Orr sees these as characteristic vehicles for a select coterie of French actresses, including Isabelle Huppert, where the lead female is caught in 'a schizophrenic oscillation between the romantic and the abject'.[37] The key here is that these are not melodramatic stories where events overtake the heroine. Rather, these heroines freely chose their degradation, their abjection. Although Orr does not write about *Ma mère*, this surely seems an apposite way of thinking about the character of Hélène, who cannot, or will not, stop herself from choosing to embrace transgression. Hélène pushes herself as far as she can go and allows herself to face the abyss, whatever its consequences. As Orr puts it, 'she welcomes descent if descent beckons'.[38]

Huppert is particularly associated with this kind of self-abasing character (her role in Michael Haneke's 2001 film *The Piano Teacher*, for example) and has developed an acting style that perfectly conveys her characters' frustrations with ordinary life and consciousness of the meaninglessness of existence. As McKibbin notes: 'Huppert so often lacks motivation. We notice that a sense of purpose that could give one's life meaning is replaced by a bored, petulant gesture that undermines the lives of others' and that 'with Huppert any notion of social progress, sexual prowess or general assertiveness is often a move towards self-destruction or emotional collapse'.[39] Existing in a state of anomie, Hélène does not seek to conform to norms of feminine desirability and, as Grønstad suggests, the film 'imagine[s] as well as image[s] female corporeality and desire differently [...] exploring an alternative rhetoric of lust and its complex transactions'.[40]

The most complex transaction of this alternative rhetoric explores the ways in which Hélène's sexuality is tied to her deviation from the ideal of motherhood and her knowing embrace of her own deviance. Hélène's lack of 'proper' maternal feeling for her son is signalled from the very start of the film; she hides when Pierre arrives home and does not take part in the general welcome of her son. Her behaviour is contrasted with the spontaneity of the housekeeper Marthe's warm embrace of Pierre and her motherly exclamations about how he has grown. In the early scenes, Hélène has no emotional connection to Pierre and when she does warm to him, it seems only so that she can hurt or humiliate him. Her repeated offers to go out with him are never followed through, leaving him disappointed at home and then, after his father's death, she finally takes him to a restaurant, where she tells him that she is a slut and a bitch. Despite his discomfort, Hélène tells him that he has to understand that part of herself and that he must love her for it. He is disgusted and leaves. We cut to him sobbing alone on the beach. When he returns to look through the restaurant window Hélène is making a spectacle of herself carousing with a group of drunken youths, and he is ashamed for her. Returning to the surf, his mother eventually joins him, drunk and laughing. She vomits beside him, making visible her abject-ness; he needs to realise just how bad she is, although she displays no shame and she wants none of his. Indeed, her education of Pierre is focused on ensuring that her son recognises the peculiarly relation-less status of her apathy and animosity; when she defines herself as a slut she is not rejecting that part of herself nor does she suggest the world might be unfair in designating her so. This notion of depravity draws on biblical understandings where sin affects all areas of being, penetrating the very core of the self so that everything is tainted. Pierre has to embrace all of his mother's wretchedness, as she already has.

Hélène does not limit his 'education' to recognition of her failures; Pierre must be made to understand that his father was disgusting too. If her version of her son's induction into adulthood is through debauchery, her first act of training Pierre is to orchestrate his annihilation of his father. He must learn that his parents are not just flawed but, by the standards of respectability, they are depraved. In the days after his father's death, Hélène asks Pierre to clean out his study. Knowing what he will find, she hands over the keys and tells him to keep what he wants, to throw out everything else.

His father's study is dirty, full of the detritus of a life interrupted, but worse than the piles of dirty plates and empty whisky-glasses is the stash of pornography and sex aids Pierre finds in the bureau. Flinging the magazines, dildos and other items onto the floor, Pierre masturbates over his father's collection. After orgasm, he urinates on the magazines and then smashes up the office. In this symbolic annihilation of his father, the Oedipal trope is made explicit: Pierre's sexual (and libertine) awakening comes at that moment. The boy's desire for his mother is clearly a failed Oedipal complex; instead of rejecting the mother and aligning himself with the father, which Freud claims is necessary for the foundation of civilisation, Pierre 'murders' his father and unleashes his own repressed desire for his mother. Her manipulation of the discovery of his father's porn implicates Hélène and perhaps provides the motivation for Pierre's act of masturbation. It is almost too much for him; when Robert rushes in, Pierre pleads with him, 'Don't tell Mom'. Of course, he need not have worried about his mother: she has fled the villa. Again, Marthe takes on the role of motherly comforter, telling him 'Don't worry. Just the three of us in peace. Robert and I will take good care of you. We'll call grandma and tell her you're going home'. But Pierre has moved on. In an act of defiance, he whistles as he walks past Robert and Marthe on his way to the beach, his nakedness clearly signalling his intentions to move beyond their notions of respectability.

The contrasts between Hélène and Marthe highlight the proper maternal role in the healthy sexual development of the child. Marthe attempts to protect Pierre, shielding him from the full dysfunction of his parents' relationship and seeking to rescue him from Hélène and her friends. For her part, Hélène takes the idea of the mother who concerns herself with how her child comes to adulthood to the extreme, turning on its head the usual mothering role of care, education and guidance towards independence and adulthood. The all-too-close engagements in any son's sexual education are evident in his mother forcing him to recognise his parents' 'shameful' sexual interests; making her friend available for his sexual initiation; observing as he loses his virginity; watching closely as he forces himself onto Réa, then attempting to make him watch her own sexual interaction with her; and her manipulation of his relationship with Hansi.

Within the narrative, we have little sense of who Hélène is. There are glimpses of a backstory, suggestions that Hélène married young, travelled with her husband to various European cities, that Pierre did not accompany them because his mother was incapable of looking after a child and that she has been unhappy, without explaining exactly why. Avoiding more detailed explanations is perhaps a precarious strategy, allowing sympathy for Hélène by hinting at deep and buried abuses. Just as possible is a more negative response to her character. Setting the film in the liminal space of a beach resort in Spain, in the anonymity and sterility of a rented villa, Honoré isolates Hélène; her life has no other purpose than the partying and general hedonism of the beach resort. This placelessness and the attendant purposelessness of her character does seem a kind of motive for Hélène's desires where, as Orr describes it, 'motive is opaque, and transformed into narrative mystery. Why transgress? Why go down? Why suffer? Why murder? There is a gap in our knowledge that can be filled by different answers; but to know milieu, which is largely transparent is not to know reason or cause, which is anything but'.[41]

Hélène is an ambiguous figure. In the novella it is very clear that she orchestrates Pierre's debauchery but in Honoré's film, she drifts, seemingly not in control although shown to be capable of manipulation. In one of the few scenes offering some explication of her past life and perhaps interior self, Hélène tells Pierre about her meeting with his father in the woods, which she presents as a form of rape occurring when she was underage, seemingly knowing that this will garner his sympathy. In his immediately rising to put his arms about her while murmuring 'Maman, maman', she succeeds in that response. Yet she goes on to add, 'No, I wish I were 13'. The ambiguity of this scene is important, playing upon the idea of this violation as the reason for her promiscuity, but her speedy acknowledgement that it is her fantasy, not the truth, snatches that explanation away. Similarly, the earlier scene that saw Hélène collapsed by the pool (interpreted by Pierre as his father having hit her) hints at violence as the cause of her emotional distance but, again, this explanation is not confirmed – indeed, is flatly denied by Marthe. While refusing to offer us any easily understood backstory might avoid the fixing of a single truth about Hélène's past that defines her in the present, it also leaves open an unhelpful focus on her self-assessment of herself as a 'bitch'. It may, as Shaviro observes:

> motivate the mother's suicide, at the climactic moment of sexual union with her son, as a consequence of obscure feelings of guilt, combined with the ennui that results from a life of sterile and loveless pleasures. Such moralism is diametrically opposed to Bataille's own sense of fatal impossibility, of pushing things to a point of total rupture. I don't think that Honoré means to be moralistic; but he's forced into it as a result of the diminished status of transgression in the world he depicts.[42]

There is a moralistic framing of women's sexuality in *Ma mère*, explicitly mouthed by Marthe, who, refusing her husband's sexual overtures, says 'You're just like them, disgusting'. Yet, to focus on this potential moralism as solely an effect of Honoré's exposition is to lose sight of a fundamental failure at the heart of Bataille's own philosophical musings on transgression. Bataille figures women's bodies as carriers or conduits for male transgression; women cannot transgress or reach ascendance themselves. Woman carries the burden of transgression. As Downing and Gillett observe, Bataille thinks of women in entirely patriarchal terms.[43] If Hélène carries the Bataille register, it is not just through dialogue but her aging body is also a key signifier of disgust. Her sexuality is the true horror, even as the story has been updated to the twenty-first century: it is signified through her lesbian encounters, her lack of heteronormative relations with men and the copious drinking she indulges in. Using an older actress to play Hélène (in the novella she is in her early 30s while in the film she is in her 40s) means that the intergenerational aspect of the central relationship is enhanced. More than this, it plays into the novella's sense of horror towards women's bodies and specifically their aging bodies. This is made explicit in one short but important scene. Hélène and Réa go to meet a man in his hotel room, he insults Hélène, rejecting her as a sexual partner. Hélène leaves the room to smoke and, left alone, she flashes a young boy on his bike, as if to confirm that she still has sexual allure. Hélène and her self-identification as a slut, a disgusting object, pays obeisance to Bataille's problematic attitude to women:

> Picture the surprise of anyone who did not know about it and who by some device witnessed unseen the passionate lovemaking of some woman who had struck him as particularly distinguished. He would think she was sick, just as mad dogs are sick. Just as if some mad bitch had usurped the personality of the dignified hostess a little while back.[44]

Throughout the film we are offered the incestuous through contrasts between older and younger bodies, the juxtaposition of women's bodies as both disgusting and beautiful. For Bataille, the body should be seductive and repulsive; transgressive desire requires disgust.[45] But in the context of this twenty-first-century adaptation, the focus on Hélène's aging body seems a dreary cliché.

And, of course, she must die. Unable to bear the burden of transgression, Hélène commits suicide while engaging in a sexual act with Pierre. Her final action (its motivations are left unexplained but suggest shame, regret, horror at her own debauchery) stands in stark contrast to

Grønstad's positive assessment of the film as presenting an alternative rhetoric of female desire.

Something About the Boy

The novella is told from Pierre's point of view. It is a story about Pierre's willingness to breach the incest taboo. Hélène is the means by which Pierre does this; he has to recognise his desire and disgust for his mother, to recognise that he is breaking the boundaries but going forward willingly. Thus, the film asks us to think in precisely those terms that Lynch posits as wrong: to see that the incested child has desires for the mother and wishes to act on them.[46] Huppert is attractive and waif-like and Garrel is physically larger; Pierre could overpower Hélène or simply walk away, contrasting Bad Boy Bubby and the throbbing physicality of his 'Mam'. Where Bubby is often terrified of his parent and her threatened punishments, Pierre seeks connection with Hélène. This is not a tale of physical coercion, at least not straightforwardly so.

Pierre's boyishness is emphasised in the film. Garrel's body is rangy, soft, youthful and lacks the worked muscles of typical Hollywood teenage stars. His long fringe flops over his eyes, he is pale and his face is sulky. Of course he has also been estranged from his mother so that his attachment to her seems particularly childlike; he runs around the villa searching for Hélène and crying out 'Maman, maman!', emphasising his innocence and his victimisation at the hands of his cool mother. When he dresses in a suit to go out with her at night, it is inappropriately 'grown-up' for an evening at a tourist-resort nightclub, signalling a naïve attempt at sophistication. In the early part of the film, he appears to have no sexual interests of his own. They are awakened by his mother and her friend Réa and he is at their mercy. His first sexual initiations are a mix of humiliation and excitement: the infamous finger-sniffing in the back seat of a taxi; being tricked out of the promised grope of Réa's body when she moves away to be replaced by an older woman whose grotesqueness causes him visible disquiet; and finally, Réa's deflowering of him on the floor of the mall while he is almost comatose. Each of these emphasise his powerlessness in the face of an older seductress. Even so, Pierre is not deterred. Returning home, he fires Marthe and Robert, presenting his rear with the order 'Slap my arse!', both a childish insult and an assertion of independence to the two adults who have sought to care for and protect him.

Having rid the house of the moral arbiters, the scene is set for his first engagement with his mother. Pierre enters his mother's bedroom. Hélène, Réa and another man are sprawled across the bed in the aftermath of their orgy. Pierre gazes at his mother and Hansi attempts to distract him. She wakes Réa, and then Pierre, now naked, mounts Réa from behind. They struggle a little, then Réa submits and Pierre, while pumping away on Réa, begins to move towards his mother. He bites and kisses her leg. She wakes and, half sitting up, she watches as Pierre begins to orgasm. He looks back at her and then closes his eyes. As he orgasms he hides his face in a gesture of shame. The scene is intercut with Hansi's watchful face. A further cut reveals Hélène caressing Réa's body and, as she does so, she looks over to Pierre sitting sulking on the side of the bed. Purposefully, Hélène adjusts her nightgown so that her buttocks are exposed to Pierre's now attentive gaze, well aware that she has his attention. Hansi gets up, crosses the room to Pierre, covers his eyes and cradles his head. The scene is fascinating because of the ways in which it foregrounds the difference between the 'act of sex' and the experience of 'eroticism' in Bataille's formulation of transgression. In coupling with Réa, Pierre is sublimating his desire for his mother. As he overwhelms Réa he gazes at his mother, but it does not bring the sought-for Bataillean 'continuity'. Instead, it emphasises his sense of 'discontinuity'; he is still an individual and hence his sulking, his shame, his disappointment.

Thus, what is important here is that Pierre understands that he *wants* his mother and *chooses* to transgress; Hansi's attempts to shield his gaze from Hélène's congress with Réa highlights the judgments others will make of his desire. The scene cuts to Pierre running down the street, railing against God and respectability and shouting his intentions to live with the consequences. Pierre is aware of the extent of his desire and he is both repulsed and fascinated by the 'anguish' his actions will produce. Within the societal contexts of taboo, eroticism is inextricably linked to the transgression of prohibitions; the prohibition itself establishes the attractions of the acts it forbids. As Bataille wrote, 'The bounds set on freedom of action give a fresh fillip to the irresistible animal impulse'.[47]

Watching the film and finding it affecting is not necessarily about wanting to share those desires, nor to validate them. It is about being willing to acknowledge their messy human significance and the possible philosophical interest they might have for thinking about current sexual mores. It is a form of filmmaking that demands critical self-awareness in its viewers, offering no easy narrative resolutions and its effect is that it disturbs, disgusts, upsets and unsettles.

Drawing on Shaviro, Kendall suggests that *Ma mère* foregrounds 'the contradictory status of transgression in our era of global consumer capitalism', that even as the film offers us a ' "subversive", "shocking" and "taboo-busting" portrayal of mother–son incest, sadomasochism and necrophilia, it does so in terms that are in keeping with market values, and promotes such transgression to an already carefully identified and differentiated target audience'.[48] Indeed, this is one of the most repeated criticisms of the film: that it offers itself to a particularly niche interest, an audience of 'art film' appreciators who can recognise its cleverness while at the same time finding its 'eye-rolling' moments sufficiently amusing that they can deflect their attention away from the 'horror' of incestuous desires to an appreciation of the filmic qualities of its presentation. It is a cinematic form and accompanying viewing perspective that has come to be understood as offering very 'French' pleasures, where Frenchness might be described as:

> a cover for potentially dangerous and arousing experiences. [As] an art-house excuse, so that middle-class elites can get to see and relish things that aren't 'safe' for ordinary folks (rather in the manner that nineteenth-century museums allowed rich patrons to access their pornography for 'research', while damning its public circulation).[49]

Assessments of this kind often seem to seek to isolate such films from popular culture, to insist that they are too pretentious to participate in wider discussions or understandings of sexuality, their attendant concerns or popular moralising. Measuring *Ma mère* for its ability to move beyond representing commodified sex is a problem as it presupposes that there is nothing now to shock in representations of sex, no feelings that are unsettled or explored in this kind of film, that it is shock for shock's sake:

a vacuous form of connection. Yet, it seems to me that this is a film that is of interest, it intervenes in particular considerations of appropriate sexual relationships and who can have desires for whom. To think of this film only in terms of it living up to its Bataillean legacy is to insist on it having a particular message or purpose (not to say that Honoré does not) but in coming to the film, do viewers?

Given that the film is based on the Bataille short story, it is little wonder that it offers the 'cultural package of transcendence through perverse sexuality that is now a staple ingredient of the high French philosophical and literary canon'.[50] Yet, the film does have unsettling qualities that are more than simply about shock. It exposes the 'enigma of incest' not as the answer to the riddle of character motivation, as is often the case in much fiction and cinema, but as 'intricate absurdities'.[51] Making sense of characters' behaviours and motivations is a process of self-examination and questioning for viewers. That is why Huppert is such an compelling choice here, because she refuses to offer an instantly readable characterisation of Hélène. Part of the pleasure of this film lies in the effort her performance demands in thinking and arguing about what lies behind her actions. The same is true of Garrel.

Retained from Bataille is the idea that the taboo actually invites us to seek out the pleasures of transgressing it, watching a beautiful and youthful body discovering what it is to be sexual, exploring those possibilities but at the same time worrying about what that means. In this sense, I agree with Martin Barker that this has not 'been "Hollywoodized". It isn't glossy, easy, sumptuous, instantly climactic. It's complicated, messy and all too human'.[52] Ways of thinking about incest are limited by current constructions of 'the incestuous parent'. The demonisation of men and women who engage in intra-familial and intergenerational sex is often justified through mobilisation of feminist accounts of harm, sexual abuse and victimisation, as well as through recourse to ideas of 'natural' feelings for children that must never stray into the territory of the sexual. This complex and ambivalent film, in which the relationship between sexual desire and abuse is, at best, murky, and the deliberate presentation of mother–son romantic and sexual intimacy against a backdrop of the licensed thrill-seeking of the holiday resort certainly makes for uncomfortable viewing but, nonetheless, it is all the more beguiling for that. Their relationship may be deviant and criminal but in its representation as purposeful it offers a view of the 'sensualities of defilement'.[53] Without the backstory that might explain their mutual desire, we have to entertain the idea that mother and son become lovers because they *want* to, because they believe they will enjoy it and that theirs is a truly existential transgressive act, wilful and intended.

Notes

1. Steven Shaviro, 'Come, come, Georges: Georges Bataille's *Story of the Eye* and *Ma mère*', *Artforum International* 43/9 (May 2005).
2. James Quandt, 'Flesh and blood: sex and violence in recent French cinema', *Artforum International* 42/6 (February 2004), p. 126. Key titles are Gaspar Noe's *Seul contre tous/I Stand Alone* (1998) and *Irréversible* (2002), François Ozon's *Les Amants criminels/Criminal Lovers* (1999), Catherine Breillat's *Romance* (1999), Trinh Thi's *Baise-Moi* (2000), Claire Denis' *Trouble Every Day* (2001), Bruno Dumont's *Twentynine Palms* (2003).
3. Richard Falcon, 'Reality is too shocking', *Sight and Sound* 9/1 (1999), p. 11.
4. Asbjørn Grønstad, *Screening the Unwatchable: Spaces of Negation in Post-millennial Art Cinema* (Basingstoke: Palgrave Macmillan, 2012), p. 9.
5. Asbjørn Grønstad, 'Abject desire: Anatomie de l'enfer and the unwatchable', *Studies in French Cinema* 6/3 (2006), pp. 163–4.
6. Eric Henderson, '*Ma mère*', *Slant Magazine*, 12 May 2005. Available at http://www.slantmagazine.com/film/print.php?rid=1511 (accessed 22 March 2012).
7. Jessica Winter, 'The Mother and the Whore', *The Village Voice*, 3 May 2005. Available at http://www.slantmagazine.com/film/print.php?rid=1511 (accessed 22 March 2012).
8. Stephen Holden, 'A young man's education in mom's hedonistic ways', *New York Times*, 13 May 2005. Available at http://movies.nytimes.com/2005/05/13/movies/13mere.html (accessed 22 March 2012).
9. Ginette Vincendeau, 'Review of *Ma mère*', *Sight & Sound* (March 2005), p. 62.
10. Nick Rees-Roberts, *French Queer Cinema* (Edinburgh: Edinburgh University Press, 2008), p. 100.
11. Tina Kendall, 'Reframing Bataille: on tacky spectatorship in the new European extremism', in Tanya Horeck and Tina Kendall (eds), *The New Extremism in Cinema: From France to Europe* (Edinburgh: Edinburgh University Press, 2011), p. 47.
12. Grønstad, *Screening the Unwatchable*, p. 106.
13. Tony McKibbin, 'The chaos of the organs: Isabelle Huppert's reverse pygmalionism', *Studies in French Cinema* 5/1 (2005), p. 20.
14. Shaviro, 'Come, come, Georges'.
15. Georges Bataille, *Erotism: Death and Sensuality* (New York: Walker and Company, 1962).

16. Shaviro, 'Come, come, Georges'.
17. Kendall, 'Reframing Bataille', p. 53.
18. Christophe Honoré, 'An interview with Christophe Honoré', *TLA Releasing* (2004). Available at http://www.tlareleasing.com/mamere/content/christophe_honore.cfm (accessed 22 March 2012).
19. Claude Levi-Strauss, *The Elementary Structures of Kinship* (London: Eyne and Spottiswoode, 1961), p. 41.
20. James L. Peacock and A. Thomas Kirsch, *The Human Direction: An Evolutionary Approach to Social and Cultural Anthropology* (New York: Appleton-Century-Crofts, 1970), p. 100.
21. Emile Durkheim, *Incest: The Nature and Origin of the Taboo*, translated by Edward Sagarin (New York: Lyle Stuart, 1963), p. 5. Originally published 1897.
22. James B. Twitchell, *Forbidden Partners: The Incest Taboo in Modern Culture* (New York: Columbia University Press, 1987), p. ix.
23. R. Danielle Egan and Gail Hawkes, 'Imperiled and perilous: exploring the history of childhood sexuality', *Journal of the Historical Sociology* 21/4 (2008), p. 365.
24. Juul Gooren, 'Deciphering the ambiguous menace of sexuality for the innocence of childhood', *Critical Criminology* 19/1 (March 2011), pp. 32–3.
25. Gillian Harkins, *Everybody's Family Romance: Reading Incest in Neoliberal America* (Minneapolis: University of Minnesota Press, 2009), p. xii.
26. Katie Roiphe, 'Making the incest scene', *Harper's*, November (1995), p. 68.
27. Ibid.
28. Joan Driscoll Lynch, 'Incest discourse and cinematic representation', *Journal of Film and Video*, 54/2–3 (2002), p. 43.
29. Kathleen Rowe Karlyn, ' "Too close for comfort": *American Beauty* and the incest motif', *Cinema Journal* 44/1 (2004), pp. 69–93.
30. Lynch, 'Incest discourse and cinematic representation', p. 54.
31. Kendall, 'Reframing Bataille', p. 48.
32. Cas Wouters, 'Balancing sex and love since the 1960s sexual revolution', in Mike Featherstone (ed.), *Love and Eroticism* (London: Sage, 1999), p. 189.
33. Twitchell, *Forbidden Partners*, p. 54.
34. Julia Kristeva, *Powers of Horror: An Essay on Abjection* (New York: Columbia University Press, 1982), p. 64.
35. Barbara Creed, '*Alien* and the monstrous-feminine', in Annette Kuhn (ed.), *Alien Zone: Cultural Theory and Contemporary Science Fiction Cinema* (London: Verso, 1990), p. 134.
36. John Orr, 'Stranded: stardom and the free-fall movie in French cinema 1985–2003', *Studies in French Cinema* 4/2 (2004), p. 105.
37. Ibid.
38. Ibid., p. 108.
39. McKibbin, 'The chaos of the organs', p. 17.
40. Grønstad, *Screening the Unwatchable*, p. 85.
41. Orr, 'Stranded', p. 109.

42. Shaviro, 'Come, come, Georges'.

43. Lisa Downing and Robert Gillett, 'Georges Bataille at the avant-garde of queer theory?: transgression, perversion and death drive', *Nottingham French Studies* 50/3 (2011), pp. 88–102.

44. Bataille, *Erotism*, p. 106.

45. Fred Botting and Scott Wilson (eds), *The Bataille Reader* (Oxford: Blackwell, 1997), p. 253.

46. See Lynch, 'Incest discourse and cinematic representation'.

47. Bataille, *Erotism*, p. 212.

48. Kendall, 'Reframing Bataille', p. 46.

49. Martin Barker, ' "Typically French"?: Mediating screened rape to British audiences', in Dominique Russell (ed.), *Rape in Art Cinema* (New York: Continuum, 2010), p. 146.

50. Rees-Roberts, *French Queer Cinema*, p. 97.

51. Bataille, *Erotism*, pp. 197, 201.

52. Barker, 'Typically French', p. 158.

53. Jack Katz, *Seductions of Crime: Moral and Sensual Attractions of Doing Evil* (New York: Basic Books, 1988), p. 312.

IV

Sexual Infidelity: Adapting the Deviant, Re-imagining the Perverse

12

Perverting the Marquis De Sade in *Quills*

Sarah Taylor-Harman

Denounced by psychiatrist Richard von Krafft-Ebing as a 'monster', condemned by Andrea Dworkin as a 'rapist and writer' and reappraised by Angela Carter as a 'pornographer', the Marquis de Sade's reputation always precedes him.[1] Indeed, Sade's work and life, and sadomasochism (SM) more broadly, has divided feminist thought, pitching radical feminist anti-SMers (such as Dworkin) against more liberal, 'sex-positive' feminists who see the practice as subverting, rather than enforcing the hetero-patriarchy. Furthermore, while post-structural feminists including Simone de Beauvoir and Luce Irigaray and others such as Geoffrey Gorer, Georges Bataille, Roland Barthes and Marcel Hénaff have attempted to rescue Sade from the 'terror' of second-wave feminism and media moral panics, by focusing on a 'non-gendered' political and philosophical reading, the Marquis' legendary status as the father of Sadism endures nonetheless.[2]

Sade, of course, has only himself to blame. In stories such as *The 120 Days of Sodom* (1785), *Justine* (1791), *Philosophy in the Bedroom* (1795) and *Juliette* (1797), Sade catalogued and explored sexual perversion including rape, sodomy, child abuse and sexual violence. This exploration extended to his own criminal, sexually perverse practice, such as the false imprisonment, whipping and reputed candle wax torture of Rose Keller in 1768 and the (non-lethal) poisoning of Marseilles prostitutes four years later. Sade remains the spectre of sadistic sexual perversion, haunting the collective cultural conscience at large. While Pier Paolo Pasolini's adaptation and political allegory *Salò, or the 120 Days of Sodom* (1975) – 'banned' until 2000 in the UK – undoubtedly remains Sade's most notorious contribution to cinematic history, it is by no means the sole, or necessarily most enduring, example. In fact, the Marquis' on-screen presence has proliferated across a number of genres, from erotic adaptations and horror appropriations to dramatised biopics conflating both modes.

Following the Obscene Publications Act amendment of 1959, Sade's previously banned texts returned to print and circulation, now legally sanctioned according to their 'artistic merit'. This included not only what survived of Sade's vast corpus of work but further opened the door to pornographic cinematic adaptations newly legitimised by their association with his artistic yet sexually deviant novels. Yet these were, in the main, far from today's standard of hardcore texts and still had to adhere to the strict standards of the British Board of Film Classification to avoid criminalisation.[3] This infamously resulted in a softer 'English cut', enabling the films to achieve certification and thus distribution in the UK. Nonetheless, the floodgates had been opened to a tidal wave of Sadean pictures, such as the prolific pornographer and cult film hero Jess Franco's *Marquis De Sade: Justine* (1969), *Marquis de Sade's 'Philosophy in the Boudoir'* (1970) and the loosely inspired *Die Marquise von Sade* (1976) and *Justine and the Whip* (1979). Sade's reputation as deviant pornographer was thus cemented on screen.

Yet, it is not only Sade's sexually subversive writing that has penetrated cinematic history. He came back to haunt in such horror films as: *The Skull* (Freddie Francis, 1965), in which the Marquis' skull is stolen by a grave-robbing phrenologist and wreaks havoc upon those whose hands into which it falls; *Night Terrors* (Tobe Hooper, 1993), in which a descendent of Sade lures a teenage girl into a sadomasochistic cult and series of murders;

and Anthony Hickox's comic horror *Waxwork* (1988), in which Sade is re-animated in a collection of the 'most evil beings'. Interestingly in the latter, Sade is the only non-fictional character in this line-up that includes such iconic monstrous figures as the Phantom of the Opera, Count Dracula, the Invisible Man and Jack the Ripper (as part mythological character). Sade's inclusion in this grouping clearly articulates a mythical status and presence within the cultural imaginary as torturer, executioner and, to return to Krafft-Ebing's diagnosis, sadistic monster. *Waxwork*, *Night Terrors* and *The Skull* were far from commercial successes and were relegated to the annals of B-movie cult history.

Conversely, Sade has also inhabited the highbrow genre of dramatic adaptations, which in turn fall into two not-altogether-distinct categories: theatrical biopics and romantic historical bio-dramas. Peter Brook's critically lauded *Marat/Sade* (1967) is undoubtedly the most prestigious of this former category, adapted from Peter Weiss's Royal Shakespeare Company production. More recently, Philip Kaufman's *Quills* (2000) – adapted from a stage play – has straddled this theatrical legacy alongside the heritage styled fiction dramas such as *Dark Prince: Intimate Tales of Marquis De Sade* (Gwyneth Gibby, 1996), which romanticise Sade as an erotic hero of feminine desire. But how does such a filmic text reconcile the differing modes of adaptation and appropriation? How can Sade's infamy and legacy of sexual perversity – rooted in these multiple arenas and genres – co-exist alongside a highbrow, romantic re-imagining? What figure, or figures, of Sade result? Rather than the contemporary concern surrounding the mainstreaming of SM practice and/or identity, this chapter contends that *Quills* goes one step further and attempts to romanticise, rehabilitate and mainstream the Marquis, through a trajectory that ultimately takes the sadism out of Sade, elevating instead this figure as the tortured artist *par excellence*. By filtering and negotiating the perverse through character foils, the Marquis is written impotent, but for the power of his quill. Yet this finds resistance not only from critical reception but also fan reinterpretation, which negotiates *Quills'* narrative confines, re-inscribing the figure of Sade as sexual guru. Perversion here thus occupies multitudinous roles in a plethora of re-envisions, each of which construct and are ultimately bound by the contemporary politics of perversity.

'He's a writer, not a madman': Constructing Sade in *Quills*

Based on Doug Wright's Obie award-winning stage play and adapted screenplay and with an estimated budget of $13,500,000, *Quills* was a moderate success at the box office, grossing a total of $17,989,227 worldwide. Set shortly after the French Revolution, the film follows the struggle of Sade (Geoffrey Rush) against the authority of Church and State from within the walls of Charenton Asylum as he fights to write and publish his prose. Under the governance of the naive and rather ineffectual Abbé de Coulmier (Joaquin Phoenix), *Quills* presents to us a Sade whose perversity, we are told, makes him one-eyed in the land of the blind, a land extending beyond the walls of the asylum itself. Bridging both realms – the long, twisting darkened halls of Charenton and its locked cells, and the newly literate Parisian public hungry for Sade's stories – is the laundress Madeleine LeClerc (Kate Winslet). Madeleine smuggles his work out, first on parchment and later on his own sheets. While the narrative consists of many mirroring thematic strands involving character foils, it is this relationship between Sade and Madeleine (indeed pairings of the two adorn the film's promotional material) that is key, leading to their demise (see Fig. 12.1). With the unwitting assistance of the priest's literacy lessons, Madeleine is able to scribe what we are told is Sade's last tale through a 'Chinese whispers' style chain of cell-to-cell communication. So inflamed by the sexually violent material of the story, another inmate, Bouchon (Stephen Marcus), violently murders the laundress, enacting the content of Sade's tale. Overcome by grief, the Marquis opts for suicide, biting and choking upon the priest's rosary.[4] The film's dénouement sees the inmates all working in a Charenton printing press, publishing the Marquis de Sade's tomes under the guidance of the new asylum governor Dr Royer-Collard (Michael Caine).

While nominated for three Academy Awards, including Best Actor in a Leading Role for Geoffrey Rush's portrayal of Sade, the film's release met with a mixed critical response, particularly on the grounds of factual inaccuracy. As Neil Schaeffer asserts in his *Guardian* review, titled 'Perverting De Sade':

> What is the harm in misrepresenting the true nature of De Sade's life and career? [...] if a biographer makes a mish-mash

Fig. 12.1. The Marquis de Sade (Geoffrey Rush) seduces Madeleine (Kate Winslet) in *Quills* (Philip Kaufman, Fox Searchlight Pictures, 2000) – this pairing featured prominently in promotional material

of his subject, there is hell to pay. If a movie does the same, there could be talk of Academy awards for all concerned, as there has been in this case.[5]

At the time of his review, Schaeffer was still promoting his biography of Sade, hence his ire and defence of the biographer's sacred role as truth-teller.[6] However, the assertion that *Quills* perverts Sade invokes a powerful debate that has long been central to the field of adaptation studies: the importance of fidelity to its source and, thus, authenticity.[7] For screenwriter Doug Wright, this question of factual inaccuracy versus the 'true' nature of Sade's life and work was irrelevant to his vision of the Marquis:

> It was always my intention to write a story about Sade which drew on equal parts of his life and his fiction. So the movie is not a scrupulously accurate biographical account by any means. In the opening tale that the Marquis tells, he begins by saying: 'Dear Readers, I have a naughty little tale to tell. Plucked from the pages of history, true but tarted up and guaranteed

to stimulate the senses'. That's what we've done. We've plucked his story from history and tarted it up a great deal. Our own embellishments, our own shocking twists of plot. But it's all in an effort to be true to his spirit.[8]

Being 'true' to his spirit while fictionalising his story stands at odds with the marketing of the UK DVD release; the tagline reads 'The story of the infamous Marquis de Sade'. Yet Wright's line is further carried by the director Kaufman, who enthusiastically states that 'by the end [...] the actual boring biopic approach has been forsaken'.[9]

Instead, *Quills* shows us Sade as 'a writer, not a madman', as Madeleine describes him; 'writing is involuntary, like the beating of my heart. My constant erection!' Sade proclaims. Sade as artist, then, is foregrounded, a reconfiguration most clearly asserted when Sade escapes his Charenton cell, only to rush to his inmates to show them his newest work. For other critics however, the historical inaccuracies and debates over Sade's (mis)representation did not detract from the success of the film via Rush's portrayal. As Anthony Lane asserted in his review in *The New Yorker*:

> *Quills* should be seen, simply for the presence of Geoffrey Rush. Of all the lies perpetrated by the film, his alone will win you over; in place of the Marquis de Sade, perhaps the most wearisome of revolutionary writers, we have a charming combination of scoundrel, flirt, dandy, nudist, and wit.[10]

Indeed, as Lane implies, there is undoubtedly some disparity both in how the film as (non)biopic was conceived and received. This is referred to in the DVD commentary, which is largely focused upon the realism, or 'truth', of Rush's portrayal. As the director asserts, 'Geoffrey researched the Marquis de Sade extensively, and read his major works, read copious numbers of biographies of Sade and even consulted a renowned Australian psychiatrist to get a formal diagnosis of the man'.[11] Yet, while Rush's process of becoming Sade is clearly located within historical research, and is thus legitimised and authenticated, Wright's addition of fictionalised foils further problematises this question of historical fidelity versus history 'true but tarted up'.

For the makers of *Quills*, then, Sade's story is less about historical fact and more about art, violence and affect. While 'the Marquis was never actually accused of murder but various literary critics have suggested that his work is so potent and so toxic that it has inspired others to kill', Wright explains, 'we see [the fictional character of] Bouchon so inflamed by the action on stage that he begins to imitate it. The film hopes to ask the question, does violent art in our culture actually induce unstable minds to commit violent acts?'.[12] Here too lies a point of contradiction. On the one hand, characters stand in support of the anti-censorship position; 'If I wasn't such a bad woman on the page, I couldn't be such a good woman in life', Madeleine explains. Sade too asserts of his work, 'It's a fiction, not a moral treatise'. On the other hand, the narrative also departs from this position, aligning the characters' actions with direct influence from Sade's pages. This leaves little room to question such a complex ideological consideration regarding the potency of sexually violent texts, their consumption and potential impact upon the audience. By portraying Sade as the tortured genius artist, and by displacing the sadistic, violent, and indeed sexual, acts upon the character of Bouchon, Sade emerges romanticised and sanitised. Bouchon's appearance as the masked executioner of Mademoiselle Renard (Diana Morrison) – 'a ravishing, young aristocrat whose sexual proclivities ran the gamut from winsome to bestial' – to the murder of Madeleine, clearly aligns him with the narrative's ideological position on Sade and his work. Such a treatment of perversity thus obfuscates Sade, creating by contrast an ultimately aged, impotent 'fool'.

It is clear that this romanticisation and sanitisation of Sade is most overt in his relationship with Madeleine. Schaeffer notes:

> [He] apparently did not take sexual advantage of [Madeleine]. However, De Sade's last journal makes it clear that he had been having a regular sexual liaison with the 18-year-old chambermaid from her early teens until the week before he died.[13]

Certainly it would seem that, by rewriting Madeleine's character as an adult woman, her relationship with Sade offers the potential for unproblematic on-screen eroticism. The film's depiction of their relationship, while flirtatious, is ultimately sexually harmless. As Elisabeth Ladenson argues, Sade 'demonstrates his love for laundress Kate Winslet by not having sex with her'.[14] This is a fact seemingly born out in the film's exchange between Sade and Coulmier following Madeleine's death and preceding the Marquis' fictional suicide. In this scene, Sade attempts to avoid admitting that he indeed loved her, sobbing as Coulmier explains that she died a virgin: 'It's no secret that you loved her', Coulmier asserts. However, as Ladenson explains, this not only seeks to position the re-imagined Sade of Quills as a heteronormative hero of romantic love, but further works to construct a Marquis who 'talks a good game but refuses to engage in actual sex acts'. 'Sade, this Sade', he goes on to note, 'is the perfect figure for our time, the incarnation of an abstract ideal of transgression, purged of content'.[15]

While Sade's sexuality is constrained within his role as self-disciplined libertine guru, as Anette Insdorf notes in her study of Kaufman as auteur, the narrative also 'elaborates on the triangle so often found in Kaufman's films [...] rather than merely romantic, the form conveys a philosophical tension among the three "points" of priest, scientist, and artist'.[16] This triangle is instead, rather than merely philosophical, a romantic and eroticised process of libidinal displacement and projection. Wright's narrative offers a complementary cast of characters through which to refract the many facets of Sade, from 'the scientist' Royer-Collard's sexually violent relationship with his child bride Simone (Amelia Warner) to Coulmier's necrophilic fantasy of, in essence, fucking Madeleine back to life. These examples, along with the rewriting of Madeleine as an adult, obfuscate the perverse nature of the real Marquis de Sade's desires. Just as Bouchon acts as a foil by which to unproblematically displace the violent elements of Sade's character, the figures of Coulmier and Royer-Collard, the priest and the scientist, act as vehicles for Sade's own reconfigured sexuality. The resulting Sade in Wright's re-imagining is not only 'purged of content' but purged of sexual deviancy. Yet, it is exactly these narrative tensions of eroticism, deconstructed and reconstructed sexuality, which would offer fans a lens through which to re-imagine and re-write the Marquis de Sade once more.

Fans, Fan Fiction and Fantasies of Desire: Adapting *Quills'* Marquis de Sade

Cultural studies has long since been fascinated with fandom and how it may subvert, or ultimately reinforce, dominant ideologies and messages. Fan fiction, the fan practice or labour of creating new narratives inspired by favourite texts, characters and/or the 'canonical universe' of said text, is an ideal focus for the examination and understanding thereof of fan activity and their relationship to the text. That fan fiction has been seen as a practice predominantly undertaken by women demarcates it as a realm in which gender politics can be explored, as well as potentially corrected by its (assumed female) author, and this is particularly so within the categories of romance and erotica, being that this is the terrain of traditional female authorship. Central to this lies the 'slash' genre, which takes its name from the '/' symbol that separated the names of Spock and Captain Kirk first studied in Camille Bacon-Smith's 1992 study of *Star Trek* fanfics.[17] Slash fictions have been traditionally theorised as a subversive space for sexually transgressive romantic pairings, although the politics of a homoerotic pairing as a projected locale for a specifically feminine authored desire is focus for contemporary debate.[18] More recently, it has been extended to include the genre of 'femslash', yet comparatively little attention has been paid to the seemingly heteronormative area of 'het fics'.[19]

Of the 41 English-language fan-authored *Quills* 'fics' published at fanfiction.net, and uploaded between 2001 and 2007, 22 (52 per cent) can be considered erotic narratives.[20] Of these fictions, an overwhelming 77 per cent (17 fics) feature a heterosexual, or 'het', pairing most popularly between Sade and Madeleine (7 fics, 41 per cent) and closely followed by Coulmier and Madeleine (6 fics, 35 per cent). It is this former group that will be examined in the following discussion. These re-imaginings of Sade mobilise, and have a clear understanding of, current sexual politics and are crucial in relation to both *Quills'* paratexts and to the contemporary figure of Sade himself.

The fics differ from those traditionally studied both through their heterosexual pairings and to a lesser extent their fidelity to the source text rather than, for instance, utilising an Alternate Universe (AU) narrative framework. As Brigid Cherry succinctly explains, AU 'is a form of fan fiction where canonical elements of the original text are changed, allowing writers to explore different settings, plot developments or character relationships'.[21] Contrastingly, the *Quills* het fics do not seek to liberate Sade from the literal prison within which he is contained but instead write to free his libido from the confines of the film's narrative, while remaining faithful to its settings, plot developments and *heterosexual* character relationships. The fact that *Quills* fan fiction writers have largely elected not to rewrite Sade may well problematise traditional theorisations of erotic fan fiction as offering transgressive resistance by subverting the canon. As such, these fan-authored narratives downplay Sade's perversions, often displacing them onto the body of Madeleine. While this is in keeping with *Quills'* own construction of Sade, the appropriation of real and imagined scenes from *Quills'* in the fanfics works to construct him through a differing socio-political framework.

In the 2003 fanfic *Leading the Blind* by Furious Angel, the Sade of *Quills* and his lover Madeleine engage in a consensual sadomasochistic (SM) relationship, in which he is portrayed both as 'a man of control, and an experienced sensualist'.[22] Certainly this portrayal seems to be in keeping with *Quills'* construction of Sade as romantic hero and, as such, the fic enjoys a textual fidelity, expanding upon the characters' coy flirtation in the film. This is undoubtedly furthered in the culmination of the narrative in which Sade uses Madeleine's body with quill and wine as a canvas upon which to write his next work of art. Just as in *Quills* then, *Leading the Blind* privileges the construction of Sade as artiste rather than as sexual sadist. This is a recurrent theme in *Quills* fan fiction, as *Elusive Love* by Sadeness explores:

> On the cold stone ... spread your legs ... lie still ... you'll be my finest work, my pet,' he whispered, his hand combing her hair back. 'Work, Marquis?' Madelaine [sic] breathed, her naked breasts rising and falling with her excitement. 'Oh yess [sic] ...' he hissed, taking the splinter and impaling it deeply in a vein in his forearm [...] his hands roamed over her flesh, sensitizing her body, inciting a pleasure in her far greater than any sexual mechanics could ever achieve.[23]

Not only does *Elusive Love* introduce a more extreme eroticism than *Leading the Blind*, but it further ratifies a fidelity to Sade's work through the themes of bodily disruption and haematolagnia (blood play). As Marcel Hénaff notes, Sade's texts are 'hallucinated by sex and blood, making sex and blood run gratuitously through the narrative, relating blood to nothing outside themselves, and formulating this self-sufficiency as the blunt fact of sexual pleasure'.[24] While this certainly recalls the scene from *Quills* in which Sade, deprived of quill and ink, uses his own blood to pen his next story, the use of blood in *Elusive Love* could also be, conversely to Hénaff's assertion, read as metaphor. Sade's aristocratic blood herein lifts Madeleine above her working-class origins as laundress to become, by virtue of his sanguinity and artistry, his 'finest work'.[25] This in turn mirrors the description of Madeleine becoming his 'masterpiece' in *Leading the Blind*, elevating her body from the corporeal to the 'divine'. This phrase, as well as implying a lack of subjectivity in Madeleine as becoming Sade's object – with its associations of BDSM, to be 'owned' – may well additionally attempt to collapse Sade's writing with his sexual practice, for here her body bridges both realms. Furthermore, Sade's masterly instructions ('lie down ... spread your legs ... lie still') restore the Marquis to a position of both power and control in line with the traditional role of the sadist. Yet, I would argue that the controlled violence of the scene eroticises *both* characters as undergoing a sadomasochistic experience and as such they are drawn equally within the power dynamics of the situation. This would inform Sadeness' next fic, *Sub Secreto*, which foregrounds Sade as sexual sadist 'guru' – or indeed sexpert – through a hurt/comfort (h/c) framework, over his thus far usual construction as genius artist that is privileged in the film. By departing from *Quills'* original narrative, *Sub Secreto* differs in it attempts to liberate Sade from the ideological confines of his internment.[26]

The concept of hurt/comfort (or Hurt/comfort if the former dominates the narrative over the latter) can be employed to explain fan fiction wherein one character is hurt and the other provides comfort. As Judith May Fathallah notes in 'H/c and me: an autoethnographic account of a troubled love affair', the traditional theorisation of such fictions, as set forth by Bacon-Smith, closes down any potential for pleasure. Instead these approaches, she argues, pathologise the reader/writer as replicating dominant power ideologies of violence and inequality. Yet, Fathallah further states that h/c narratives are only truly problematic when the character hurt is female, which she perceives as 'uncomfortable, and too close to home'.[27] This would certainly seem to mirror the long history of feminist debates waged over the feminine masochist body as resistive or transgressive site, versus dominant ideology echo chamber.[28,29] Indeed, as Alex Dymock has noted about female submission, 'femsub is broken too', inseparable from 'sexual compliance, compliance not only with the wishes and desires of another, but with the assimilation of feminine masochism into the system of *heteronormativity itself*.[30] Hurt/comfort's traditional location within homoerotic slash, I would argue then, obfuscates these correlative debates by ensconcing BDSM desire within an egalitarian and ultimately depoliticised system of safety and comfort. But do these *Quills* het fics actually offer any alternative?

Sub Secreto attempts to navigate these complex sexual politics of female submission. After being flogged by Royer-Collard for visiting Coulmier's room late in the night (a point of narrative fidelity), Madeleine calls upon the Marquis in his cell for comfort, and an implied masochistic display of her wounds, and thus the pain she has undergone. The characters are immediately established as located within an equal power paradigm: 'She hesitated. "I question your motives, Marquis, not your expertise". "If it makes you feel any better, dearest, you yourself has [sic] stated that you could easily overwhelm me should a struggle ensue".[31] Again, however, this works to reinforce notions of class difference between the two characters; hers is a power entrenched in her physicality – the working-class labouring body – his the power of intellectual and aristocratic privilege. This in turn informs the power dynamics of their sadomasochist student/teacher relationship:

> Perhaps [...] you do not wish to admit that you actually enjoyed the fine edge between pleasure and pain, hmm? I only mourn the fact Doctor Royer-Collard had the fancy of introducing you to this concept. Perhaps under my hands, you would not be so distracted by shame...' [...] 'I've dressed wounds before,' he said. 'If you permit me, I will mind yours. I need only a needle, a candle and thread.[32]

Sade simultaneously occupies the roles of both the comforter and potential future inflictor of sadistic pleasure/pain. From a contemporary perspective however, this is in keeping with the BDSM community's legitimising notion of 'safe, sane and consensual' sexual practice, in which the 'responsible top', we are told, must both care for and comfort their submissive, ensuring emotional as well as physical wellbeing. Nonetheless it is far removed from Sade's own practice and works.

To rewrite Sade as carer and nurse of Madeleine's wounds, however, may well work to not just romanticise, but also feminise Sade within this particular fic, again thus negating the complex sexual politics of heterosexual BDSM (and indeed h/c) at hand. Indeed, *Sub Secreto*'s sexual dénouement shows Madeleine as the sexual aggressor, thus further ratifying both her own sexual power and consensual involvement within their sexual relationship:

> 'Feel this, Marquis', she rasped, shoving his hand under her skirts. He gasped faintly at the evidence of her own arousal [...] In the darkness of the curtained bed, the Marquis rejoiced at his sudden turn of luck and whispered, 'Oh my dearest Madelaine [sic]... I've such lessons to teach you...'.[33]

Yet *Quills* het fics do not always portray Madeleine as the character in need of comfort. Returning to Furious Angel's *Leading the Blind* through the lens of h/c, we see an inversion in which it is the Marquis who is hurt and requires Madeleine's comfort:

> de Sade was acutely aware of how savagely illness can grip a body. He was impossibly miserable. Until there came the timid knock on his door, and the familiar voice that followed it. 'Marquis? Marquis. They said you weren't well. I've ... well I've brought you something. Don't know if it will help' [...] 'Madeleine, my peach. You know that anything you bring me will aid my recovery. Your mere presence will be sure to lift my spirits, among many other things'.[34]

This is very much in keeping with Mirna Cicioni's assertion that erotic fan fictions are often the 'eroticization of nurturance'[35] and additionally would appear to conform to Christine Gledhill's figure of 'The Wounded Man', in which she proposes such narratives 'make the male figure accessible to the female imagination'.[36] Yet *Quills*' Sade, as I have argued, is already made accessible by a process of romanticisation precisely through the removal of his libido, his sexually sadistic desire. By re-eroticising Sade, *Elusive Love*, *Sub Secreto* and *Leading The Blind* reject the process of desexualisation, yet adhere and conform – whether via a h/c framework, or contemporary BDSM politic – to a Sade whose sadism is entirely sanitised, purged of its transgressive, sexually perverse potential. While such fictions depart from the desexualised Sade, they do so mostly following a heteronormative, romanticised re-envisioning of the Marquis, in line with Wright's screenplay. The ultimate result of such narratives is both oscillating and contradictory; these are stories that transgress *Quills'* sterilisation, yet also stop short of completely re-imagining *Quills'* Marquis de Sade.

Conclusion: The Cultural Re-imaginings of the Marquis de Sade

Quills as historical romantic drama may offer one view on the life and work of Sade, conflated into what is arguably a biopic, wherein notions of censorship, art and liberty are foregrounded. Its relationship with Sade's sexuality is more complex, however, since transgressive views of gender and sexuality are negated, confined within Rush's performance and Kaufman and Wright's text. Sade is thus not simply 'purged of content'[37] but instead distilled, refracted and projected into a series of narrative foils: Coulmier is the priest, lover and would-be necrophile; Royer-Collard is the torturer and violator of his child bride; and Bouchon is the violent, sadistic killer. 'There is in each of us such beauty and such abomination', Coulmier asserts in a final scene where Sade's soul is prayed for by the priest, simultaneously speaking of both himself and the Marquis.

The process of re-imagining the Marquis de Sade is not limited to this cinematic adaptation alone but is further articulated in critic and fan responses alike. While critical responses question the validity of Sade as a subject for such a genre piece, or the fidelity of the adaptation process, fans choose to re-read (and indeed re-write) him in a process of re-articulating their own desires, eroticising Sade while remaining faithful to the source text. The resulting fictions, predominantly heterosexual with a BDSM twist, attempt to navigate the complexity of sexual politics, re-writing Sade as the romantic lover and, perhaps most curiously, the responsible 'top'. Far from transformative or progressive, perversion and transgression are anchored within the ratification, rather than disavowal, of dominant ideologies and sexual norms. By largely constricting the Marquis' sexuality to that of romantic heteronormativity, they ultimately succumb to the mainstream palatable, non-perverse.

The fictions – just as with *Quills* – belong to a long practice of re-imagining the Marquis de Sade, whose political, literary and historical legacy is fluid; a concurrent number of Sades co-exist within the cultural imagination, not limited to the official text/s, nor indeed to history. The Marquis de Sade's cinematic legacy, then, lies not within the adaptations of his vast corpus of work alone but in himself becoming an appropriated, adapted and 'perverted' figure in film history, whether in sexploitation adaptations, horror appropriations or mainstream cinema re-imaginings, which seek to negotiate his notoriously sexually subversive character.[38]

Notes

1. Richard von Krafft-Ebing, *Psychopathia Sexualis: A Medico Forensic Study*, translated by Franklin S. Klaf (New York: Arcade Publishing, 1965), p. 105. Originally published 1886; Andrea Dworkin, *Pornography: Men Possessing Women* (New York: Pedigree Books, 1981), p. 70; Angela Carter, *The Sadeian Woman: An Exercise in Cultural History* (London: Virago, 1979), p. 36.

2. See Simone De Beauvoir, 'Must we burn Sade?' in Austryn Wainhouse and Richard Seaver (eds) and (trans.) *The 120 Days of Sodom and Other Writings* (New York: Grove Press, 1987), pp. 3–64; Luce Irigaray, *This Sex Which Is Not One* (New York: Cornell University Press, 1985); Geoffrey Gorer, *The Life and Ideas of the Marquis de Sade* (London: P. Owen, 1953); Georges Bataille, *Erotism: Death and Sensuality* (New York: Walker and Company, 1962); Roland Barthes, *Sade, Fourier, Loyola*, translated by Richard Miller (New York: Hill and Wang, 1976) and Marcel Hénaff, *Sade: The Invention of the Libertine Body* (Minneapolis, MN: University of Minnesota Press, 1999).

3. For an extended discussion of 'Sadean' hardcore see Xavier Mendik, 'That's l'Amorte: Joe D'Amato and the Sadean Art of Love', in Xavier Mendik (ed.), *Peep Shows: Cult Film and the Cine-erotic* (London: Wallflower, 2012), pp. 95–108.

4. As I will go on to discuss, Sade's death in *Quills* is one of many fictionalisations. This suicide is a romanticisation of the Marquis' own death, for as Schaeffer notes, 'De Sade's hideous death in the movie is nothing like the truth, for he died in his sleep, in his 74th year'. Neil Schaeffer, 'Perverting De Sade', *Guardian* (2001). Available at http://www.guardian.co.uk/books/2001/jan/13/biography.film (accessed 31 May 2012).

5. Schaeffer, 'Perverting De Sade'.
6. Neil Shaeffer, *The Marquis De Sade: A Life* (New York: Knopf, 1999).
7. See Deborah Cartmell and Imelda Whelehan (eds), *Adaptations: From Text to Screen, Screen to Text* (London: Routledge, 1999).
8. Doug Wright, Audio commentary, *Quills* (DVD), Twentieth Century Fox 2001.
9. Quoted in Mark Morris, 'How to erect a marquis', *Observer*, 2012. Available at http://www.guardian.co.uk/film/2001/jan/14/awardsandprizes.features (accessed 31 May 2012).
10. Anthony Lane, 'Body of writing', *The New Yorker*, 27 November 2000, p. 181.
11. Wright, 'Audio commentary', 2001.
12. Ibid.
13. Schaeffer, 'Perverting De Sade'.
14. Elisabeth Ladenson, *Dirt for Arts Sake: Books on Trial from Madame Bovary to Lolita* (London: Cornell University Press, 2007), p. 232.
15. Ibid., p. 234.
16. Anette Insdorf, *Philip Kaufman (Contemporary Film Directors)* (Champaign, IL: University of Illinois Press, 2012), p. 54.
17. See Camille Bacon-Smith, *Enterprising Women: Television Fandom and the Creation of Popular Myth* (Philadelphia, PA: University of Pennsylvania Press, 1992).
18. See Henry Jenkins, *Textual Poachers* (London: Routledge, 1992); Constance Penley, 'Feminism, psychoanalysis and the study of popular culture', in Lawrence Grossberg, Cary Nelson and Paula A. Treichler (eds), *Cultural Studies* (New York: Routledge, 1992), pp. 479–500; Sarah Gwenllian-Jones, 'The sex lives of cult television characters', *Screen* 43/1 (Spring 2002), pp. 79–90; Elizabeth Woledge, 'Decoding desire: from Kirk and Spock to K/S', *Social Semiotics* 15/2, (2005), pp. 235–50.
19. Bethan Jones, 'Normal female interest in vampires and werewolves bonking: slash and the reconstruction of meaning', in Wickham Clayton and Sarah Harman (eds), *Screening Twilight: Critical Approaches to a Cinematic Phenomenon* (London: I.B.Tauris, 2014).
20. For purposes of clarity, I have used the term 'erotic' herein to denote any fiction including a sexual pairing, whether 'het' (heterosexual) or 'slash'.
21. Brigid Cherry, 'Defanging the vampire: projected interactivity and all human *Twilight* fanfic', in Wickham Clayton and Sarah Harman (eds), *Screening Twilight: Critical Approaches to a Cinematic Phenomenon* (London: I.B.Tauris, 2014).
22. Furious Angel, *Leading the Blind*, 2003. Available at http://www.fanfiction.net/s/1513376/1/Leading_The_Blind (accessed 31 May 2012). Unfortunately neither Furious Angel nor Sadeness – two of the authors of fanfics on fanfiction.net discussed herein – were available to interview for this chapter; both accounts have selected to not accept private messages, and neither list an alternate contact method. Further, both user accounts have been dormant for around a decade, and as such the users appear inactive.
23. Sadeness, *Elusive Love*, 2001. Available at http://www.fanfiction.net/s/266824/1/Elusive_Love (accessed 7 July 2012).

24. Hénaff, *Sade: The Invention of the Libertine Body*, p. 5. For an interesting discussion of the application of this theory to Sadean themes in vampire films, see Lindsay Anne Hallam, *Screening the Marquis de Sade: Pleasure, Pain and the Transgressive Body in Film* (Jefferson, NC: McFarland & Co, 2012).
25. Sadeness, *Elusive Love*.
26. Sadeness, *Sub Secreto*, 2001.
27. Judith May Fathallah, 'H/c and me: an autoethnographic account of a troubled love affair', *Transformative Works and Cultures* 7 (2011). Available at http://journal. transformativeworks.org/index.php/twc/article/view/252/206 (accessed 15 March 2013).
28. See Kate Millett, *Sexual Politics* (New York: Avon Books, 1970); Andrea Dworkin, *Woman Hating* (New York: E. P. Dutton, 1974); Robin Ruth Linden, Darlene R. Pagano, Diana E.H. Russell and Susan Leigh Star (eds), *Against Sadomasochism: A Radical Feminist Analysis* (California: Frog in the Well, 1982).
29. See Pat Califia, 'Feminism and sadomasochism' in *Public Sex: The Culture of Radical Sex* (San Francisco, CA: Cleis Press, 1980), pp. 168–81; Pat Califia, 'Beyond leather: expanding the realm of the senses to latex', in *Public Sex: The Culture of Radical Sex* (San Francisco, CA: Cleis Press, 1984).
30. Alex Dymock, 'But femsub is broken too!: On the normalisation of BDSM and the problem of pleasure', *Psychology & Sexuality* 3/1 (2012), p. 6. Original emphasis.
31. Sadeness, *Elusive Love*.
32. Ibid.
33. Sadeness, *Sub Secreto*.
34. Furious Angel, *Leading the Blind*.
35. Mirna Cicioni, 'Male pair-bonds and female desire in fan slash writing', in Cheryl Harris and Alison Alexander (eds), *Theorizing Fandom. Fans, Subculture, and Identity* (Cresskill, NJ: Hampton, 1998), p. 163.
36. Christine Gledhill, 'Women reading men', in Pat Kirkham and Janet Thumim (eds), *Me Jane: Masculinity, Movies and Women* (New York: St Martins Press, 1995), pp. 86–7.
37. Ladenson, *Dirt for Arts Sake*, p. 234.
38. I am indebted to the advice of Bethan Jones, whose support and knowledge on the subject of fan fiction has been crucial to this chapter.

13

'Something Sweet': *Little Children*, the Sex Offender and Emma Bovary's Eyes

Guy Barefoot

At the end of *Little Children* (Todd Field, 2006), Sarah Pierce (Kate Winslet) and her three-year-old daughter Lucy (Sadie Goldstein) make a night-time visit to the playground. Sarah has arranged to meet Brad Adamson (Patrick Wilson), with whom she has planned to elope. However, Brad has been distracted by a group of teenage skateboarders whose encouragement for him to join in leads to his hospitalisation. Instead, Sarah encounters Ronnie McGorvey (Jackie Earle Haley), a known local sex offender, who tearfully tells her his mother has died. A distracted Sarah realises Lucy has wandered away and she rushes off to find her. Her departure is followed by the arrival of ex-policeman Larry Hedges (Noah Emmerich), organiser of the 'Committee of Concerned Parents' campaign. Larry's campaign has led him to call for Ronnie's castration, but it has also brought him into conflict with Ronnie's mother May (Phyllis Somerville), a conflict that has ended with her hospitalisation and death. On approaching him to apologise, Larry notices Ronnie is bleeding. In a perverse fulfilment of Larry's campaign proposal, and his mother's dying wish that he 'be a good boy', Ronnie has castrated himself.

While Ronnie's story is introduced at the very beginning, he only properly appears a third of the way into the film. The film is primarily about Sarah, her dissatisfaction with her husband, the suburban world in which she has found herself and the resulting affair she has with Brad. Yet when Ronnie does appear, he transforms the film, disrupting a story of suburban conformity and marital infidelity. The strongest note at the close of *Little Children* is not Sarah's unrealised elopement or Brad's skateboarding injury, but Ronnie's more extreme self-mutilation. There is no such scene in the 2004 Tom Perrotta novel on which the film is based, which ends with a confession, not a castration. At different stages in Perrotta's novel, Ronnie is linked to the disappearance of nine-year-old Holly Colapinto and eventually admits that he sexually assaulted and murdered her, a storyline that does not exist in the film.

When subsequently asked about differences between novel and film, Perrotta reported that 'the one thing that the studio said when we began the project was that they didn't like my book ending. There was going to have to be a new ending'.[1] Perrotta, who co-wrote the screenplay with director Todd Field, did not initially think much of the new ending that was adopted. He came to see that it had a certain rationale as an internalisation of the community's judgement on Ronnie, but also to view its adoption as the moment when the project became Field's film and not his book.[2] One approach to this might be to understand it as an illustration of how even a screenwriting credit cannot prevent the novelist from losing creative control to the business of filmmaking. A more productive approach is to see the new ending as part of a wider process of recycling and modification in adaptation that can tell us about the relationship between novel and film and the place of controversial material within contemporary cinema.

It is not that there is no place in Hollywood for the predatory paedophile. Indeed, Jackie Earle Haley went on to play one in *A Nightmare on Elm Street* (Samuel Bayer, 2010) and Patrick Wilson had just played one in *Hard Candy* (David Slade, 2005). It is rather that *Little Children* defines itself as different from those films in which the narrative as a whole revolves around a sex offender or his victim. The cover of the British DVD release quoted Michael Phillips from the *Chicago Tribune* on 'this "beautiful, provocative and compelling" [...] adult drama'.[3] The label is not just an ironic play on the story's title but also an indicator of status, formal complexity and thematic permissiveness. It has some of the characteristics that Robert J. Thompson had identified in 'quality television', including an ensemble cast, a tendency to be literary and writer-based as well as controversial subject matter.[4] For *Variety* it was part of a trend towards ensemble casts.[5] As a film, *Little Children* performs a balancing act, juggling different narrative strands, invoking and transforming material from Perrotta's novel and addressing paedophilia at explicit and implicit levels. The result is a film that has a complex relationship to its source material and subject matter.

Aside from the ending, there are minor differences between the novel and the film, such as the change of Sarah's lover's name from Todd to Brad, but in many respects the novel and film are remarkably close. The novel's first paragraph ends with the following lines: 'Smiling politely to mask a familiar feeling of desperation, Sarah reminded herself to think like an anthropologist. *I'm a researcher studying the behavior of boring suburban women. I am not a boring suburban woman myself*.'[6] The film's first shot of Sarah is accompanied by the voice of an off-screen narrator (Will Lyman) repeating those lines in third person with 'boring' becoming 'typical'. That is, the film (here and elsewhere) quotes from the novel and utilises the words of an omniscient narrator in a manner that is more common in literature than film. This has the effect of giving the visuals a literal and literary quality but also of adding an ironic and temporal distance, suggesting not the present tense commonly ascribed to film but that we are looking back at the recent past.[7]

This strategy of telling as well as showing is accompanied by a wider emphasis on literature, marking Sarah out as distinct from the typically suburban. She is seen with a book in her hands at the playground, park and swimming pool, or in her book-filled study at home, where Brad discovers the depth of her interest in him through finding his photograph in a copy of Shakespeare's sonnets (with 'my love is a fever' underlined in blue). As in the novel, she is invited to a local book group to discuss Flaubert's *Madame Bovary*, where she distinguishes herself through her nuanced contribution to the discussion, and where both film and novel spell out the comparison between Sarah's marital infidelities and those of

Emma Bovary. Novel and film contrast Sarah to another young mother also invited to the book group, Mary Ann (Mary B. McCann), who condemns Emma Bovary as a 'slut' and who ends the conversation by asking: 'I mean, did she really think a man like that was going to run away with her' (194–5). In the novel, this prompts Sarah to recall the previous day's discussion with Todd about divorcing their respective spouses. In the film, the connection with Flaubert's novel is emphasised through the insertion of shots of Sarah having sex and discussing Brad's wife.

According to Robert Stam, 'Flaubert never tells us the exact colour of Emma Bovary's eyes, but we colour them nonetheless. A film, by contrast, must choose a specific performer'.[8] In doing so, film appears to limit the relative openness of the literary text. Individual novels can of course vary in the amount of descriptive detail they provide. In Perrotta's novel, Sarah's jealousy of Todd's wife prompts her to ask him what she looks like. He attempts 'to describe Kathy as if she were a criminal suspect: five-nine, straight brown hair, brown eyes, no visible scars or tattoos'. Yet these dry details leave Sarah unsatisfied: she asks him if he has a picture (183). Adapting *Little Children* meant providing a picture and a performer (Jennifer Connelly). However, if this means that the audience's image of Kathy is restricted to the particular interpretation that Connelly gives, the process of adaptation opened up the narrative of the novel in other ways.

While Perrotta's novel lacks the film's visual precision, it provides more sexual detail, placing Sarah's affair with Todd and Ronnie's paedophilia in the context of a range of sexualities and sexual practices, from Sarah's graduate-school affair with a Korean-American woman to Todd's heterosexual frat-party memories. Sarah's husband Richard is obsessed with internet porn star Slutty Kay in both novel and film, but this is developed further in the novel, in which Richard abandons Sarah and travels to Beachfest 2001, the summer meeting of the Slutty Kay Fan Club. The removal of this and similar material from the film can partly be explained in terms of a need to simplify the narrative to fit it into a running time of just over two hours and partly in terms of a toning down of the explicit and varied sexual content. Sex plays an important role in the film but with certain limits. Richard (Gregg Edelman) masturbating with Slutty Kay's (Sarah Buxton) panties over his head makes it into the film but Todd and Kathy's son Aaron masturbating while watching a video of

Clifford the Big Red Dog (PBS Kids 2000–2003) does not. Sarah's heterosexual affair is performed in front of the camera, but her lesbian affair disappears along with most of the rest of her backstory. Childhood masturbation can be mentioned in a novel but not presented in a mainstream film, and while the same level of taboo does not exist for adult same-sex relationships, in the film Sarah's desires are made less complicated by being made exclusively heterosexual.

As Joan Faber McAlister notes, the film also goes some way towards 'pathologizing the "normal" residents of suburbia', as well as 'normalizing the pathologies represented as the biggest threats to the dream of a happy family life in the suburbs'.[9] Perversity is named in both novel and film and most closely associated with Ronnie, but particularly emphasised in the novel, which is also more insistent on linking it to the community at large. Larry distributes leaflets warning the neighbours that 'THERE IS A PERVERT AMONG US!' (27); the film changes this to 'ARE YOUR CHILDREN SAFE?' In one scene he struggles with 'the grinning pervert' (Ronnie), who then turns and shouts at Larry: 'You're the pervert!' (252–3). Flying to San Diego, the novel's Richard imagines his obituary if his plane crashes: 'Pierce, a successful branding consultant for Namecheck Inc., was on his way to a gathering of the Slutty Kay Fan Club, a web-based group of perverts that he had recently joined' (299).[10] Novel and film share the scene in which Larry surprises Brad/Todd who is thinking of Sarah while watching the skateboarders, by shouting: 'Hey, pervert! Like little boys do you?' (46). However, the novel's nine to 13-year-old skateboarders have grown to young adulthood in the film. Here and elsewhere the film treads more carefully than the novel. McAlister suggests that, in removing Sarah's bisexuality, the film limits the narrative's subversive potential, and it is true that the central male–female couple are straightened out in the film in line with sexual norms and narrative linearity.[11] Yet, in providing less of Ronnie's story it becomes a more open text. In the film, Ronnie acquires a less stable identity, as he shifts between the sympathetic and the sinister, documentary subject and folk devil. Here the film almost subverts its own narrative, as Ronnie disturbs the story of Sarah and Brad's affair.

In both novel and film, Ronnie, under pressure from his mother, advertises in a Lonely Hearts column. The film retains the novel's line:

'What he needed was a girlfriend, and May intended to help him find one', but retains sympathy for Ronnie by dropping the next sentence: 'If he had a nice girl in his life, maybe he wouldn't spend so much time alone in his room, spying on the neighbourhood kids through his binoculars' (67). In the novel, but not the film, Ronnie initially proposes for the advert: 'Likes kiddie porn and quiet nights in front of the television'. 'That's not funny', says May; 'It wasn't a joke', he replies (63). In the novel he switches from being uncooperative, giving his mother 'that hard, pitiless look, the one that scared her sometimes', to 'doing his best to be a good boy' (64). In the equivalent film scene, his concern for his mother's health leads into a series of close-ups of mother and son that are as affectionate as anything in the film. May is presented as concerned for her son in both novel and film, but while in the novel that concern is about what he might do, in the film her clearest concern is with how he will get by when she is gone. When his date, Sheila, tells him about her breakdown, in the novel he initially seems interested, but then yawns in her face; when the check arrives he says he has forgotten his wallet. Visiting his mother in the hospital, he shoots dirty looks at a Puerto Rican family who get on his nerves. In the equivalent film scenes he causes the clinically depressed Sheila (Jane Adams) to smile when he tells her she's 'not so bad', and shares a sympathetic moment in the hospital waiting room with an Hispanic woman who gives him a coffee and shows him a photograph of her mother.

By omitting references to spying on the local kids, child pornography and the abuse and killing of a nine-year-old, and adding moments in which Ronnie is allowed to relate emotionally to others, we are left with a character who can seem as much a victim of hysteria as a threat. Thus, the film was regarded as 'the first mainstream Hollywood movie to depict a community's victimisation of a convicted child sex offender'.[12] This is accentuated by the way in which the film places the action within what is signalled as a more paranoid time. The novel's setting is moved slightly forward from summer 2001 to 2003, a point emphasised when the vigilant Larry asks Brad: 'You ever think of homeland security?' In this distrustful, post-9/11 world, Ronnie is harassed by Larry (who is himself a killer, having retired from the police force after accidentally shooting a teenager at the mall), and ostracised by the community.

However, removing this material also serves to make Ronnie a more ambiguous figure. In the production notes for *Little Children*, Field is quoted as accounting for his script contribution on the grounds that:

> There were things for the film I would want to change. Primarily, knowing for certain what the sex offender, Ronnie, had, or hadn't done, that led to his incarceration. He should represent an almost fairytale-like archetype from the Brothers Grimm: The troll under the bridge, or Beowulf's *Grendel*. Serving as an alibi, and distraction for the other characters – a receptacle to rationalize their own fear and desire without the burden of self-examination.[13]

It is not exactly accurate to say that we do not know what led to Ronnie's incarceration. At the beginning of the film we are shown a local news report on the sex offender who, the reporter announces, has returned to the quiet residential neighbourhood of Woodward Court, 'after serving a two-year prison service for indecent exposure to a minor'. Yet, while this provides clear factual information, presented in a documentary style, it is framed by shots of the interior of the Woodward Court house to which Ronnie has returned that provide a different tone. First, a montage of shots of antique clocks and Hummel-style figurines against a sombre background precede the news report. Then, during the report the camera pulls back from the television screen on which it is being played, bringing into view the curtained room, the back of a chair, a glass of soda and an arm that lifts the glass to the mouth of the indistinctly seen viewer. Ronnie is watching himself being discussed on television, but we do not see him clearly at this point. For the first third of the film he exists only as a shadowy figure, lurking behind the Woodward Court façade. The scene functions to introduce the bare facts (along the lines of Todd's 'criminal suspect' description of his wife in the novel) but also the folk devil in his lair, disturbingly surrounded by little children in shorts or short skirts.

Ronnie's initial absence lends some weight to Field's point about the character being a modern-day folk devil. In the early part of the film he is an absent figure against whom other characters measure themselves, from a distance. Initially, the closest view we get of him is his mugshot, seen on the 'Committee of Concerned Parents' leaflets. 'He should be castrated', says Mary Ann when given one of the leaflets. 'You know what else you should do', mocks Sarah, 'Nail his penis above the entrance to the elementary school'. Sarah distinguishes herself from Mary Ann and the other mothers in the playground in her response to Ronnie, establishing herself as liberal and rational within this alarmist and alarmingly normal suburban world. However, while the editing of the scene in which Sarah disagrees with Mary Ann over *Madame Bovary* directly links the stories of Emma Bovary and Sarah Pierce and suggests that Flaubert's novel leads Sarah to self-examination, at this stage the reference to Ronnie barely makes her take her eyes off the book she is reading. The leaflet prompts one of the other mothers to volunteer that her brother used to expose himself to her but this only leads to Mary Ann's 'It's not the same thing' and the laughter of everyone else, Sarah included. As Field suggests, at this stage Ronnie is a distraction rather than an individual, allowing the characters to demonstrate their differences but not seeming to inhabit their world.

This begins to shift when he does make a proper appearance, causing panic at the local swimming pool. Ronnie's ambiguous role is again evident in this scene. A number of reviewers made the link to the beach scene in *Jaws* (Steven Spielberg, 1975), in which underwater shots of the legs of swimmers are seen from the predator's viewpoint and there is a panic-driven exit from the water.[14] Yet, the scene also echoes *The Graduate* (Mike Nichols, 1967), another film about alienation in suburbia, featuring an awkward man who dives into a swimming pool in a ridiculous outfit surrounded by unsympathetic parents and children. The anxieties about suburbia expressed in *The Graduate* film have changed into the anxieties of suburbia presented but partially undercut in *Little Children*. The fact that we have already witnessed an earlier minor panic (when Sarah horrifies the other mothers by kissing Brad in the playground) undercuts the effect of the panic caused by Ronnie in the pool and links Sarah to Ronnie as a fellow outsider. As he is escorted away by the police he turns to protest: 'I only wanted to cool off!' Here, the actor's performance helps to open up the reading further; Haley's exasperated delivery makes his desire seem reasonable.

In changing Ronnie's persona and crime the film shifts the novel's subplot about child murder towards a reflection on paranoia and conformity. However, the filmmakers' concern not to present too much sex-offender detail and at letting a murder mystery dominate the adult drama is accompanied by a concern not to present an overly sympathetic portrayal of a paedophile. Thus, while the film avoids both the child-killer narrative and the relentless negativity of the novel's Ronnie, it also periodically reassures us that it is not totally dismissing the fears about Ronnie.

This is most clearly demonstrated in a scene when Ronnie asks Sheila to 'make a little stop' on the drive home. 'You seem like a nice person', she tells him after recounting a previous unhappy date. Looking towards him, the camera cuts to a shot of Ronnie, framing him from the waist up and quite clearly masturbating. He appears to be staring at her with something akin to the hard, pitiless look mentioned in the novel. A pull focus, however, reveals the actual source of his attention: the playground across the street from where they are parked. There are similarities here to the opening of *Happiness* (Todd Solondz, 1998), a film presenting a more detailed and even less judgemental portrait of a paedophile and begins with a dinner date that moves from awkward apparent sympathy to the humiliation of a woman (again played by Jane Adams). In a different way, *The Naked Kiss* (Samuel Fuller, 1964) constructs an apparently benevolent portrait of the man the heroine is about to marry so as to make the revelation of his paedophilia all the more jarring, particularly in a 1960s Hollywood movie. In *Little Children*, Ronnie's perversion is performed in front of us precisely at the moment when Ronnie might seem redeemable.

The use of a racking focus is evident in other scenes in the film. At the pool, a shot of a boy wearing an uneasy expression reveals that he is looking towards Ronnie, initially shown out of focus on the edge of the frame, but then in focus, moving to look away from the now out-of-focus boy. The implication is that Ronnie does not only want to cool off, he wants to look and be looked at, in line with the nature of the offence for which he was imprisoned and his final act of exposure. The restaurant scene begins with a shot of two giggling children to the left of the frame, one shown out-of-focus, the other in focus. An indistinct figure appears in the right half of the frame. Ronnie is then brought into focus, looking in the direction of the children, now both out-of-focus (see Fig. 13.1). In subsequent shots Sheila is the focus of the discussion and the lens but the

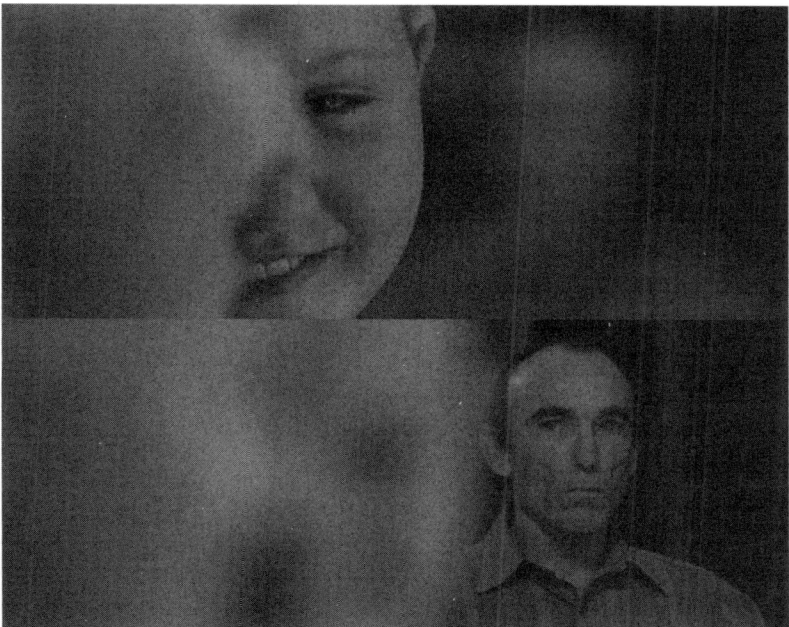

Fig. 13.1. Shallow and deep focus identifies the desiring gaze of convicted sex offender Ronnie McGorvey (Jackie Earle Haley) in *Little Children* (Todd Field, New Line Cinema, 2006)

out-of-focus children can be seen behind her, by Ronnie and the audience. The children exist as a background reminder of Ronnie's gaze, who Ronnie is, what he has done and what he might do.

The dialogue at the restaurant also contains a crucial motif. 'What do you say, Sheila, do you want to share something sweet?' asks Ronnie. The question is motivated by the waiter asking if they wanted dessert. However, framed as it is by a shot of Sheila with the children in the background, and delivered with Haley's slightly sinister inflection, it can easily be connected to other films featuring sex offenders, from the obviously cautionary *Never Take Sweets from a Stranger* (Cyril Frankel, Hammer Films, 1960) to *The Woodsman* (Nicole Kassell, 2004) with the 'bad paedophile' nicknamed Candy (Kevin Rice). In *The Naked Kiss*, candy serves as a euphemism for the sex for sale at Candy's brothel, accentuating the significance of the candy that 'Uncle Grant' (Michael Dante) gives to the little girl he abuses.

In *Little Children*, when one of the parents at the swimming pool refuses her daughter's request for a snack, she turns to her companions to say, 'All they want is sugar. Constantly'. The camera cuts to a shot of Ronnie approaching the pool. The children's fondness for sugar makes them vulnerable to predators such as Ronnie. Ronnie is himself sweet-toothed and child-like in his appetite for soda and dessert, though this serves to make him sinister as well as vulnerable.

There are other ways in which the film works through suggestion. The masturbating in the car scene ends with Ronnie saying, 'You'd better not tell on me. You hear me. You'd better not tell or I'll fucking get you'. There is an equivalent scene in the novel in which Ronnie says, 'You're not going to tell on me [...] Because I don't like tattletales' (208). The film scene also anticipates lines that come at the end of the novel. Having confessed to the murder of Holly Colapinto, Ronnie goes on to say, 'I didn't want to... She said she was going to tell on me' (352). In the novel, Ronnie is a compulsive paedophile whose fear of 'tattletales' will take him as far as child murder. The film avoids this clear establishment of guilt. The closest it gets to speaking of Ronnie as a murderous threat is the moment when an anxious mother warns Sarah about 'the pervert', adding 'I guess they're just waiting for him to kill someone'. The warning is undercut by the speaker's delivery (she shrugs) and Sarah's response (an offer of a cup of tea). Yet, Ronnie's '...or I'll fucking get you' remains an identification of a potential threat, emphasised by the fact that it is spoken by a convicted sex offender to a vulnerable adult in front of an empty playground.

In the course of a discussion of the films of Wes Craven, Bernice Murphy cites Freddy Krueger as 'that most hated of suburban bogeymen: the murderous child molester', going on to note 'the spectre of the suburban child-murderer/abuser recurs fairly often in the Suburban Gothic, particularly in literary depictions of the milieu', such as Shirley Jackson's *The Road Through the Wall* (1948), Suzanne Berne's *A Crime in the Neighbourhood* (1997), Alice Sebold's *The Lovely Bones* (2002) and Perrotta's *Little Children*.[15] It is an interesting shift from film to literature and in fact highlights what the film of *Little Children* does *not* show. In the novel, Ronnie worked as a school janitor, just as Freddy worked as the school gardener, but the film distances itself from the more sensationalist play on paedophilia and vigilantism evident in the *Nightmare on Elm Street* films. Because it was so central to the plot, the film adaptation of *The Lovely Bones* (Peter Jackson, 2009) could not remove the abuse and murder at the centre of novel, although Xan Brooks noted they could avoid showing the murder and even mentioning the rape.[16] The murder in Perrotta's novel was more easily excised, although traces of the novel's secondary plot can be seen behind the adult drama of *Little Children*.

Warning against prioritising the literary source over the resulting film, Imelda Whelehan notes 'the potential cinema audience of even the most widely read classic will be largely made up of individuals who haven't read the text'.[17] Yet, it is also important to consider what was brought to the narrative by those viewers of *Little Children* familiar with the book. The film features a scene in which Sarah and Richard are invited to dinner by Kathy and Brad, and Kathy becomes increasingly suspicious that Sarah is having an affair with her husband. The narrator continues: 'On a hunch, Kathy dropped her fork, in the hope that she would catch Sarah and Brad playing footsie. But she was mistaken'. She goes on to crawl under the table and stare for a while at Sarah's blue-painted toenails, described in the novel as:

> a hideous metallic blue, the kind of color a trashy twelve-year-old would have loved, nothing you would expect to find on the feet of a grown woman, the mother of a young child. You would have to be crazy to wear nail polish like that, or so deeply in love that you were beyond caring (271–2).

In the film, Kathy's reason for looking under the table is spelled out by the narrator, but her reason for staring so long at Sarah's toenails is not. Adaptations invariably filter out lines from their source material; the fact that Kathy realises that Sarah and Brad are having an affair has anyway already been signified to viewers of the film, and there are other scenes in the film to indicate the child/adult connection made in the novel's 'trashy twelve-year-old' reference. Retaining the shot of Kathy looking at Sarah's painted toenails also contributes to the film's comic tone. The film is full of quirky details, from a man with panties on his head to a woman under the table, partially explained but also made stranger by the deadpan voiceover. But in addition it suggests that the novel could provide further details not offered by the film. A viewer who watches *Madame Bovary* (Vincente Minnelli, 1949) having read the novel will see Jennifer Jones reflected through the light of Flaubert's prose (whether or not that viewer measures one against the other). The same could be said of a reader of Vladimir Nabokov's 1955 novel *Lolita*, who subsequently watches Stanley Kubrick's 1962 adaptation (MGM). Those who read and then watched *Little Children* may have been inclined to explain Ronnie's actions in the film in the light of what they had learned through reading the novel.

The film version of *Little Children* contains different stories, is open to different interpretations and hints at material it does not depict. It shows us the exact colour of Sarah's toenails but leaves us to make the connection with her child-like romanticism, the colour she uses to express desire (the blue ink used to underline 'my love is a fever') or the words found in the novel but not the film. It is at its most ambiguous at the very beginning. The barely audible opening line, 'Want to take a walk with me?' appears to be delivered by Sarah's daughter, Lucy, but the recipient is not revealed and the words are neither in the novel nor directly related to the plot of the film. They suggest the vulnerability of children but also a film striving for a degree of ambiguity and opacity.

The adaptation of *Little Children* involved a rejection of the novel's child-murder subplot. Removing references to the killing of a nine-year-old child allows the film to accentuate the portrayal of neighbourhood panic and to present an alternative portrayal of Ronnie. However, allusions to abuse and murder were retained. Rather than a murder confession, we end with the narrator telling us: 'He knew Ronnie had done some bad things in the past, but so had Larry', as they rush to the hospital. As the camera juxtaposes Kathy meeting Brad outside the hospital with Sarah protectively hugging Lucy in bed, the narrator continues, 'You couldn't change the past. But the future could be a different story. And it had to start somewhere'. The last line is spoken as the camera cranes out of Lucy's bedroom window and up towards the night sky. But this penultimate moment of uplift is followed by a night-time shot of the playground, the empty swings squeaking ominously in the breeze, almost as if we are on Elm Street. The imagery here and at the beginning (when we are shown the 'sweet' child figurines in the Woodward Court house) serves to both remind us of the (non-adult) children of the title and also to mark their absence.

The thematic permissiveness of the adult drama and literary adaptation gave *Little Children* a licence to address but not always show controversial material. Like other films in which child abuse is part of the narrative, it relies on metaphor, allusion and the unseen. The empty swings, cryptic comments and unfocused images in *Little Children* can be linked to the red ball in *The Woodsman* or the balloon caught in the telephone wires in *M* (Fritz Lang, 1931). The filmmakers never show us the exact nature of the crimes, but we colour in the details nonetheless. In the film version of *Little Children*, this reliance on the imagination of the viewer is complicated and unsettled by the uncertain role of Ronnie as victim as well as victimiser, self-castrator rather than self-confessed murderer. Far from closing down the narrative, in Ronnie the film provides us with a sex offender who invites sympathy as well as condemnation.

Notes

1. Ruth Maxey, 'Tom Perrotta in conversation about literary adaptation', *Literature/Film Quarterly* 38/4 (2010), pp. 270, 272.
2. Ibid., p. 272.
3. *Little Children*, region 2 DVD, Eiv (2007).
4. Robert J. Thompson, *Television's Second Golden Age: From* Hill Street Blues *to* ER (Syracuse, NY: Syracuse University Press, 1997), pp. 13–16.
5. Dave McNarry, 'Band in the run: ensemble pics may not deliver big paydays, but they can polish a resume with shiny kudos', *Variety*, 11–17 December 2006, pp. B1–2.
6. Tom Perrotta, *Little Children* (London: Allison & Busby, 2004), p. 3. Original emphasis. Subsequent page references in text appear in parentheses.
7. Imelda Whelehan, 'Adaptations: the contemporary dilemmas', in Deborah Cartmell and Imelda Whelehan (eds), *Adaptations: From Text to Screen, Screen to Text* (London and New York: Routledge, 1999), p. 11.
8. Robert Stam, 'Beyond fidelity: the dialogics of adaptation', in James Naremore (ed.), *Film Adaptation* (New Brunswick, NJ: Rutgers University Press, 2000), p. 55.
9. Joan Faber McAlister, 'Unsafe houses: the narrative inversion of suburban morality in popular film', *Liminalities: A Journal of Performance Studies* 4/1 (2008), p. 10.
10. Original emphasis.
11. McAlister, 'Unsafe houses', p. 23.
12. Ben Hoyle, 'Winslet plays role in breaking taboo over child sex offenders', *The Times*, 27 October 2006, p. 16.

13. Todd Field, *Little Children*, Production notes (2006). Available at change to http://www.cinemareview.com/production.asp?prodid=3642 (accessed 11 July 2017).

14. See Peter Bradshaw, '*Little Children*', *Guardian*, 3 November 2006. Available at http://www.guardian.co.uk/film/2006/nov/03/comedy.katewinslet (accessed 31 May 2011).

15. Bernice Murphy, *The Suburban Gothic in American Popular Culture* (Basingstoke: Palgrave Macmillan, 2009), pp. 151–2.

16. Xan Brooks, '*Lovely Bones*', *Guardian*, 24 November 2009. Available at http://www.guardian.co.uk/film/2009/nov/24/the-lovely-bones-film-review (31 May 2011).

17. Whelehan, 'Adaptations,' p. 4.

14

Let the *Right One In* and the Wrong One Go: Paedophilia and Film Culture

Darren Kerr

Patrick Süskind's 1985 novel *Perfume: The Story of a Murderer* tells the story of Jean Baptiste Grenouille, a young, scentless apprentice who acquires the skills of a master perfumer in France during the mid-eighteenth century. His picaresque problems and pleasures in this world eventually converge on his killing of young girls in order to capture, distil and bottle the scent of the just-pubescent. As the manhunt grows, Grenouille cannot help but continue to quietly extinguish the life of the girls, wrapping them in a pomade and oil-soaked linen from which their scent is drawn. Eventually captured and sentenced to the scaffold, the mood of the execution crowd turns as he appears, lightly adorned with a drop or two of the fragrance. They declare that there must be a mistake; he cannot possibly be guilty and he should be freed. Grenouille is 'innocence personified'.[1] Overcome with infatuation and explicit arousal, the crowd embarks on 'the largest orgy the world had seen since the second century before Christ' (247). Returning to Paris, an unnoticed Grenouille enters the Cimetière des Innocents and, as night falls, he pours the remains of the perfume over himself. A nearby crowd, on smelling the fragrance, experience escalating desire as rapture envelopes them. Consequently, the now-scented Grenouille is touched, grabbed, molested and attacked. The crowd continues in its uninhibited need to take, have and possess Grenouille and, 'driven by voluptuous lust', dismember and devour him (263). The young perfumer disappears, along with the scent, as the crowd proudly walk away having 'done something out of Love' (sic, 263).

The quietly guarded work of Süskind's antihero and the actions of the crowd confront us with a very provocative illustration of perverse longing and an attraction to the nature of desire, motivated by the innocence of the child and the experience of the adult. Tom Tykwer's 2006 film adaptation of Süskind's novel takes Grenouille on a rather less perilous path, casting a captivating Ben Whishaw as the troubled antihero, pathologised by his performance and ravaged by a largely female-led crowd at the film's dénouement. This depiction of Grenouille's end is the demise of a melancholy romantic whose lost love leaves him consumed by those desiring him, rather than hacked to pieces by those compulsively driven by lust. In spite of muting the brutal effect of this story's end, the film cannot entirely escape the air of intent behind Süskind's writing and the scent created.

Richard Maltby claims that, in the shift from literary text to screen, 'the industry was less concerned with the adaptation of a work than with its adaptation to a set of external political conditions'.[2] This proves illuminating not only in exploring the contexts in which omissions in adapting texts are made but also how such external political conditions and cultural sensibilities appear to influence decisions about what is also introduced, included and even added to the stories told. When looking at the relationship between novel and film, rather than review them as distinct separate works, the shift from text to screen in adaptation is not so much a movement from one medium to another but a series of interrelated choices leading to the excavation of certain ideas and themes that go on to dominate a character-based screenplay. Screenwriter Andrew Davies claimed to metaphorically split the page when adapting for film and television in order to find the scene, sequence or moment that the novelist had overlooked for a variety of reasons, including self-censorship in response to social or political sensitivities.[3]

Cultural sensibilities surrounding taboo practices and perversions are repeatedly encountered within film adaptations of horror novels that have been a firm part of cinema's history. In adapting John Ajvide Lindqvist's 2004 novel of the same name, Tomas Alfredson's film *Let the Right One In* (2008) appears to be no different in its exploration of child vampirism and violence in the Stockholm suburb of Blackeburg. In this adaptation, the explicit erasing of a central character's paedophilia and the implications such an omission has when adapting the book for the screen speaks of historical and contemporary anxieties that circulate around sexual attraction towards children. It also draws attention to the ways in which film has tried to navigate the language and politics of paedophilia.

Adapting the Paedophile in *Let the Right One In*

Like many cases of novel-to-film adaptations, the film version of *Let the Right One In* closes down the scale of the narrative in focusing on the relationship between bullied schoolboy Oskar (Kåre Hedebrant) and child-vampire Eli (Lina Leandersson), who initially appears to have been a girl but is revealed in the novel to be a boy. The character who procures blood for Eli is the aging Håkan (Per Ragnar), a symbolic father in the film and, in the book, a paedophile whose longing for Eli charges his desire (and occasionally repulsion) towards fantasising, sexualising and sexually exploiting children. In adapting the novel for the screen, Lindqvist and Alfredson consciously and collectively decided to omit Håkan's paedophilia because they did not want the film to be *about* paedophilia. Lindqvist's observation that 'it is not the idea behind the story at all'[4] goes some way towards demonstrating how paedophilia in film is seen to consume its narrative, regardless of its relevance to the story or, indeed, characters.

The novel is explicit in detailing Håkan's paedophilic desire and closely aligns it to what Lindqvist says is essentially his love for Eli.[5] Part One of the novel – 'Lucky Is He Who Has Such A Friend' – introduces each key character while being a section that belongs to Håkan. Key themes and ideas are encapsulated in these first 89 pages of the 500-page novel but have Håkan as the perverse moral centre to the story. It is his thoughts, his point of view, his concerns, desires and wishes that determine the narrative, establishing an affinity between him, the reader's knowledge of events and Oskar's actions, all of which offer narrative companionship to Håkan. In the opening section, the repetition of literary motifs (a forest; murderous anticipation; being taunted; attraction/repulsion; arousal and dismissal; reality and fantasy) – alternating between Håkan and Oskar's narratives – offers a congruence of character. The simultaneity of events confronts the reader with a sense of equivalence between an adult and child who can each appear on first reading to be independent characters, rather than related in a reciprocal way.

We are also presented with numerous contradictions that circulate around Håkan's personality and actions that repeatedly place him as in-between. This may be of little surprise in a novel about a 12-year-old vampire-child who has been alive for 200 years and whose identity is conflicted by abuse and violence that defines the character. Håkan is situated in spaces where the fantasies of child-sex-made-real are often ruptured by the desperate and bleak environments in which they are about to take place. The chance of oral sex in the novel is twice thwarted by the grimness of the situation. Once, after paying for sex, Håkan looks on at his friend's ejaculate still glistening on the cheek of a 12-year-old boy, leaving him feeling that 'the whole situation was too disgusting'.[6] It becomes apparent that Håkan's desire is compromised by him becoming a witness rather than participant in the sexual exploitation of children. The second occurrence takes place in a public urinal stall. A boy 'about eleven or twelve [...] blonde hair, heart-shaped face' (47–8) attempts to perform oral sex on Håkan, but it becomes apparent to him that the child has had his teeth forcibly removed to 'make him more fit for his work' (48). Such attraction and repulsion, arousal and dismissal often leaves Håkan subjected to the boys that he fixes on rather than them being subjected to him. It is a confrontational narrative of a paedophile lacking control, predatory persuasion and aggressive sexual success. While the narrative *belongs* to Håkan, it is not his voice but an omniscient narrator who tells us of Håkan's obeying, following orders and not being 'the one doing this' (48). This displacement may be part of the paedophile's fantasy of complicity, yet Lindqvist writes a character that thwarts his own desire due to a love for Eli that is not governed by the immediacy of sexual gratification.

Håkan's desire exists between intimacy and intrusion as his unconditional yearning to touch Eli is met with conditional demands that lead to pleasurable exchanges for blood. For Håkan, it is love. As Lindqvist says of his novel, this enables the reader 'to pity [Håkan, to] understand the monster. And it's still love, in a twisted sense'.[7] Lindqvist's assertion that this twisted love is designed to solicit understanding, sorrow and compassion is a rather courageous claim considering the climate of antagonism in which the paedophile is immersed in popular culture.[8] We are presented with a character that is not pathologised by their sexual preference but instead draws attention to the often ignored distinction between sexual attraction and physical abuse in discourses of paedophilia. Håkan's love is made perverse by its proximity to father–child relations, a desire linked to the development of child sexuality and intergenerational intimacy. It is a love that leaves Håkan conflicted.

Alfredson's adaptation not only attempts to dismiss Håkan's paedophilia but also takes away a perspective that helps to narrate the experiences encountered in the first part of the book. In the film, Håkan remains influential as a modern-day bogeyman that moves through woodlands, schools and changing rooms after dark in his attempts to find blood young enough to satisfy his needs and Eli's thirst. When considered alongside knowledge of his actions, his aged, pock-marked and largely unassuming physicality lends itself to the ways in which culture has written adult sexual deviance onto the body. The novel similarly captures an anxiety of appearance made suspicious with Håkan's 'incipient beer belly, a receding hairline and an address unknown to the authorities' (12). Håkan's demise further maps his being onto that of the demonised monster that wider culture would have him be. Pouring acid onto his own face after a failed abduction in both book and film, Håkan makes his humanity anonymous, even though his self-mutilating actions are motivated by protecting Eli. In the film, Håkan is rendered largely silent and is often presented on screen through a series of intimate gestures towards Eli: a smile, the opening of a door, a disapproving glance, a look of sadness and dissatisfaction when failing to succeed in his role (see Fig. 14.1). These moments become the visual language that communicates his intimacy and desire to please Eli. His longing is implicit in the film but then so too are the meanings behind his actions.

Fig. 14.1. Håkan (Per Ragnar) is comforted by Eli (Lina Leandersson) in *Let the Right One In* (Tomas Alfredson, EFTI, 2008)

In the film, he remains a man who seeks out young boys, using, abusing and exploiting them, albeit for Eli. Similarly, like in the two instances of sexual failure in the novel, he twice fails to use the boys in the way he feels compelled in his attempts to procure blood. The replicating of Håkan's behaviours, which imprints a deviant associative relationship to children upon him, is further illustrated in a scene in which he uncomfortably rejects the invitation to join a group of local drinkers, casting him as an adult incapable of socialising with adults. His ability to communicate does not extend beyond his relationship with Eli, a relationship that is not so much regressive as it is in stasis, denied the dynamics of a normal adult–child relationship. The picture of Håkan emerging in the cinematic narrative establishes sympathy for a rather pathetic character who is subjected to the child, rather than Eli being subjected to him and his actions. This thematically mirrors the novel but lacks the overt sexual references and depictions that, as in much vampire film and fiction, cannot ever be entirely negated.[9] It is not until the end of the film that his character, or more clearly the provenance of his character, is fully realised in the adaptation. In focusing the script on Oskar and Eli's relationship, we see Oskar's coming-of-age effectively rewrite our understanding of Håkan as one who assists Eli to document the birth of a relationship that would see Oskar mature into adulthood, while always drawn by desire to Eli.[10] The film essentially makes a discomforting distinction between paedophilia and abuse. This is further illustrated when, in the novel,

Håkan is accidentally turned by Eli after a fall from the hospital window fails to kill him.[11] As a vampire he compulsively pursues and attempts to rape Eli and is later killed by a local youth. While his death in the novel may be read as an act of literary poetic justice, it is complicated by the conflation of his history, which casts him as a tragic figure, and by his newly sociopathic un-dead existence, which is deserving of his death. In his un-dead state, Håkan effectively becomes the predatory violator in the novel that in his human state, in spite of his sexual orientation, he is not.

The attempted displacement of paedophilia in adapting *Let the Right One In* is a case in point. Studies of adult sexual interest in children begin to highlight how provocative the conflation of Håkan/Oskar in the adaptation actually is. In reviewing studies of sexual offences against children, Max Taylor and Ethel Quayle note that typologies of offenders were broadly divided between what termed the 'regressed offender' and the 'fixated offender'.[12] The regressed offender is someone who has age-appropriate sexual relations 'but could regress to sexual involvement with children' given the circumstances.[13] The fixated offender is theorised as 'one whose primary sexual interest was children, *and who never developed psychosexually beyond that level*'.[14] The film adaptation offers up Håkan/Oskar as the latter, destined to fail to develop age-appropriate relations having moved into what will become a predetermined state of desire for the child, who in the guise of Eli is not a quite a child but retains the physical form of the pre-pubescent.

This complication of the child-vampire poses a challenge to the discourses and terminology that envelop discussions of the paedophile and his actions. According to Patricia Phelan – whose work belongs to literature exploring offender perspectives – the child capable of adult sexual engagement is a common fantasy for offenders whose misperception of compliance is read as consent.[15] What the film offers in its conclusion is a reflection on Håkan conflicted by this and Oskar about to journey into it through his love for Eli. As noted by Taylor and Quayle, studies in offender behaviour often emphasise the adult as perpetrator and child as victim. The shift from text to screen begins to reveal Eli's complicated role and illustrates the limitations of such reductionist approaches when exploring the subject. Instead, when considering the child-vampire it may be more productive, for all its layered connotations, to explore it in the context of Western cultures that have increasingly valorised and eroticised the image and body language of children/youth while trying to sustain the idea of innocence that 'creates a sexualised child whom we pretend to protect.'[16]

In considering the behaviour and actions of offenders, Sarah D. Goode's research on paedophilia and society explicitly aims to 'counter the emotionality surrounding the topic in the popular media', in order to develop a better-informed cultural understanding and thereby produce more effective social policy to assist child protection.[17] Central to Goode's exceptionally courageous work is the need to challenge the concept of the paedophile as pathological, acknowledge the failure of criminal-justice interventions and, crucially, recognise the distinction between desire and action, attraction and abuse. As Goode states, 'paedophilia, as we currently understand it, is the medical diagnosis of a fixed sexual orientation which may or may not manifest itself in actual behaviour towards a child.'[18] The history of defining and determining paedophilia from Richard von Krafft-Ebing's *Psychopathia Sexualis* to the ongoing and revised editions of the *Diagnostic and Statistical Manual of Mental Disorders* has constantly lead to the fostering of clinical solutions to cure as well as legal solutions to prevent or punish, which is inextricably related to this 'medical condition similar to other psychosexual disorders or "paraphilias"'.[19] Goode effectively draws out the sensitivities around the widespread existence of paedophilia as well as the need to look closely at child sexuality.

Let the Right One In offers a narrative that is sensitive to the complexities of adult sexual attraction to children as well as an emerging child sexuality and the terror of abuse. Lindqvist and Alfredson's adaptation is just one film in a marginal history of cinema that confronts the politics of paedophilia. The ways in which filmmakers have directed and presented paedophilia on screen has been largely defined by what I would argue are three 'structures of feeling', to borrow Raymond Williams' useful term that succinctly captures the shared values and perceptions of a culture in its artistic forms.[20] These are: firstly, a struggle to find a coherent language for adult sexual attraction to children; secondly, the impact of the cultural demonisation of paedophilia; and thirdly, the presentation of more openly dialogic narratives that can engineer better-informed social debate. Cumulatively, this demonstrates how film engages the problematic politics of paedophilia on screen, which connects effectively to Goode's social scientific research on understanding sexual attraction to children.

Screening Paedophilia: Language, Retribution and Reflection

The struggle to find an adequate language of comprehension for paedophilia, like the sexual politics of the time, is found across a number of films from the 1970s. Nicholas Gessner's French-Canadian co-production *The Little Girl Who Lives Down the Lane* (1976) casts Jodie Foster as Rynn Jacobs, a 13-year-old girl protecting her family home from numerous intrusions, including that of local 'pervert' Frank Hallet (Martin Sheen). Set in the small coastal town of Wells Harbor, Maine, married man Frank appears one Halloween, escorting his two young stepsons, who are trick-or-treating for the holidays. Sheen presents Frank as an agitated, excitable and confident man whose sexually coercive approach to Rynn is constantly evident in their exchanges. The discourse that broadly revolves around Frank centres on how well-known his perversion is and that his predilection for children is seemingly ignored in the community. The inhabitants of Wells Harbor and its authorities appear ill-equipped to manage Frank outside of the conceit that every town has one such pervert. Rynn wonders why he is 'never arrested', noting that if he was killed, local law enforcement would simply be relieved. As Rynn develops an age-appropriate relationship with Mario (Scott Jacoby), Frank's desire for her increases until a revelation about her family allows him to sexually blackmail her. Rynn eventually poisons Frank less for his sexual proclivities than to protect her secret, leaving the actions of his deviant sexuality as a problem without a perceived strategy for solution.

This struggle to 'speak' paedophilia also informs two films whose focus on child sexual abuse is inflected through a confession within the legal system. US director Sydney Lumet's British drama *The Offence* (1973) and Robert M. Young's US prison film *Short Eyes* (1977) were both adapted from the stage and focus on characters with impulses that can neither be controlled nor adequately explained. In *The Offence*, Detective Sergeant Johnson (Sean Connery) is investigating a series of rapes against schoolgirls that lead to the arrest and interrogation of suspect Kenneth

Baxter (Ian Bannen). During the interrogation, the accused recounts a tale of how victims of school bullying can actually feel needed by the bullies who abuse them. The subtext is clearly presenting a morally perverse perspective on the power a victim can give to an abuser. During the interrogation, however, it is the detective Johnson who suffers a breakdown during the questioning of Baxter, effectively confessing to the accused child-rapist his own compulsion to enact the very sex crimes he investigates. The accused Baxter declaims:

> Oh, you've found it haven't you? Eh? Something a little like the truth. Does it surprise you? Does it shock you? It's there in everyone. You must know that better than anyone.

This rewrites the significance of Johnson's protective proximity to the victims and pursuit of violators in the film, which concludes with an associative struggle to articulate what is in his head:

> I can't stop thinking. Is it like that? Is it the same for you? Is your mind full of things all the time? Thoughts. Pictures. Shadows. Darkness. White. Smooth white legs, thighs, breasts, blood and pain.

Johnson begins to weep and asks the accused Baxter for help. He responds by telling him to help himself and, in an act of mutual wish-fulfilment, Johnson's failed pursuit for empathy and understanding compels him to violently assault Baxter, beating him to death in the interrogation room.

Moral complexity around managing knowledge of inappropriate desire and physical abuse similarly informs the prison drama *Short Eyes*, in which Clark Davis (Bruce Davison) is imprisoned after being accused of raping a girl. He eventually befriends Juan (José Pérez), who refuses to treat him with the indignities that the 'short eyes', that is paedophile, inmates suffer. In a remarkable and extended confession, Davis confides in Juan that he has no recollection of the rape he is accused of but does molest and have sex with children:

> It seemed like I almost had a second sense about children, you know? I would sit there on that park bench for hours and then

I'd talk to a little girl for a minute, I'd know right way whether
we were gonna do it or not. The little Puerto Rican girls and the
black girls were the easiest. Little white girls would masturbate
you right there in the park for a quarter or whatever, depending
on how much emphasis the parents put on money. I couldn't
stop myself. I couldn't stop myself.

Juan is left furious at being inadvertently made 'father confessor'.
Davis knows it is wrong but cannot stop what he describes as his 'flash
fever' desire that leaves both him and Juan knowing that seeking legal
or psychiatric help is futile. Just as violence overcomes Johnson in *The
Offence*, the inmates of *Short Eyes* collude to cut the throat of Davis, whose
desire for children is understood by them through a reductive series
of homophobic epithets. The struggle to find a suitable grammar and
coherent language persists and is intricately linked to the demonising of
the subject, which has historically informed discourses on paedophilia.
This has arguably escalated since the popularising of sexual offender
legislation, illustrated in the US by Megan's Law and in the UK by Sarah's
Law, respectively.[21]

Alongside two US dramas, Nicole Kassell's *The Woodsman* (2004)
and Todd Field's *Little Children*,[22] which explore social vilification of the
paedophile, the Australian exploitation film *Daddy's Little Girl* (Chris Sun,
2012) and French-Canadian thriller *7 Days* (Daniel Grou, 2010) present
extreme examples of retribution as strategy. Both films have something to
say about the cultural demonisation of the paedophile and focus on the
capture and subsequent torture of an offender by fathers of young girls
who have been sexually abused and murdered. *Daddy's Little Girl* can be
varyingly described as domestic horror, Ozploitation and torture-porn,
in which Derek (Michael Thompson) incarcerates and slowly tortures his
brother Tommy (Christian Radford), who is responsible for the death of
his six-year-old daughter Georgia (Billi Baker). The narrative of torture
that is written on Tommy's body by Derek is incited by tabloid rhetoric
and numerous emotive reports he has come across in the media. Derek
even conflates the case of James Bulger with the need for revenge on sex
offenders.[23]

The convergence of extreme physical violence and verbal outrage
echoes the emotive velocity that child abuse and murder elicits. *7 Days*

takes a less exploitative approach than *Daddy's Little Girl* but is equally driven by validating physical and psychological torture in recourse to the personal impact of child rape on a surviving parent. After his daughter Jasmine (Rose-Marie Coallier) is found dead, Bruno Hamel (Claude Legault) abducts the accused, Anthony Lemaire (Martin Dubreuil), from custody. In a secluded location, Bruno tortures Lemaire and eventually secures the confession he seeks before police track him down and arrest him. As retribution, Bruno's most telling moment is in the final lines of the film that focus on a reporter asking him whether vengeance was the right course of action. As he is escorted away by police, the grieving father Bruno simply states 'no'. The reporter follows this up with 'do you regret what you did?' and again the reply is simply 'no'. The violence enacted on the body of the paedophile in the film is personally and intimately satisfying but it does not succeed as retributive justice.[24] This observation equally lends itself to *Daddy's Little Girl*, which similarly concludes with the successful arrest of the torturer and bereft parent Derek. While *7 Days* quietly lets Bruno's sadness and loss prevail, *Daddy's Little Girl* intercuts the final credit sequence with fictional newspaper cuttings of vigilante attacks inspired by Derek's case. Both films indicate cynicism towards criminal-justice systems that struggle to apprehend or adequately deal with violators while failing to protect and support victims and their families.

While the films above illustrate perspectives on demonisation and retribution, they do not necessarily demystify the media-fuelled problem of paedophilia. The third structure of feeling predominantly concerns narratives in which a stronger dialogic position is presented. German production *The Silence* (Baran bo Odar, 2010), Austrian drama *Michael* (Markus Schleinzer, 2011) and Danish film *The Hunt* (Thomas Vinterberg, 2012) evoke a more explicit need to address the politics of paedophilia in their narratives that see community response, the figure of the paedophile and police procedure scrutinised to significant effect. A notable approach on behalf of the filmmakers here is the move away from narratives centring on the abused and instead they take a closer look at the culture of other contexts that impact on comprehension, conflict and understanding.

Baran bo Odar's *The Silence* and Thomas Vinterberg's *The Hunt* examine levels of affect and responsibility across a range of characters and circumstances beyond the dichotomous relationship of victims and violators. The police procedural drama that informs *The Silence* links the rape and murder of two girls across 23 years to the same killer, Peer Sommer (Ulrich Thompson), triggering the conscience of Timo Friedrich (Wotan Wilke Möhring), his companion who was present at the first killing. The film presents varying complications around complicity, guilt and responsibility through the investigating officers and especially Timo, whose struggles concerning his sexual attraction to children are clearly differentiated from Sommer's, who appears to have raped and killed again without conscience.

Both Sommer and Timo, whose differences are manifested in attraction and abuse, are outwardly 'normal' members of society, which reflects the approach taken by Markus Schleinzer in directing *Michael*. The film presents the modest routine of Michael (Michael Fuith), who incarcerates and sexually abuses ten-year-old Wolfgang (David Rauchenberder). Michael's abuse of Wolfgang, which takes place off-screen, is interspersed with rituals of the everyday: mealtime, haircutting, a trip to the zoo, watching television. Their behaviour is painfully ordinary and mirrors the intimacy of parent–child relations. The abuse is treated as an unremarkable part of their routine muting what could be melodramatic, as it does when Michael dies in a car crash at the end of the film and when Wolfgang is accidentally discovered and rescued. The persona of the paedophile and the way in which the narrative deals with abuse is confrontational because paedophilia just *is*. Consequently, there is a need to look differently at the subject to understand the actions of the paedophile, the nature of abuse and the varying levels of agency linked to the cultural and social welfare of a sexual society.

As a central antagonistic motif in the narratives of *Michael* and *The Silence*, levels of agency similarly confront the cultural understanding of paedophilia and abuse in Vinterberg's *The Hunt*. After comments from a pupil lead to him being questioned by local authorities, kindergarten teacher Lucas (Mads Mikkelsen) is falsely accused of indecent exposure. Although released without charge, opprobrium is cast upon Lucas, who is marginalised by the immediate suspicions and retrospective determinism of school teachers, a child psychologist and a community crafting a version of truth from false attribution. While *The Silence*,

Michael and *The Hunt* offer up a more dialogic approach to paedophilia in the course of their narratives, they all end on desperate notes of forewarning as cultural attitudes remain steeped in logical fallacy, compromising social understanding and detracting from the roles and responsibility of a multi-agency approach. This forewarning also encapsulates *Let the Right One In* at a time that saw these four films, and one significant other, released across a five-year period between 2008 and 2012.

The other film released during this time – in 2010 – was Matt Reeves' US version *of Let the Right One In*, titled *Let Me In*. Set in Los Alamos, New Mexico in the early 1980s, Lindqvist's novel is adapted to different effect compared to Alfredson, with a stronger focus on the story as a coming-of-age tale. Eli, renamed Abby (Chloe Grace Moretz), is more clearly a victim in this version, whose turning left her corrupted, infected and addicted. The Håkan character in Reeves' film, Thomas (Richard Jenkins), is tired, more resigned to failure and his relationship with Abby has diminished. Reeves notes that there is a 'hint at the tenderness that existed once between them'.[25] Thomas is more like Bram Stoker's Renfield, serving his vampire master, than someone with a longing for intimacy. The focus in Reeves' adaptation is more a survivor story for Abby, whose apparent precocious berating of Thomas is motivated by the need to continue to live under conditions that are not of her own doing. This is most evident in a scene shot for the film that was never included in the final cut.[26] Inspired by a flashback sequence in the novel, the turning of Abby plays out as a violent sexual assault when an aging cloaked man approaches her as she sleeps. Alternating in and out of focus, the sequence sees Abby dragged from her bed screaming and being forced face down on the floor. With her naked legs flailing, she cries 'no' while he bears down on her. The frantic vigour with which her body moves, and the repeated screams, clearly plays as a brutal child rape. Essentially adapted from the book, Reeves decided to cut the scene because the moment of Abby's turning looked too much like a sexual assault.[27] Even with the scene cut, Abby is an assaulted girl who enacts her own form of violence to survive. A key inspiration that Reeves drew on, supporting this notion of a survivor's story, are the photo essays of Mary Ellen Mark, who published images of child prostitutes and addicts in *Life* magazine during the 1980s.[28] The US version's contribution to discourses of abuse and paedophilia focuses on a coming-of-age tale corrupted by the sexual assault of a child. Consequently, this trauma never allows her to come of age but forces her to repeat abusive assaults on others in order to survive.

Cinema, Reparation and Responsibility

Notably, a significant number of these films share a degree of commonality concerning a period in history – the 1970s and early 1980s – which saw collective forms of contentious sexual-political activism emerge. Some of the films were produced during this period, others are set, or have sequences taking place in this time, while several focus on characters that came of age during these decades. As Véronique Mottier notes, the activism in question demanded the recognition and 'legalization of consensual sexual relationships between children and adults'.[29] The Netherlands' Dutch Society for Sexual Reform petitioned its government to legalise sex with children and promoted material dealing with research 'which was widely drawn upon in paedophile political activism across Western Europe'.[30] Such direct action is evident in the public petitions in France, which called on the government to decriminalise consensual sex. One such 1977 petition calling for 'the decriminalization of all consenting relations between adults and minors was signed by prominent public intellectuals including Jean-Paul Sartre, Simone de Beauvoir, Michel Foucault, Jacques Derrida, and Roland Barthes'.[31] During this period, PIE (Paedophile Information Exchange) emerged in the UK in 1974, the internationally-recognised NAMBLA (North American Man/Boy Love Association) formed in 1978 and the DPE (Danish Paedophile Association) was established in 1985. The central debate incorporated ideas and research on the legitimacy of child sexuality. At the same time, numerous journals, newsletters, erotic magazines and hardcore pornography featuring paedophilia were widely distributed across Denmark, France, the Netherlands, Czech Republic, Italy, UK and Sweden, exploiting the absence of legislation forbidding child sexual imagery.[32] Pornographic and non-pornographic paedophilic magazines such as *Pan: A Magazine about Boy-Love*, *Piccolo Boy*, *Lollitots* and *Nudist Moppets* all eventually ceased publication by the mid-1980s, largely down to the introduction of new legislation across Europe and the US. As Mottier notes of the time:

> in contrast to the World Health Organization's characterization of paedophilia as a sexual and mental disorder, paedophile activists argued for greater legitimacy, declassification of paedophilia as a mental illness, children's sexual rights, and the decriminalization of (consensual) inter-generational sex.[33]

Collectively, these films, which are widely from the liberal West and often dominated by Eurocentric voices, confront a past not by simply revising it, nor by denying it, but by dealing with the reductive approaches of the present. They clearly and rightly do not accept the activism espousing consent over harm but they do cinematically revisit the complexities of the subject that extends back to the anguish spoken by the titular figure of Fritz Lang's *M* (1931) whose cry for help – 'I can't help what I do. I can't help it. I can't' – is taken by the gathered mob as a pronouncement of his death sentence. At the same time, and in spite of prevailing cultural anxieties, they do not ignore the curiosity children have about sex and sexuality nor do they undervalue the harmful impact that adult sexual contact has on the child who has 'no developmental boundaries to protect against'. Instead, a heightened awareness is called for to better understand paedophilia and better protect children.[34]

The dialogic qualities of *Let the Right One In* and the films discussed above present troubled but honest confessions, punishments ranging from tortuous excess to little more than a subtle guilt-informed freedom for those who do escape conviction. The films offer up barely noticeable behaviours of offenders in their narratives that rail against media constructions of monstrous predators that determine the paedophile in popular culture. They point towards the inadequacies of welfare, law and legal systems while at the same time drawing attention to how acts of violence satisfy but vengeance does not. Finally, they are bold enough to indicate the need for extended knowledge on understanding differences between sexual attraction and sexual abuse.

What *Let the Right One In* does in adapting Håkan's character is not erase the paedophile as intended but writes paedophilia as desire, making the shift from novel to film a shift from *depicting* paedophilia and abuse to *thinking* about paedophilia and abuse. The adaptation asks us to consider the possibility of an emerging paedophilia in Oskar's character as an issue in the same way that the novel presents us with a conflicted Håkan. Considered alongside these other films, *Let the Right One In* illustrates how managing the erotopathic is not merely a carefully orchestrated reductive moment but illustrates the politics of paedophilia at a time when the screen is exploring in greater detail the desires and attitudes towards such a problematic and variant sexual identity.

Notes

1. Patrick Süskind, *Perfume: The Story of a Murderer*, translated by John E. Woods (London: Penguin, 1986), p. 244. Subsequent page references in text appear in parentheses.
2. Richard Maltby, 'To prevent the prevalent type of book: censorship and adaptation in Hollywood, 1924–1934', in Frances G. Couvares (ed.), *Movie Censorship and American Culture*, second edition (Amherst: University of Massachusetts Press, 2006), p. 101.
3. Andrew Davies, *South Bank Show*, ITV, 17 November 2002.
4. Virginie Selavy, '*Let The Right One In*: interview with John Ajvide Lindqvist', *Electric Sheep* (Spring 2009), p. 11.
5. Ibid.
6. John Ajvide Lindqvist, *Let the Right One In* (London: Quercus, 2007), p. 44. Subsequent page references in text appear in parentheses.
7. Selavy, '*Let The Right One In*: interview', p. 11.
8. See Chapter 5 in this collection.
9. See Tim Kane, *The Changing Vampire of Film and Television: A Critical Study of the Growth of a Genre* (Jefferson, NC: McFarland 2006) and Lorna Piatti-Farnell, *The Vampire in Contemporary Popular Literature* (London: Routledge, 2014).
10. Lindqvist went on to write an account of what subsequently happened to Oskar and Eli in a collection of short stories titled *Let the Old Dreams Die* in 2012. In the preface, Lindqvist acknowledges the suggestion that Oskar may become a paedophile, stating that it is 'a fair interpretation of the story and the deliberately open ending I left in the book. But it isn't *my* ending'. In his version, Oskar is turned by Eli so that he remains a child. Lindqvist, *Let the Old Dreams Die*, translated by Marlaine Delargy (London: Quercus, 2012), p. 285.
11. In the film, the fall from the hospital window kills Håkan.
12. Max Taylor and Ethel Quayle, *Child Pornography: An Internet Crime* (Hove and New York: Brunner–Routledge, 2003), pp. 49–50.
13. Ibid., p. 50.
14. Ibid. My italics.

15. Phelan cited in Taylor and Quayle, *Child Pornography*, p. 64.
16. Taylor and Quayle, *Child Pornography*, p. 47.
17. Sarah D. Goode, *Understanding and Addressing Adult Sexual Attraction to Children: A Study of Paedophiles in Contemporary Society* (Routledge: London, 2010), p. 1.
18. Ibid., p. 10.
19. Ibid. See this collection's introduction for a discussion of Krafft-Ebing and the *DSM*.
20. Raymond Williams and Michael Orrom, *A Preface to Film* (London: Film Drama, 1954).
21. Legally recognised as The Sexual Offender Act 1994 and The Child Sex Offender's Disclosure Law 2008, respectively.
22. See Chapters 5 and 13 in this collection.
23. Two-year-old James Bulger was abducted and killed by two ten-year-old boys, Robert Thompson and John Venables, in 1993. For a detailed account that attempts to ask why this happened see Blake Morrison, *As If* (London: Granta Books, 1997).
24. The film's original title on release – *Les 7 Jours du Retalion* (7 Days of Retaliation) – is a more accurate summation of the film's attitude towards its subject.
25. Director commentary, *Let Me In* (DVD), Region 2 (Icon Home Entertainment, 2011).
26. A still image from the scene does, however, feature on the originally released DVD cover.
27. Peter Sciretta, 'Exclusive deleted scene: *Let Me In*', Matt Reeves explains why the intense sequence was cut', */Film*, 5 October 2010. Available at http://www.slashfilm.com/exclusive-deleted-scene-let-me-in-matt-reeves-explains-why-the-intense-sequence-was-cut (accessed 17 November 2012).
28. Director commentary, *Let Me In*. For examples of Mary Ellen Mark's work see Cheryl McCall, 'Streets of the lost: runaway kids eke out a mean life in Seattle', *Life*, July 1983. Available at http://www.maryellenmark.com/text/magazines/life/905W-000-021.html (accessed 17 November 2012).
29. Véronique Mottier, *Sexuality: A Very Short Introduction* (Oxford: Oxford University Press, 2008), p. 105.
30. Ibid., p. 104.
31. Ibid., p. 105.
32. Ibid.
33. Ibid.
34. Goode, *Understanding and Addressing Adult Sexual Attraction to Children*, p. 181.

Filmography

7 Days/Les 7 jours du talion (Daniel Grou, 2010), Canada.

Anatomy of Hell/Anatomie de l'enfer (Catherine Breillat, 2004), France.

Augustine (Alice Winocour, 2012), France.

Bad Boy Bubby (Rolf de Heer, 1993), Australia/Italy.

Blue Velvet (David Lynch, 1986), USA.

Bondage (Lasse Braun, 1972), Netherlands.

Bully (Larry Clark, 2001), USA/France/UK.

Captivity (Roland Joffé, 2007), USA/Russia.

Chasing Amy (Kevin Smith, 1997), USA.

Closer (Mike Nichols, 2004), USA/UK.

Come Play with Me/Grazie zia (Salvatore Samperi, 1968), Italy.

Crash (David Cronenberg, 1996), Canada/UK.

Daddy's Little Girl (Chris Sun, 2012), Australia.

A Dangerous Method (David Cronenberg, 2011), US/Germany/Canada/Switzerland.

Dark Prince: Intimate Tales of Marquis De Sade (Gwyneth Gibby, 1996), USA/Russia.

The Dark Side of Love/Fotografando Patricia (Salvatore Samperi, 1984), Italy.

Deep Arse (Lasse Braun, 1973), Netherlands.

Desiring Julia/Desiderando Giulia (Andrea Barzini, 1986), Italy.

The Devil's Honey/Il miele del diavolo (Lucio Fulci, 1986), Spain/Italy.

Die Marquise von Sade (Jess Franco, 1976), Switzerland.

Don't Ride on Late Night Trains/L'ultimo treno della notte (Aldo Lado, 1975), Italy.

Edward II (Derek Jarman, 1991), UK/Japan.

Erotic Games in a Respectable Family/Giochi erotica di una famiglia per bene (Francesco Degli Espinosa, 1975), Italy.

Evil Senses/Sensi (Gabriele Lava, 1986), Italy.

Fatal Attraction (Adrian Lyne, 1987), USA.

Festen (Thomas Vinterberg, 1998), Denmark/Sweden.

Finnish Girls in Stockholm/Suomalaistyttöjä Tukholmassa (Roland af Hällström, 1952), Finland.

Fireworks (Kenneth Anger, 1947), USA.

Language of Love/Ur kärlekens språk (Torgny Wickman, 1969), Sweden.

Girl, Interrupted (James Mangold, 1999), USA/Germany.

The Girlfriend Experience (Steven Soderbergh, 2009), USA.

The Girl Next Door (Luke Greenfield, 2004), USA.

The Graduate (Mike Nichols, 1967), USA.

Happiness (Todd Solondz, 1998), USA.

Hard Candy (David Slade, 2005), USA.

Harold and Maude (Hal Ashby, 1971), USA.

Henry: Portrait of a Serial Killer (John McNaughton, 1986), USA.

Hostel (Various, 2005–2011), USA/Germany/Czech Republic/Slovakia/Iceland.

The Hunt (Thomas Vinterberg, 2012), Denmark/Sweden.

I Am Curious (Yellow)/Jag är nyfiken: en film i gult (Vilgot Sjöman, 1967), Sweden.

In the Cut (Jane Campion, 2003), Australia/USA/UK.

In the Realm of the Senses/Ai no korîda (Nagisa Ôshima, 1976), Japan/France.

Intimate Relations/La nuora giovane (Luigi Russo, 1975), Italy.

JFK (Oliver Stone, 1991), France/USA.

Justine and the Whip (Jess Franco as Dave Tough, 1979), Italy.

Ken Park (Larry Clark, 2002), USA/Netherlands/France.

Kids (Larry Clark, 1995), USA.

Kissed (Lynne Stopkewich, 1996), Canada.

Lady of the Night/La signora della notte (Piero Shivazappa, 1986), Italy.

La noia/The Empty Canvas (Damiano Damiani, 1963), Italy/France.

Last Tango in Paris (Bernardo Bertolucci, 1972), France/Italy.

Labyrinth of Passion/Laberinto de pasiones (Pedro Almodóvar, 1982), Spain.

The Law of Desire (Pedro Almodóvar, 1987), Spain.

L'ennui/Boredom (Cédric Kahn, 1998), France/Portugal.

Les Dames du Bois de Boulogne (Robert Bresson, 1945), France.

Let the Right One In/Låt den rätte komma in (Tomas Alfredson, 2008), Sweden.

Let Me In (Matt Reeves, 2010), UK/USA.

L.I.E. (Michael Cuesta, 2001), USA.

Life During Wartime (Todd Solondz, 2009), USA.

Little Children (Todd Field, 2006), USA.

The Little Girl Who Lives Down the Lane (Nicholas Gessner, 1976), Canada/France.

Lolita (Stanley Kubrick, 1962), UK/USA.

Love in Scandinavia (Lasse Braun, 1971), Sweden.

The Lovely Bones (Peter Jackson, 2009), UK/USA/New Zeland.

Luna (Bernardo Bertolucci, 1979), Italy/USA.

M (Fritz Lang, 1931), Germany.

Ma mère (Christophe Honoré, 2004), France/Portugal/Austria/Spain.

Marat/Sade (Peter Brook, 1967), UK.

Marquis De Sade: Justine (Jess Franco, 1969), Italy/USA/West Germany/Liechtenstein.

Marquis de Sade's 'Philosophy in the Boudoir' (Jess Franco, 1970), Spain/West Germany.

Matador (Pedro Almodóvar, 1986), Spain.

Michael (Markus Schleinzer and Kathrin Resetarits, 2011), Austria.

Murmur of the Heart (Louis Malle, 1971), France/Italy/West Germany.

My Father's Nurse/L'infermiera… di mio padre (Mario Bianchi, 1975), Italy.

Mysterious Skin (Gregg Araki, 2004), USA/Netherlands.

Mystic River (Clint Eastwood, 2003), USA/Australia.

The Naked Kiss (Samuel Fuller, 1964), USA.

Natural Born Killers (Oliver Stone, 1994), USA.

Never Take Sweets from a Stranger (Cyril Frankel, 1960), UK.

A Nightmare on Elm Street (Samuel Bayer, 2010), USA.

Night Terrors (Tobe Hooper, 1993), Canada/Egypt/USA.

O Fantasma/Phantom (João Pedro Rodrigues, 2000), Portugal.

The Offence (Sidney Lumet, 1973), UK/USA.

One Summer of Happiness/Hon dansade en sommar (Arne Mattson, 1951), Sweden.

Palindromes (Todd Solondz, 2004), USA.

Perfume: The Story of a Murderer (Tom Tykwer, 2006), Germany/France/Spain/USA.

Perversion (Lasse Braun, 1971), Denmark.

The Piano Teacher/La pianiste (Michael Haneke, 2001), Austria/France/Germany.

Play Misty For Me (Clint Eastwood, 1971), USA.

Pornography in Denmark: A New Approach (Alex de Renzy, 1970), USA.

Querelle (Rainer Werner Fassbinder, 1981), West Germany/France.

Quills (Philip Kaufman, 2000), UK/Germany/USA.

The Reader (Stephen Daldry, 2008), USA/Germany.

Road of Temptations/Viettelysten tie (Kaarlo Nuorvala, 1955), Finland.

Roberto Succo (Cédric Kahn, 2001), France/Switzerland.

Romance (Catherine Breillat, 1999), France.

Salò, or the 120 Days of Sodom (Pier Paolo Pasolini, 1975), Italy/France.

Saw (Various, 2004–2017), USA/Australia.

Scandalous Gilda/Scandalosa Gilda (Gabriele Lava, 1985), Italy.

Scorpio Rising (Kenneth Anger, 1964), USA.

The School Teacher (Nando Cicero, 1975), Italy.

The School Teacher Goes to Boys' High/L'insegnante va in collegio (Mariano Laurenti, 1978), Italy/France.

Sebastiane (Derek Jarman and Paul Humfress, 1976), UK.

Secretary (Steven Shainberg, 2002), USA.

Sensations (Lasse Braun as Alberto Ferro, 1975), France/Netherlands.

A Serbian Film (Srdjan Spasojevic, 2010), Serbia.

Sexual Freedom in Denmark (M.C. von Hellen, 1970), USA.

Shocking (Lasse Braun, 1972), Netherlands.

Short Eyes (Robert M. Young, 1977), USA.

Silence/Tystnaden (Ingmar Bergman, 1963), Sweden.

The Silence (Baran bo Odar, 2010), Germany.

The Silence of the Lambs (Jonathan Demme, 1991), USA.

The Skull (Freddie Francis, 1965), UK.

Sleepers (Barry Levinson, 1996), USA.

Sombre (Philippe Grandrieux, 1998), France.

Spanking the Monkey (David O. Russell, 1994), USA.

Storytelling (Todd Solondz, 2001), USA.

Summer with Monika/Sommaren med Monika (Ingmar Bergman, 1953), Sweden.

Summer of '42 (Robert Mulligan, 1971), USA.

Sweet Teen/L'adolescente (Alfonso Brescia, 1976), Italy.

Talk to Her/Hable con ella (Pedro Almodóvar, 2002), Spain.

Tea and Sympathy (Vincente Minnelli, 1956), USA.

Teenage Caveman (Larry Clark, 2002), USA.

Terror Express/La ragazza del vagone letto/ (Ferdinando Baldi, 1980), Italy.

Tie Me Up! Tie Me Down! (Pedro Almodóvar, 1989), Spain.

The Trap/La gabbia (Giuseppe Patroni Griffi, 1985), Italy/Spain.

Vice in the Family/Il vizio di famiglia (Mariano Laurenti, 1975), Italy.

A Virgin in the Family/Una vergine in famiglia (Luca Degli Azzeri, 1975), Italy.

The War Zone (Tim Roth, 1999), Italy/UK.

Waxwork (Anthony Hickox, 1988), USA/West Germany/UK.

Welcome to the Dollhouse (Todd Solondz, 1995), USA.

The Woodsman (Nicole Kassell, 2004), USA.

Select Bibliography

Adler, Amy, 'The perverse law of child pornography', *The Columbia Law Review* 101/2 (March 2001), pp. 209–73.

American Psychiatric Association, *Diagnostic and Statistical Manual of Mental Disorders* (Washington, DC: Author, 1952).

—— *Diagnostic and Statistical Manual of Mental Disorders*, second edition (Washington, DC: Author, 1968).

—— *Diagnostic and Statistical Manual of Mental Disorders*, third edition (Washington, DC: Author, 1980).

—— *Diagnostic and Statistical Manual of Mental Disorders*, third edition-revised (Washington, DC: Author, 1987).

—— *Diagnostic and Statistical Manual of Mental Disorders*, fourth edition Washington, DC: Author, 1994).

—— *Diagnostic and Statistical Manual of Mental Disorders*, fourth edition-revised (Washington, DC: Author, 2000).

—— *Diagnostic and Statistical Manual of Mental Disorders*, fifth edition (Washington, DC: Author, 2013).

Attwood, Feona (ed.), *Mainstreaming Sex: The Sexualisation of Western Culture* (London: I.B.Tauris, 2009).

Barker, Martin, ' "Typically French"?: Mediating screened rape to British audiences', in Dominique Russell (ed.), *Rape in Art Cinema* (New York: Continuum, 2010).

Barker, Meg and Darren Langdridge (eds), *Safe, Sane and Consensual: Contemporary Perspectives on Sadomasochism* (Basingstoke: Palgrave Macmillan, 2007).

——, 'Silencing accounts of silenced sexualities', in Róisín Ryan-Flood and Rosalind Gill (eds), *Secrecy and Silence in the Research Process: Feminist Reflections* (Abingdon: Routledge, 2009).

Bataille, Georges, *Erotism: Death and Sensuality* (New York: Walker and Company, 1962).

Berlant, Lauren, 'Structures of Unfeeling: *Mysterious Skin*', *Journal of Politics, Culture and Society* 28/3 (September 2015), pp. 191–213.

Best, Victoria and Martin Crowley, *The New Pornographies: Explicit Sex in Recent French Fiction and Film* (Manchester and New York: Manchester University Press, 2007).

Björklund, Elisabet, 'This is a dirty movie': *Taxi Driver* and "Swedish sin" ', *Journal of Scandinavian Cinema* 1/2 (2011), pp. 163–76.

Botting, Fred and Scott Wilson, 'Sexcrash', in Jane Arthurs and Iain Grant (eds), *Crash Cultures: Modernity, Mediation and the Material* (Bristol and Portland, OR: Intellect, 2003).

271

Breillat, Catherine, *Pornocracy*, translated by Paul Buck and Catherine Petit (Los Angeles: Semiotext(e), 2008).

Brinkema, Eugenie, 'Celluloid is sticky: sex, death, materiality, metaphysics (in some films by Catherine Breillat)', *Women: A Cultural Review* 17/2 (2006), pp. 147–70.

Bristol, James E., 'Free expression and a satisfied society: what child pornography laws really protect', *bepress Legal Series*, working paper 1870 (8 November 2006). Available at http://law.bepress.com/expresso/eps/1870.

Bronfen, Elizabeth, *The Knotted Subject: Hysteria and Its Discontents* (Princeton, NJ: Princeton University Press, 1998).

Bucknill, J.C. and D.H. Tuke, *A Manual of Psychological Medicine* (Philadelphia, PA: Blanchard and Lea, 1858).

Burr, Viv and Jeff Hearn (eds), *Sex, Violence and the Body: The Erotics of Wounding* (Basingstoke: Palgrave Macmillan, 2008).

Butler, Judith, *Gender Trouble: Feminism and the Subversion of Identity* (New York: Routledge, 1990).

———, *Bodies that Matter: On the Discursive Limits of 'Sex'* (New York: Routledge, 1993).

Cettl, Robert, *Offensive to a Reasonable Adult: Film Censorship and Classification in 'Secular' Australia* (Adelaide: Wider Screenings, 2011).

Cossman, Brenda, 'Sexuality, queer theory and "feminism after": reading and re-reading the sexual subject', *McGill Law Journal* 49/4 (2004), pp. 847–76.

Cowburn, Malcolm and Lena Dominelli, 'Masking hegemonic masculinity: reconstructing the paedophile as the dangerous stranger', *British Journal of Social Work* 31/3 (2001), pp. 399–415.

Cross, Simon, 'Paedophiles in the community: inter-agency conflict, news leaks and the local press', *Crime, Media, Culture* 1/3 (December 2005), pp. 284–300.

Davis, Jon, 'Imagining intergenerationality: representation and rhetoric in the pedophile movie', *GLQ: A Journal of Lesbian and Gay Studies* 13/2–3 (2007), pp. 369–85.

Dean, Tim, *Beyond Sexuality* (Chicago, IL: Chicago University Press, 2000).

de Lauretis, Teresa, *The Practice of Love: Lesbian Sexuality and Perverse Desire* (Bloomington, IN: Indiana University Press, 1994).

Demazeux, Steeves, and Patrick Singy, *The DSM-5 in Perspective: Philosophical Reflections on the Psychiatric Babel* (New York: Springer, 2015).

Doty, Alexander, 'Queer theory', in John Hill and Pamela Church Gibson (eds), *The Oxford Guide to Film Studies* (Oxford: Oxford University Press, 1998).

Downing, Lisa, 'French cinema's new "sexual revolution": postmodern porn and troubled genre', *French Cultural Studies* 15/3 (2004), pp. 265–80.

———, 'Beyond safety: erotic asphyxiation and the limits of S/M discourse', in Langdridge and Barker (eds), *Safe, Sane and Consensual: Contemporary Perspectives on Sadomasochism* (Basingstoke: Palgrave Macmillan, 2007).

De Block, Andreas, and Pieter R. Adriaens, 'Pathologizing sexual deviance: A history', *Journal of Sex Research* 50/5–3 (2013), pp. 276–98.

Downing, Lisa and Dany Nobus (eds), *Perversion: Psychoanalytic Perspectives/ Perspectives on Psychoanalysis* (London: Karnac, 2006).

Downing, Lisa and Libby Saxton, *Film and Ethics: Foreclosed Encounters* (London and New York: Routledge, 2009).

Downing, Lisa, and Robert Gillett, 'Georges Bataille at the avant-garde of queer theory?: transgression, perversion and death drive', *Nottingham French Studies* 50/3 (2011), pp. 88–102.

Durkheim, Emile, *Incest: The Nature and Origin of the Taboo*, translated by Edward Sagarin (New York: Lyle Stuart, 1963), p. 5. Originally published 1897.

Dyer, Richard, *The Culture of Queers* (London: Routledge, 2002).

——, *Now You See It: Studies is Lesbian and Gay Film*, second edition (London: Routledge, 2003).

Dymock, Alex, 'But femsub is broken too!: On the normalisation of BDSM and the problem of pleasure', *Psychology and Sexuality* 3/1 (2012), pp. 54–68.

Egan, R. Danielle and Gail Hawkes, 'Imperiled and perilous: exploring the history of childhood sexuality', *Journal of the Historical Sociology* 21/4 (2008), pp. 355–67.

Farmer, Brett, *Spectacular Passions: Cinema, Fantasy, Gay Male Spectatorships* (Durham, NC: Duke University Press, 2000).

Fathallah, Judith May, 'H/c and me: an autoethnographic account of a troubled love affair', *Transformative Works and Cultures* 7 (2011). Available at http://journal. transformativeworks.org/index.php/twc/article/view/252/206.

Fink, Bruce, 'Perversion', in Molly Anne Rothenberg, Dennis A. Foster and Slavoj Žižek (eds), *Perversion and the Social Relation* (Durham, NC: Duke University Press, 2003).

Foucault, Michel, *History of Sexuality. Volume 1: An Introduction*, translated by Robert Hurley (New York: Pantheon Books, 1978).

——, 'Sex, power and the politics of identity', in Sylvére Lotringer (ed.), *Foucault Live: Collected Interviews, 1961–1984*, revised second edition (New York: Semiotext(e), 1996).

——, *Abnormal: Lectures at the Collège de France, 1974–1975*, Valerio Marchetti and Antonella Salomoni (eds), translated by Graham Burchell (New York: Picador, 2003).

Foucault, Michel, Jean Danet and Guy Hocquenghem, 'The danger of child sexuality', *Semiotext(e) Magazine* 40–4, summer issue, translated by Daniel Moshenberg (1980).

Freud, Sigmund, *Three Essays on the Theory of Sexuality*, translated by James Strachey (New York: Basic Books, 1962). Originally published 1905.

——, 'From the history of an infantile neurosis', *Three Case Studies* (New York: Touchstone, 1963), pp. 161–280. Originally published 1918.

Fromm, Erich, *The Anatomy of Human Destructiveness* (London: Cape, 1973).

Giroux, Henry, 'Teenage sexuality, body politics, and the pedagogy of display', in Jonathon S. Epstein (ed.), *Youth Culture: Identity in a Postmodern World* (Oxford: Blackwell, 1998).

Goffman, Erving, *Frame Analysis* (New York: Harper & Row, 1974).

Select Bibliography

Goode, Sarah D., *Understanding and Addressing Adult Sexual Attraction to Children: A Study of Paedophiles in Contemporary Society* (Routledge: London, 2010).

Gooren, Juul, 'Deciphering the ambiguous menace of sexuality for the innocence of childhood', *Critical Criminology* 19/1 (March 2011), pp. 29–42.

Grønstad, Asbjørn, 'Abject desire: Anatomie de l'enfer and the unwatchable', *Studies in French Cinema* 6/3 (2006), pp. 161–9.

———, *Screening the Unwatchable: Spaces of Negation in Post-millennial Art Cinema* (Basingstoke: Palgrave Macmillan, 2012).

Halberstam, Judith, *Female Masculinity* (Durham, NC and London: Duke University Press, 1998).

Hale, Frederick, 'Time for sex in Sweden: enhancing the myth of the "Swedish sin" during the 1950s', *Scandinavian Studies* 75/3 (2003), pp. 351–74.

Harkins, Gillian, *Everybody's Family Romance: Reading Incest in Neoliberal America* (Minneapolis, MN: University of Minnesota Press, 2009).

Harman, Sarah, Bethan Jones and Ruth Deller, 'Reading the *Fifty Shades* phenomenon', *Litro*, 28 February 2013. Available at http://www.litro.co.uk/2013/02/reading-fifty-shades/.

Harrop, John, *Acting* (London: Routledge, 1992).

Hilliard, Robert J., *Hollywood Speaks Out: Pictures That Dared to Protest Real World Issues* (Oxford: Wiley–Blackwell, 2009).

Hooper, Carol-Ann and Ann Kaloski, 'Rewriting "the paedophile": a feminist reading of *The Woodsman*', *Feminist Review* 83 (2006), pp. 149–55.

hooks, bell, *Reel to Real: Race, Sex, and Class at the Movies* (London and New York: Routledge, 1996).

Horeck, Tanya and Tina Kendall (eds), *The New Extremism in Cinema: From France to Europe* (Edinburgh: Edinburgh University Press, 2011).

Karlyn, Kathleen Rowe, '"Too close for comfort": *American Beauty* and the incest motif', *Cinema Journal* 44/1 (2004), pp. 69–93.

Katz, Jack, *Seductions of Crime: Moral and Sensual Attractions of Doing Evil* (New York: Basic Books, 1988).

Keesey, Douglas, *Catherine Breillat* (Manchester: Manchester University Press, 2009).

Kerr, Darren and Claire Hines (eds), *Hard To Swallow: Reading Pornography On Screen* (London and New York: Wallflower, 2010).

Khan, Ummni, 'A woman's right to be spanked: testing the limits of tolerance of S/M in the socio-legal imaginary', *The Journal of Sexuality and the Law* 18 (2009), pp. 79–119.

Kirkland, Ewan, 'Romantic comedy and the construction of heterosexuality', *Scope* 9 (2007), available at http://www.scope.nottingham.ac.uk/article.php?issue=9&id=957.

Kitzinger, Jenny, 'The ultimate neighbour from hell? Stranger danger and the media framing of paedophiles', in Bob Franklin (ed.), *Social Policy, the Media and Representation* (Abingdon: Routledge, 1999).

Krafft-Ebing, Richard von, *Psychopathia Sexualis: A Medico Forensic Study*, translated by Franklin S. Klaf (New York: Arcade Publishing, 1965). Originally published 1886.

Kristeva, Julia, *Powers of Horror: An Essay on Abjection* (New York: Columbia University Press, 1982).

Krzywinska, Tanya, *Sex and the Cinema* (London: Wallflower, 2006).

Kulick, Don, 'Four hundred thousand Swedish perverts', *GLQ: A Journal of Lesbian and Gay Studies* 11/2 (2005), pp. 205–35.

Ladenson, Elisabeth, *Dirt for Arts Sake: Books on Trial from Madame Bovary to Lolita* (London: Cornell University Press, 2007).

Loughnane, Rory and Edel Semple (eds), *Staged Transgression in Shakespeare's England* (Basingstoke: Palgrave Macmillan, 2013).

Lynch, Joan Driscoll, 'Incest discourse and cinematic representation', *Journal of Film and Video*, 54/2–3 (2002), pp. 43–55.

MacCormack, Patricia, *Cinesexuality* (Aldershot: Ashgate, 2008).

Maines, Rachel P., *The Technology of Orgasm: 'Hysteria', the Vibrator and Women's Sexual Satisfaction* (Baltimore, MD and London: The John Hopkins University Press, 1999).

Mainon, Dominique and James Ursini, *Cinema of Obsession: Erotic Fixation and Love Gone Wrong in the Movies* (New York: Limelight Editions, 2007).

McAlinden, Ann-Marie, 'Deconstructing victim and offender identities in discourses on child sexual abuse: hierarchies, blame and the good/evil dialectic', *The British Journal of Criminology* 54 (2014), pp. 180–98.

McAlister, Joan Faber, 'Unsafe houses: the narrative inversion of suburban morality in popular film', *Liminalities: A Journal of Performance Studies* 4/1 (2008), pp. 2–25.

McClintock, Anne, 'Maid to order: commercial fetishism and gender power', *Social Text* 37, special issue on sex work (Fall 1993), pp. 87–116.

McNair, Brian, *Striptease Culture: Sex, Media & the Democratisation of Desire* (London: Routledge, 2002).

Miller, William Ian, *The Anatomy of Disgust* (Cambridge: Harvard University Press, 1997).

Mottier, Véronique, *Sexuality: A Very Short Introduction* (Oxford: Oxford University Press, 2008).

Newmahr, Staci, *Playing on the Edge: Sadomasochism, Risk, and Intimacy* (Bloomington, IN: Indiana University Press, 2011).

Oosterhuis, Harry, 'Richard von Krafft-Ebing's step-children of nature: psychiatry and the making of homosexual identity', in Kim M. Phillips and Barry Reay (eds), *Sexualities in History: A Reader* (New York: Routledge, 2002).

O'Toole, Laurence, *Pornocopia: Porn, Sex, Technology and Desire* (London: Serpent's Tale, 1998).

Paasonen, Susanna, Kaarina Nikunen and Laura Saarenmaa (eds), *Pornification: Sex and Sexuality in Media Culture* (Oxford: Berg, 2007).

Palmer, Tim, 'Style and sensation in the contemporary French cinema of the body', *Journal of Film and Video* 58/3 (2006), pp. 22–32.

Peakman, Julie, *The Pleasure's All Mine: A History of Perverse Sex* (London: Reaktion Books, 2013).

Phillips, Kim M. and Barry Reay (eds), *Sexualities in History: A Reader* (New York: Routledge, 2002).

Primoratz, Igor, *Ethics and Sex* (London: Routledge, 2003).

Quandt, James, 'Flesh and blood: sex and violence in recent French cinema', *Artforum International* 42/6 (February 2004), pp. 126–32.

Rechy, John, *The Sexual Outlaw: A Documentary* (London: Futura, 1977).

Rich, B. Ruby, 'Beyond doom: Gregg Araki's *Mysterious Skin*', *New Queer Cinema: The Director's Cut* (Durham, NC and London: Duke University Press, 2013).

Rothenberg, Molly Anne and Dennis Foster, 'Introduction. Beneath the skin: perversion and social analysis', in Molly Anne Rothenberg, Dennis Foster and Slavoj Žižek (eds), *Perversion and the Social Relation* (Durham, NC: Duke University Press, 2003).

Rubin, Gayle, 'Thinking sex (1984)', in Carole S. Vance (ed.), *Pleasure and Danger: Exploring Female Sexuality* (London: Pandora, 1989).

Russo, Vito, *The Celluloid Closet: Homosexuality and the Movies* (New York: Harper and Row, 1981.

Schofield, Karin, 'Collisions of culture and crime: media commodification of child sexual abuse', in Jeff Ferrell, Keith Hayward, Wayne Morrison and Mike Presdee (eds), *Cultural Criminology Unleashed* (London: The Glasshouse Press, 2004).

Stevenson, Jack, *Scandinavian Blue: The Erotic Cinema of Sweden and Denmark in the 1960s and 1970s* (Jefferson, MD: McFarland, 2010).

Stockton, Kathryn Bond, *The Queer Child, or Growing Sideways in the Twentieth Century* (Durham, NC and London: Duke University Press, 2009).

Stoller, Robert, *Perversion: the Erotic Form of Hatred* (New York: Pantheon Books, 1975).

Taylor, Max and Ethel Quayle, *Child Pornography: An Internet Crime* (Hove and New York: Brunner–Routledge, 2003).

Thomas, Calvin, *Straight with a Twist: Queer Theory and the Subject of Heterosexuality* (Urbana and Chicago, IL: University of Illinois Press, 2000).

Twitchell, James B., *Forbidden Partners: The Incest Taboo in Modern Culture* (New York: Columbia University Press, 1987).

Weeks, Jeffery, *Sexuality and Its Discontents* (London: Routledge and Kegan Paul, 1985).

Whitebook, Joel, *Perversion and Utopia: A Study in Psychoanalysis and Critical Theory* (Cambridge, MA: MIT Press, 1995).

Williams, Linda, *Hard Core: Pornography and the 'Frenzy of the Visible* (Berkeley, CA: University of California Press, 1989).

———, 'Film bodies: gender, genre, excess', in Leo Braudy and Marshall Cohen (eds), *Film Theory and Criticism* (Oxford: Oxford University Press, 1991).

———, 'Second thoughts on *Hard Core*: American obscenity law and the scapegoating of deviance', in Pamela Church Gibson and Roma Gibson (eds), *Dirty Looks: Women, Pornography, Power* (London: British Film Institute, 1993).

———, (ed.), *Porn Studies* (Durham, NC: Duke University Press, 2004).

———, *Screening Sex* (Durham, NC: Duke University Press, 2008).

Williams, Linda Ruth, *The Erotic Thriller in Contemporary Cinema* (Edinburgh: Edinburgh University Press, 2005).

Wood, Robin, 'The murderous gays: Hitchcock's homophobia', in Alexander Doty and Corey Creekmur (eds), *Out in Culture: Gay, Lesbian, and Queer Essays on Popular Culture* (Durham, NC: Duke University Press, 1995).

Wouters, Cas, 'Balancing sex and love since the 1960s sexual revolution', in Mike Featherstone (ed.), *Love and Eroticism* (London: Sage, 1999).

Wyatt, Justin, 'Selling "atrocious sexual behavior": revisiting sexualities in the marketplace for adult films in the 1960s', in Hilary Radner and Moya Luckett (eds), *Swinging Single: Representing Sexuality in the 1960s* (Minneapolis, MN: Minnesota University Press, 1999), pp. 105–31.

Yarom, Nitza, *Matrix of Hysteria: Psychoanalysis of the Struggle Between the Sexes as Enacted in the Body* (London and New York: Routledge, 2005).

Contributors

Sarah Arnold is Lecturer in Gender and Production Studies at Maynooth University, Ireland and has previously worked at universities including Falmouth University and as a project manager in interactive television technologies. She publishes on gender and sexuality in film and television and is currently preparing the monograph *Television, Technology and Gender: New Platforms and New Audiences*. Her previous books include *Maternal Horror Film: Melodrama and Motherhood* (2013) and the co-authored book *The Film Handbook* (2013). She is also a contributor to the *Critical Studies in Television* blog.

Guy Barefoot is Associate Professor in Film Studies and member of the Centre for American Studies at the University of Leicester. His publications include *Gaslight Melodrama: From Victorian London to 1940s Hollywood* (2001) and *The Lost Jungle: Cliffhanger Action and Hollywood Serials of the 1930s and 1940s* (2017) as well as contributions to *Adaptation: The Journal of Literature on Screen Studies*, *Historical Journal of Film, Radio and Television*, *The Cinema Book* and the *Oxford Dictionary of National Biography*.

Lisa Downing is Professor of French Discourses of Sexuality at the University of Birmingham. She is a specialist in sexuality and gender studies, film, and critical theory. Her book-length publications include: *Desiring the Dead: Necrophilia and Nineteenth-Century French Literature* (2003), *Patrice Leconte* (2004), *Perversion: Psychoanalytic Perspectives/Perspectives on Psychoanalysis* (co-edited with Dany Nobus, 2006), *The Cambridge Introduction to Michel Foucault* (2008), *Film and Ethics* (co-authored with Libby Saxton, 2010), *Queer in Europe* (co-edited with Robert Gillett 2011), *The Subject of Murder* (2013) and *Fuckology: Critical Essays on John Money's Diagnostic Concepts* (co-authored with Iain Morland and Nikki Sullivan, 2015).

Martin Fradley is Lecturer at the University of Brighton and has taught widely across the UK university sector. He is a regular contributor to *Film Quarterly*, and his work has also appeared in *Screen*, *Journal of British Cinema and Television*, *Journal of Canadian Studies* and *Film Criticism*. He is co-editor of the anthology *Shane Meadows: Critical Essays* (2013), and his recent published work has appeared in the collections *Postfeminism and Contemporary American Cinema* (2013) and *Directory of World Cinema: American Independent 3* (2016).

Contributors

Helen Hester is Associate Professor of Media and Communications at the University of West London. Her research interests include technofeminism, sexuality studies and theories of social reproduction, and she is a member of the international feminist working group Laboria Cuboniks. She is the author of *Beyond Explicit: Pornography and the Displacement of Sex* (2014), co-editor of the collections *Fat Sex: New Directions in Theory and Activism* (2015) and *Dea ex Machina* (2015), and series editor for Ashgate's 'Sexualities in Society' book series. She has two texts forthcoming: *After Work: What's Left and Who Cares?* (with Nick Srnicek) and *Xenofeminism*.

Beth Johnson is Associate Professor of Film and Media at the University of Leeds. Her research interests include representations of class and region on screen, feminist media, screen authorship and sex on screen. Her books include *Paul Abbott* (2013) and *Television, Sex and Society* (2012). Beth has recently completed co-editing (with David Forrest, University of Sheffield) a collection of essays entitled *Social Class and Television Drama in Contemporary Britain* (2017).

Darren Kerr is Senior Lecturer and Head of Film at Southampton Solent University. He is a member of the editorial board for *Porn Studies*, the first international peer-reviewed journal dedicated to pornography. His research and publications have explored autoerotic asphyxiation, paedophilia and 1970s porn culture. He is co-editor of *Hard to Swallow: Hard-core Pornography on Screen* (2012) and co-curator of the academic blog *Screening Sex*. Darren has also written and published research on transnational horror, screen violence and literary adaptations.

Xavier Mendik is Professor of Cult Cinema Studies and Director of the Cine-Excess International Film Festival at Birmingham City University. He has written extensively on cult film traditions, and some of his books (as author/editor/co-editor) include: *Bodies of Desire and Bodies in Distress: The Golden Age of Italian Cult Cinema* (2015), *Peep Shows: Cult Film and the Cine-Erotic* (2012), *100 Cult Films* (with Ernest Mathijs, 2011), *The Cult Film Reader* (with Ernest Mathijs, 2008), *Underground USA: Filmmaking Beyond the Hollywood Canon* (2002), *Dario Argento's Tenebrae* (2000) and *Unruly Pleasures: The Cult Film and its Critics* (2000).

John Mercer is Professor of Gender and Sexuality at the Birmingham Centre for Media and Cultural Research. His research interests include film and television genres, celebrity and stardom, the pornography debate, masculinity and the sexualisation of contemporary media culture and contemporary cultural theory. He is the author of *Gay Porn: Representations of Masculinity and Sexuality* (2017), *Rock Hudson* (2015) and *Melodrama: Genre Style Sensibility* (with Martin Shingler, 2013). John is co-editor of the *Journal of Gender Studies*, one of the editorial founders of *Porn Studies* and a member of the editorial board of *Sexualities* and *Celebrity Studies*.

Contributors

Susanna Paasonen is Professor of Media Studies at University of Turku, Finland. With an interest in studies of popular culture, sexuality, affect and media theory, she is most recently the author of *Carnal Resonance: Affect and Online Pornography* (2011) and co-author of the forthcoming *Not Safe for Work: Sex, Humor and Risk in Social Media* (with Kylie Jarrett and Ben Light), as well as co-editor of *Working with Affect in Feminist Readings: Disturbing Differences* (2010) and *Networked Affect* (2015).

Donna Peberdy is Senior Lecturer in Film and Television at Southampton Solent University. She is the author of *Masculinity and Film Performance: Male Angst in Contemporary American Cinema* (2011) and co-curator of the academic blog *Screening Sex*. Donna has written about acting and performance in contemporary US film and television, film noir, transnational cinema, voice and vocal performance, and the performance of sex, sexuality and masculinity. She is particularly interested in the relationship between screen acting and the performance of identity.

Clarissa Smith is Professor of Sexual Cultures in the Centre for Research in Media & Cultural Studies at the University of Sunderland. She researches sex, sexual identities and sexual representations in contemporary culture and is a founding editor of the Routledge journal *Porn Studies*.

Sarah Taylor-Harman is an early career researcher and educator in the final stages of completing her doctoral research at Brunel University London. Her thesis focuses upon BDSM and gender in the adaptations of 1950s female authored 'pornographic' novel *Story of O*. She is co-editor of *Screening Twilight: Critical Approaches to a Cinematic Phenomenon* (2014) and editorial board member for the journal *Porn Studies*. Her research interests include: adaptations, representations of gender and sexuality, feminism, queer theory, BDSM and pornography.

Caroline Walters is Visiting Lecturer in Media and Cultural Studies at Middlesex University London and a research associate for BiUK (The UK Organisation for Research on Bisexuality). Her AHRC funded PhD explored discourses of heterosexual female masochism and submission from the 1880s to the present day. She is co-editor of *Fat Sex: New Directions in Theory and Activism* (2015) and her other research interests include sexual ethics, mental health and public engagement. She is currently working on a manuscript titled 'Raced White: Female Masochism, Class and Race'.

Index

Index

Index

Index

Index

Index

Index